GUIDE TO START AND GROW YOUR SUCCESSFUL TAX BUSINESS

Charles E. McCabe, MBA

Founder, Peoples Tax & The Income Tax School

Foreword By Roger Russell
Senior Editor, Accounting Today

Editor & Designer, Terry McCabe Judge

 ITS Books

ITS Books, a division of The Income Tax School, Inc.

10120 W. Broad St., Suite. A, Glen Allen, VA 23060

ISBN: 978-1-947413-00-9

August 2020 Revised Edition.

First edition published in both electronic form and in print form as a trade paperback - printing August 2017.

 is a registered trademark of The Income Tax School, Inc.

For information regarding special discounts for bulk

purchases, please contact ITS Books at 1-800-984-1040.

Printed in the U.S.A. by the ITS Books Print Shop

Table of Contents

Acknowledgements   i

Foreword – By Roger Russell, Senior Editor for Tax and Accounting Today   iii

Evolution of Taxation and the Income Tax Industry   v

Introduction   xii

Chapter 1 – Learning Tax Preparation and Obtaining Credentials   1

    Your Purpose and Role as a Tax Preparer   2

    Start with the Basics   3

Federal and State Education Requirements   3

    California and Oregon   3

    Maryland   3

    New York   4

    Voluntary IRS Regulations   4

Tax Education Options   4

    Advantages of Learning Tax Preparation Online   5

    Important Numbers You'll Need as a Tax Preparer   7

    The Voluntary IRS Annual Filing Season Program (AFSP)   7

The Big Tax Preparer Myth   10

Tax Industry Credentials   10

    The Benefits of Becoming an IRS Enrolled Agent   11

    About the IRS Special Enrollment Exam (SEE)   12

    The Perfect Pathway to Becoming an Enrolled Agent   14

Conclusion   16

Chapter 2 – Developing a Business Plan   17

Table of Contents

Why a Business Plan?	**18**
Identify Your Mission and Commit to It	**18**
Writing Your Business Plan	**20**
Sample Tax Firm SWOT Analysis	21
Trade Names	24
Spreading Out Seasonality and Diversifying Your Business	25
Your Short-term Plan	25
Implementation of Your Plan	**26**
Tracking What Works and What Doesn't Work	**26**
Analysis of Results	**26**
Grow with an Advisory Board	**26**
Example of Advisory Board Membership Criteria	28
Conclusion	**29**
Chapter 3 – Risk Management	**31**
Types of Business Insurance	**32**
Why You Really Need a Data Breach Policy	**35**
Know the Scams	36
IRS Security Campaigns	36
IRS Safeguards	38
IRS Fact Sheet Identity Theft Information for Tax Professionals	**40**
What is Tax-Related Identity Theft?	40
How to Know if a Client is a Victim of Tax-Related Identity Theft	40
What Can Preparers Do if a Client is a Victim of Identity Theft?	41

Table of Contents

How Can Preparers Protect Clients' Sensitive Information?   41

Related Resources: 41

Conclusion   **42**

Chapter 4 – Getting Started as a Tax Business Owner   **43**

Key Considerations if You Want to Open a Tax Business   44

Buying a Tax Franchise   45

Becoming an Independent Tax Business Owner   47

Tax Preparation as a Part-Time Business   47

Legal Forms of Organizing Your Business   **49**

Sole Proprietor   49

Limited Liability Company (LLC)   49

C-Corporation   49

Partnership   49

Bank Financing   **51**

Conclusion   **51**

Chapter 5 – Establishing Your Tax Office   **53**

Home-Based Office   **54**

Brick and Mortar Business   **55**

Professional Office Building   **56**

Executive Suites Office   **56**

Virtual Tax Service   **57**

Retail Storefront Office   **58**

Table of Contents

Storefront Office Site-selection   58

Storefront Office Leasing   59

Conclusion   **61**

Chapter 6 – Tax Office Operating Systems   **63**

Systematic Operating Methods   **64**

Tools to do the Job   **65**

Tax Season Equipment & Supplies   **66**

Tax Office Set-up   **67**

Benefits of Adopting Systematic Operation Methods   **72**

Conclusion   **73**

Chapter 7 – Buying a Tax Practice   **75**

Valuation and Payment Terms   **76**

Research and Due Diligence   **77**

Purchase of Practice Agreement   **77**

Sample Letter to Seller's Clients   78

Open House Invitation   79

Employing the Seller   00

Transferring the Client Files   80

Conclusion   **80**

Exhibit A - Tax Practice Purchase Agreement   **81**

Exhibit 1 - Non-Compete, Non-Solicitation Agreement   **82**

Table of Contents

Chapter 8 – Market Planning   85

Hiring a Marketing Consultant   86

Strategies and Tactics   86

Establish Your Marketing Budget   86

Identify Your Target Clients   87

Determine Your Competitive Positioning   87

Develop an Action Plan   88

Conduct Test Marketing   88

Conclusion   89

Chapter 9 – Pricing Your Services   91

Determining Your Fees   92

Check Out the Competition   92

Pricing Policies   93

    Charging by the Forms   93

    Pricing by the Hour   94

Quoting Fees in Advance   94

    Sample Rates for a Home-based Tax Business   95

    Sample Rates for a Brick and Mortar Tax Business   96

Invoices   97

Accepting Payments   97

Offering a Satisfaction Guarantee   98

Conclusion   100

Table of Contents

Chapter 10 – Mass Media Advertising   **101**

Segmenting Your Targeted Clients   **102**

Network Television   104

Media Buying   104

Cable TV   105

Radio Advertising   105

Print   106

Mass Mailing   108

Outdoor Advertising   108

Mass-Transit Advertising   109

Cinema Advertising   109

Telemarketing   109

Internet Marketing   110

Conclusion   **110**

Chapter 11 – Digital Marketing   **111**

Search Engine Optimization (SEO)   **113**

Your Website's Content   114

Improving Your User Experience   114

Mastering On-page Optimization   115

Quality Links   115

Pay-Per-Click Advertising (PPC)   **115**

Search Engine Marketing (SEM)   **115**

Display Advertising   **117**

Table of Contents

Conclusion   120

Chapter 12 – Your Website   121

Start with a Basic Website   122

Being Mobile Friendly   125

Communication Tools   125

Your Domain Name   129

Hosting   129

Website Maintenance Issues   130

Search Engine Optimization (SEO)   131

Legal Considerations   132

Conclusion   133

Chapter 13 – Social Media Marketing   135

Managing Your Social Media Marketing   136

Connecting through Social Media   136

    Facebook   136

    LinkedIn   138

    Twitter   140

    Blog   141

Management Tools   141

    Social Media Checklist   143

Advertising through Social Media   144

Conclusion   148

Table of Contents

Chapter 14 – Neighborhood Marketing   **150**

Marketing with Limited Resources   **150**

    Seminars   150

    Bartering   151

    Client Refer-A-Friend Program   151

    Public Speaking   152

    Public Relations (PR) and Publicity 152

    Community Service   155

    Group Tax Program   160

    Become an Author   160

    Friends, Family, Neighbors   160

    Churches   161

    Networking   161

    Influencer Marketing   163

    Become a Connector   165

    Host an Open House   167

Conclusion   **169**

Chapter 15 – Client Retention Strategies   **171**

Distinction Between Customer and Client   **172**

Client Retention   **172**

13 Tips to Retain Your Clients and Grow Your Tax Business: **173**

Service Guarantee   **175**

Guarantee Example   **176**

Table of Contents

Positive Experience   177

Encourage Clients to File Their Tax Returns Early   177

Year-round Service   178

Year-End Tax Planning   179

Convenience (Appointments, Walk-ins, Drops Offs, Off-site)   180

Letters and Postcards   180

Essentials for Developing a Client Newsletter   181

Loyal Client Discount   182

Client Brochures   183

Giving Away Free Services and Information   183

Handling Paperwork Professionally   185

Managing Client Expectations   185

Associates' Sales Efforts   185

Phone Etiquette   186

Build Better Client Relationships During Tax Season and Beyond   187

Seven Ways to Build Client Relationships   187

How and When to Fire Problem Clients   189

Why Client Surveys are Important   192

Conclusion   193

Chapter 16 – Recruiting & Training Tax Preparers   196

Today's Personnel Challenge   196

Operating Your Own Tax School   197

Identifying the Best Tax Preparer Prospects   197

Table of Contents

Why People Skills are Paramount   197

Buy-in to Your Company Philosophy   198

Finding the Right People   198

Sources of Experienced Tax Preparers   198

Long-term Seasonal Career Candidates   199

Low-cost Ways to Recruit Tax School Students   200

How to Set Up a Tax School   205

Alternatives to Operating Your Own Income Tax School   209

Guerilla Tactics   210

Conclusion   211

Exhibit A – Tax Preparer Sample Job Description   184

Chapter 17 – Employee Pre-work Training   213

Tax Preparer Training   214

Tax Preparation and Client Interview Training   214

Providing World-Class Service   220

On the Job Training   223

Conclusion   223

Chapter 18 - Motivating & Retaining Employees   225

Tax Preparer Employment Agreements   226

Tax Preparer Compensation   227

Table of Contents

Training and Tools to do the Job   228

Company Culture   228

Benefits   228

Recognition   229

Communication   229

Having Fun to Boost Morale   229

Consider Adopting a Servant Leadership Model for Your Tax Business 232

Conclusion   233

Chapter 19 – Continuing Education   235

Preparing More Complicated Tax Returns   236

10 Reasons to Earn CE and Tax Pro Credentials   236

Tax Business Owners   240

Conclusion   241

Chapter 20 – Diversification for Year-Round Revenue   243

How Will You Earn Money After Tax Season?   244

Conclusion   248

Chapter 21 – IRS Circular 230, Due Diligence & Fraud Protection   249

Have a Set of Written Policies   250

Most Common Errors   250

The Penalties   250

Confidentiality   251

Table of Contents

Tax Preparer Circular 230 Regulations   251

Checking Tax Returns   252

Fraud   **256**

Warning Signs of Fraud   256

Verifying Taxpayer Identification Numbers   257

Signatures   **260**

IRS e-file Signature Authorization   **261**

Identity Verification Requirements   264

Acknowledgements of Transmitted Return Data   **265**

Resubmission of Rejected Tax Returns   267

Due Diligence   **267**

Suggested Additional Safeguards   **269**

Conclusion   **276**

Chapter 22 - Helping Your Clients Deal with the IRS   **277**

Examination of Returns   **278**

If You Agree   279

If You Do Not Agree   279

IRS Notices   **279**

Tips on Responding to the IRS   **284**

Payment Plans and Issues   **285**

Interest and Penalties   **286**

Payment Methods   **287**

Statutory Collection Period   **288**

Table of Contents

Bankruptcy 288

EIC and Head of Household Questionnaires 289

Tips for Clients Who are Likely to be Audited 291

Non-Filers 297

Offer in Compromise 298

Audit Preparation 302

Post-Audit Action 305

Glossary 306

Conclusion 308

Chapter 23 – Peer Support and Tax Professional Associations 309

Seeking Support and Assistance 310

Keep Abreast of Tax Industry News 310

Ways Tax Preparers Can Stay on the Cutting Edge 313

Conclusion 318

Acknowledgements

My success as a tax industry executive would not have been possible without the support of my wife, Marilyn McCabe, co-owner and Vice President of H.R. & Administration and a driving force of our family business, to whom I owe the deepest debt of gratitude. Marilyn sees all of the details to which I am oblivious.

This book reflects my four decades of tax industry experience, as well as the collective efforts of many members of our Peoples Income Tax Family, who have helped to develop systematic methods to operate and expand our successful tax business. We are making these proven methods available to readers of this book to help them achieve success as tax business owners.

The following people, who made significant contributions to our business, have also made major contributions to the creation of this book.

Terry McCabe Judge, our daughter, co-owner, and Director of Marketing & Sales for Peoples Tax and The Income Tax School, has been a driving force for the growth of our business; often by keeping me from making snap decisions that would yield negative results. I am very fortunate to have the pleasure of Terry working with me over the years. Terry has served as a contributing author, and as the primary editor of this book.

Sheila Clark, Director of The Income Tax School, and many times our unofficial staff counselor providing both business and personal support. Sheila has been a loyal colleague for more than two decades and she also served as a contributing author and assisted in editing this book.

Cathy Mueller, EA, Director of Peoples Tax & Business Services, and our "Tax Guru," who helped to write and edit early drafts of sections of this book. Cathy has also been a trusted advisor and valued confidante to me during the 25 years that we have worked together.

Ashley Ray, Social Media Manager and "Chief Blogger" for our business, who served as a contributing author of early drafts of sections of this book.

Foreword
By Roger Russell, Senior Editor for Accounting Today

It's a tough task to start a tax business on your own. However, managing a successful tax business can be enjoyable and profitable, if you know what you're doing. But getting from startup status to running a well-organized and profitable enterprise is not intuitive. At some point, the prospective preparer is likely to ask "Why doesn't somebody write a book about it?"

Well, somebody has, and that somebody is Chuck McCabe.

In this important nuts and bolts explanation, Chuck McCabe provides everything you need to know, whether you're a neophyte or a seasoned preparer. He's been there and done it all. From learning tax preparation, getting your credentials, licensing requirements, to developing a business plan and opening and running a business, pricing your services, marketing, and dealing with the IRS – it's all here, and more!

While Chuck graduated summa cum laude and #1 in his college class, and has degrees in marketing, finance, organizational development and communications, everything he teaches is the result of experience. After a series of family set-backs he cut short his education to care for his younger siblings. Only later was he able to pursue his education. As a result of a job-related railroad accident, he was temporarily disabled, which led him to take a tax course and begin working for H&R Block. He started as an entry-level tax preparer, and worked his way up to become Regional Director for H&R Block, responsible for more than 225 offices and more than 1,500 people in the New York City Region and Mid-Atlantic-Baltimore/Washington Region. Later he became chief operating officer of an H&R Block franchise in Virginia.

And then he decided to put to work the knowledge he gained working for someone else. Chuck founded Peoples Income Tax in 1987, building it to 26 offices in central Virginia. A year later, he founded The Income Tax School, initially as a means of educating his preparers, and then helping other independent tax preparation businesses. Chuck served as Chair of the Better Business Bureau of Central Virginia, and emphasizes the importance of "giving back" by providing community service while forging ties with other local businesses. A look at his Tax Business Owners blog underscores his commitment to educating and mentoring other independent business owners.

There's literally nothing he doesn't know about tax preparation as a profession and as a business, and he's put everything he knows – plus his heart and soul – into this book. It is destined to become the bible for the tax preparation business.

The Evolution of Taxation in the United States

To understand taxation, it's helpful to understand how and why taxation began in the United States.

Many taxpayers wonder how taxation began in the United States. Most think that taxation began in the 20th century, while others think that the idea of taxation is as old as the world. The truth is that taxation became a way of life in the United States after the Revolutionary War. The United States was faced with tremendous war debt and a need to create economic stability and prosperity. As a means of funding these financial issues, Congress placed an excise tax on the sale of whiskey.

Farmers in western Pennsylvania felt that their livelihoods were threatened by the tax, and many refused to pay it. As a protest to the tax, the farmers took part in the 1794 Whiskey Rebellion. President George Washington sent militias into western Pennsylvania, and the rebellion was defeated.

The Whiskey Rebellion was the first test of the government's constitutional power to tax. Some criticized Washington for sending troops to face American citizens, yet his actions enforced the Federal Government's authority. Washington made the point that the Constitution is the law of the land and must be obeyed.

Over the years that followed the Whiskey Rebellion, tariffs and taxes were placed on various goods and services. The taxes were used primarily to promote revenue for wars or national crisis. In 1862, President Abraham Lincoln and Congress passed the first federal income tax law, *The Revenue Act of 1862,* to ease the burden of the Civil War debts. *The Revenue Act of 1862,* created the nation's first Commissioner of Internal Revenue and The Bureau of Internal Revenue.

This early tax was a progressive tax. It applied only to people who earned more than $600 per year, ensuring that the tax was based on a citizens' ability to pay. The government relied on voluntary compliance with the income tax. This federal income tax provided nearly a quarter of the war revenue.

The federal income tax that resulted from *The Revenue Act of 1862* was repealed 10 years later (in 1872). The Supreme Court declared *The Revenue Act of 1862* unconstitutional in 1895. The federal income tax was later reinstated in 1913 under the 16th Amendment, which gave Congress the authority to enact an income tax. That same year, the first Form 1040 (a copy appears at the end of this chapter appeared after Congress levied a 1% tax on personal net incomes above $3,000 with a 6% surtax on incomes of more than

The Evolution of Taxation in the United States

$500,000. As the nation sought greater revenue to finance World War I, the top rate of the income tax rose to 77% in 1918. It dropped sharply in the post-war years, down to 24% in 1929, and rose again during the Depression. During World War II, Congress introduced payroll withholding and quarterly tax payments.

In the 1950s, The Bureau of Internal Revenue was reorganized to replace the patronage system (private taxation enforcement) with career professional employees. The Commissioner of Internal Revenue was replaced with an Internal Revenue Service Commissioner, who is selected by the President and confirmed by the Senate. To emphasize service to the taxpayers, the Bureau's name was changed to the Internal Revenue Service.

Since the 1950s, the Internal Revenue Service and our tax laws have undergone many changes to modernize the Service and to protect taxpayers. The tax law changes have been necessary to keep up with our nation's ever changing policies and economy. Changes will continue to be made and tax preparers will continue to have a need for continuing tax law education.

The Evolution of the Income Tax Preparation Industry

Henry and Richard Bloch can be credited with creating the mass market income tax preparation industry. Below is an excerpt from Wikipedia on the history of H&R Block.

> During World War II, Henry W. Bloch was a young Army Air Forces navigator who wanted to start a family business with his brothers in Kansas City. Home from the war in 1946, Henry saw a pamphlet suggesting a bright future for companies serving small businesses, and it fired his imagination. That year, Henry and his older brother, Leon, borrowed $5,000 and opened a small bookkeeping business on Main Street in downtown Kansas City. However, four months later, they had few clients and Leon decided to seek a law degree.

> Henry wanted to keep trying with the fledgling business and placed a newspaper ad for help-wanted.[1] He got an unexpected response—from his mother—who proposed that Henry hire his younger brother, Richard, for the job. Henry and Richard Bloch jointly ran their United Business Company, which focused on bookkeeping, but also did some income tax work for clients. The brothers found that doing taxes was time consuming

and they decided to end that type of service. One of their clients, John White, an ad salesman for The Kansas City Star newspaper, had a different idea; he suggested the Blochs make tax preparation a separate business and developed an ad announcing $5 tax services. The Blochs were not convinced, but they agreed to run the ad in January 1955. The next day, the brothers had an office full of tax clients, and H&R Block was born.

H&R Block began to expand, initially through franchising and then by the addition of many company-owned offices. Eventually, Block became a national business with thousands of company and franchise offices in every state. Block even expanded to Australia, which is one of the few countries in the World that has an income tax system similar to that of the U.S. Block also established offices on U.S. military basis worldwide. The author of this book, Chuck McCabe, co-founded the first Block offices in Brazil by opening four Block franchise offices in Sao Paulo. Over the years, many of the income tax firms that sprung up were founded by former employees of H&R Block, including Chuck McCabe, who also founded Peoples Income Tax, Inc. and The Income Tax School, Inc. (ITS). Many accounting firms derive a significant portion of their revenue from income tax preparation.

The First Form 1040 introduced in 1913, shown below, was comprised of only four pages, including one page of instructions! Today the US Tax Code includes aproximately 74,000 pages!

The Evolution of Taxation in the United States

Form 1040.

INCOME TAX.

List. No. ....

.... District of ....

Date received ....

THE PENALTY
FOR FAILURE TO HAVE THIS RETURN IN
THE HANDS OF THE COLLECTOR OF
INTERNAL REVENUE ON OR BEFORE
MARCH 1 IS $20 TO $1,000.
[SEE INSTRUCTIONS ON PAGE 4.]

File No. ....

Assessment List ....

Page .... Line ....

UNITED STATES INTERNAL REVENUE.

RETURN OF ANNUAL NET INCOME OF INDIVIDUALS.

(As provided by Act of Congress, approved October 3, 1913.)

RETURN OF NET INCOME RECEIVED OR ACCRUED DURING THE YEAR ENDED DECEMBER 31, 191 ....

(FOR THE YEAR 1913, FROM MARCH 1, TO DECEMBER 31.)

Filed by (or for) .... of ....

(Full name of individual.)   (Street and No.)

in the City, Town, or Post Office of .... State of ....

(Fill in pages 2 and 3 before making entries below.)

1. GROSS INCOME (see page 2, line 12)	$				
2. GENERAL DEDUCTIONS (see page 3, line 7)	$				
3. NET INCOME	$				

Deductions and exemptions allowed in computing income subject to the normal tax of 1 per cent.

4. Dividends and net earnings received or accrued, of corporations, etc., subject to like tax. (See page 2, line 11) . . .	$					
5. Amount of income on which the normal tax has been deducted and withheld at the source. (See page 2, line 9, column A)						
6. Specific exemption of $3,000 or $4,000, as the case may be. (See Instructions 3 and 19)						
Total deductions and exemptions. (Items 4, 5, and 6)	$					
7. TAXABLE INCOME on which the normal tax of 1 per cent is to be calculated. (See Instruction 3) .	$					

8. When the net income shown above on line 3 exceeds $20,000, the additional tax thereon must be calculated as per schedule below:

						INCOME.				TAX.			
1	per cent on amount over $20,000 and not exceeding $50,000 .	$						$			
2	"	"	50,000	"	"	75,000 .							
3	"	"	75,000	"	"	100,000 .							
4	"	"	100,000	"	"	250,000 .							
5	"	"	250,000	"	"	500,000 .							
6	"	"	500,000									

Total additional or super tax	$			
Total normal tax (1 per cent of amount entered on line 7) . .	$			
Total tax liability	$			

GROSS INCOME.

This statement must show in the proper spaces the entire amount of gains, profits, and income received by or accrued to the individual from all sources during the year specified on page 1.

DESCRIPTION OF INCOME.	A. Amount of income on which tax has been deducted and withheld at the source.				B. Amount of income on which tax has NOT been deducted and withheld at the source.			
1. Total amount derived from salaries, wages, or compensation for personal service of whatever kind and in whatever form paid	$				$			
2. Total amount derived from professions, vocations, businesses, trade, commerce, or sales or dealings in property, whether real or personal, growing out of the ownership or use of interest in real or personal property, including bonds, stocks, etc.								
3. Total amount derived from rents and from interest on notes, mortgages, and securities (other than reported on lines 5 and 6)								
4. Total amount of gains and profits derived from partnership business, whether the same be divided and distributed or not								
5. Total amount of fixed and determinable annual gains, profits, and income derived from interest upon bonds and mortgages or deeds of trust, or other similar obligations of corporations, joint-stock companies or associations, and insurance companies, whether payable annually or at shorter or longer periods								
6. Total amount of income derived from coupons, checks, or bills of exchange for or in payment of interest upon bonds issued in *foreign countries* and upon *foreign mortgages* or like obligations (not payable in the United States), and also from coupons, checks, or bills of exchange for or in payment of any dividends upon the stock or interest upon the obligations of foreign corporations, associations, and insurance companies engaged in business in foreign countries								
7. Total amount of income received from fiduciaries								
8. Total amount of income derived from any source whatever, not specified or entered elsewhere on this page								
9. TOTALS								
NOTES.—Enter total of Column A on line 5 of first page.								
10. AGGREGATE TOTALS OF COLUMNS A AND B					$			
11. Total amount of income derived from dividends on the stock or from the net earnings of corporations, joint-stock companies, associations, or insurance companies subject to like tax (To be entered on line 4 of first page.)					$			
12. TOTAL "Gross Income" (to be entered on line 1 of first page)					$			

The Evolution of Taxation in the United States

3

GENERAL DEDUCTIONS.

1. The amount of necessary expenses actually paid in carrying on business, but not including business expenses of partnerships, and not including personal, living, or family expenses .	$	....	....	....
2. All interest paid within the year on personal indebtedness of taxpayer	....	....	....	....
3. All national, State, county, school, and municipal taxes paid within the year (not including those assessed against local benefits)	....	....	....	....
4. Losses actually sustained during the year incurred in trade or arising from fires, storms, or shipwreck, and not compensated for by insurance or otherwise	....	....	....	....
5. Debts due which have been actually ascertained to be worthless and which have been charged off within the year	....	....	....	....
6. Amount representing a reasonable allowance for the exhaustion, wear, and tear of property arising out of its use or employment in the business, not to exceed, in the case of mines, 5 per cent of the gross value at the mine of the output for the year for which the computation is made, but no deduction shall be made for any amount of expense of restoring property or making good the exhaustion thereof, for which an allowance is or has been made . . .	....	....	....	....
7. Total "GENERAL DEDUCTIONS" (to be entered on line 2 of first page)	....	....	....	....

AFFIDAVIT TO BE EXECUTED BY INDIVIDUAL MAKING HIS OWN RETURN.

I solemnly swear (or affirm) that the foregoing return, to the best of my knowledge and belief, contains a true and complete statement of all gains, profits, and income received by or accrued to me during the year for which the return is made, and that I am entitled to all the deductions and exemptions entered or claimed therein, under the Federal Income-tax Law of October 3, 1913.

Sworn to and subscribed before me this ....

day of .... , 191

SEAL OF OFFICER TAKING AFFIDAVIT.	....
	(Official capacity.)

....
(Signature of individual.)

AFFIDAVIT TO BE EXECUTED BY DULY AUTHORIZED AGENT MAKING RETURN FOR INDIVIDUAL.

I solemnly swear (or affirm) that I have sufficient knowledge of the affairs and property of .... to enable me to make a full and complete return thereof, and that the foregoing return, to the best of my knowledge and belief, contains a true and complete statement of all gains, profits, and income received by or accrued to said individual during the year for which the return is made, and that the said individual is entitled, under the Federal Income-tax Law of October 3, 1913, to all the deductions and exemptions entered or claimed therein.

Sworn to and subscribed before me this ....

day of .... , 191

....
(Signature of agent.)

ADDRESS IN FULL {
....
....

SEAL OF OFFICER TAKING AFFIDAVIT.	....
	(Official capacity.)

[SEE INSTRUCTIONS ON BACK OF THIS PAGE.]

X

INSTRUCTIONS.

1. This return shall be made by every citizen of the United States, whether residing at home or abroad, and by every person residing in the United States, though not a citizen thereof, having a *net income* of $3,000 or over for the taxable year, and *also* by every *nonresident alien* deriving income from property owned and business, trade, or profession carried on *in the United States* by him.

2. When an individual by reason of minority, sickness or other disability, or absence from the United States, is unable to make his own return, it may be made for him by his *duly authorized* representative.

3. The *normal tax* of 1 per cent shall be assessed on the total net income less the specific exemption of $3,000 or $4,000 as the case may be. (For the year 1913, the specific exemption allowable is $2,500 or $3,333.33, as the case may be.) If, however, the normal tax has been deducted and withheld on any part of the income at the source, or if any part of the income is received as dividends upon the stock or from the net earnings of any corporation, etc., which is taxable upon its net income, such income shall be deducted from the individual's total *net income* for the purpose of calculating the amount of income on which the individual is liable for the normal tax of 1 per cent by virtue of this return. (See page 1, line 7.)

4. The *additional or super tax* shall be calculated as stated on page 1.

5. This return shall be filed with the Collector of Internal Revenue for the district in which the individual resides if he has no other place of business, otherwise in the district in which he has his *principal place of business;* or in case the person resides in a foreign country, then with the collector for the district in which his principal business is carried on in the United States.

6. This return must be filed on or before the first day of March succeeding the close of the calendar year for which return is made.

7. The *penalty for failure to file the return within the time specified by law* is $20 to $1,000. In case of refusal or neglect to render the return within the required time (except in cases of sickness or absence), 50 per cent shall be added to amount of tax assessed. In case of *false or fraudulent return,* 100 per cent shall be added to such tax, and any person required by law to make, render, sign, or verify any return who makes any false or fraudulent return or statement with intent to defeat or evade the assessment required by this section to be made shall be guilty of a misdemeanor, and shall be fined not exceeding $2,000 or be imprisoned not exceeding one year, or both, at the discretion of the court, with the costs of prosecution.

8. When the return is not filed within the required time by reason of sickness or absence of the individual, an extension of time, not exceeding 30 days from March 1, within which to file such return, *may be* granted by the collector, *provided* an application therefor is made by the individual within the period for which such extension is desired.

9. This return properly filled out must be made under oath or affirmation. Affidavits may be made before any officer *authorized by law* to administer oaths. If before a justice of the peace or magistrate; not using a seal, a *certificate of the clerk of the court as to the authority* of such officer to administer oaths should be *attached to the return.*

10. Expense for medical attendance, store accounts, family supplies, wages of domestic servants, cost of board, room, or house rent for family or personal use, *are not expenses that can be deducted from gross income.* In case an individual owns his own residence he can not deduct the estimated value of his rent, neither shall he be required to include such estimated rental of his home as income.

11. The farmer, in computing the net income from his farm for his annual return, shall include all moneys received for produce and animals sold, and for the wool and hides of animals slaughtered, provided such wool and hides are sold, and he shall deduct therefrom the sums actually paid as purchase money for the animals sold or slaughtered during the year.

When animals were raised by the owner and are sold or slaughtered he shall not deduct their value as expenses or loss. He may deduct the amount of money actually paid as expense for producing any farm products, live stock, etc. In deducting expenses for repairs on farm property the amount deducted must not exceed the amount actually expended for such repairs during the year for which the return is made. (See page 3, item 6.) The cost of replacing tools or machinery is a deductible expense to the extent that the cost of the new articles does not exceed the value of the old.

12. In calculating losses, only such losses as shall have been actually sustained and the amount of which has been definitely ascertained during the year covered by the return can be deducted.

13. Persons receiving fees or emoluments for professional or other services, as in the case of physicians or lawyers, should include all actual receipts for services rendered in the year for which return is made, together with all unpaid accounts, charges for services, or contingent income due for that year, if good and collectible.

14. Debts which were contracted during the year for which return is made, but found in said year to be worthless, may be deducted from gross income for said year, but such debts can not be regarded as worthless until after legal proceedings to recover the same have proved fruitless, or it clearly appears that the debtor is insolvent. If debts contracted prior to the year for which return is made were included as income in return for year in which said debts were contracted, and such debts shall subsequently prove to be worthless, they may be deducted under the head of losses in the return for the year in which such debts were charged off as worthless.

15. Amounts due or accrued to the individual members of a partnership from the net earnings of the partnership, whether apportioned and distributed or not, shall be included in the annual return of the individual.

16. United States pensions shall be included as income.

17. Estimated advance in value of real estate is not required to be reported as income, unless the increased value is taken up on the books of the individual as an increase of assets.

18. Costs of suits and other legal proceedings arising from ordinary business may be treated as an expense of such business, and may be deducted from gross income for the year in which such costs were paid.

19. An unmarried individual or a married individual not living with wife or husband shall be allowed an exemption of $3,000. When husband and wife live together they shall be allowed jointly a total exemption of only $4,000 on their aggregate income. They may make a joint return, both subscribing thereto, or if they have separate incomes, they may make separate returns; but in no case shall they jointly claim more than $4,000 exemption on their aggregate income.

20. In computing net income there shall be excluded the compensation of all officers and employees of a State or any political subdivision thereof, except when such compensation is paid by the United States Government.

Introduction

During the past 40+ years, I have managed hundreds of income tax preparation offices, both directly, and indirectly through colleagues working with me. Throughout these decades, our team has developed and adopted numerous proven best practices, and employed them to achieve success both professionally and systematically.

Since founding Peoples Income Tax in 1987, we have helped thousands of people become independent tax business owners and achieve their own business success in this rewarding profession. We have helped these tax entrepreneurs by enabling them to adopt the proven best practices comparable to those used by the national tax firms.

Accounting Today has kindly recognized me for multiple years in their "Top 100 Most Influential People in Accounting." Their foundation for this recognition is: "As a veteran in the tax preparation industry, McCabe had the vision to offer support to other tax business owners who opt to remain independent by providing them with tax education and business skills so they can be successful on their own."

The Income Tax School

In September, 1988, one year after founding Peoples Income Tax, I founded The Income Tax School as a division of Peoples Income Tax. The sole purpose of the tax school was to train tax preparers to work for Peoples Income Tax. The following year, our tax software sales representative noted that there was no other independent tax firm that had a tax school comparable to that of H&R Block. He suggested making this best practice available to other independent tax firms. Soon after, we began packaging our basic tax course with an instructor guide and a Tax School Operations Manual, and licensing this turn-key system to tax firms nationwide. Over the next several years, we added an advanced individual tax course and a small business tax course to teach corporate and partnership tax preparation. We supported more than 150 tax business owners nationwide with this best practice in just our first few years.

In 2003, I decided we needed to start teaching students directly, nationwide, through eLearning, to enable more people to become employed or self-employed as tax professionals. We continued to add tax courses and Continuing Education (CE) seminars, as well as more students and more tax school licensees. The Income Tax School, Inc. (ITS), now a separate legal entity, also became a publisher with an in-house print shop. ITS is now a private career school certified by the State Council of Higher Education for Virginia (SCHEV). ITS educates thousands of students annually in every state and more than a dozen foreign countries where U.S. expatriates need tax services. We also partner with colleges and career schools, in addition to other tax industry vendors.

Introduction

Tax Practice Management

As time went on, we also developed a set of four comprehensive Tax Practice Management Manuals (TPMs) for independent tax business owners, and a smaller set of business start-up guides for home-based tax businesses. Our TPMs cover Tax Office Operations, Marketing, Personnel, and Expansion.

The Mission of this Book

During a recent strategic planning session, our management team adopted the following mission statement for ITS. ***We empower people with a professional career to fulfill their dreams and serve others as industry leaders.*** We hope that this book will help us fulfil our mission of enabling you to succeed as a tax entrepreneur!

One thing I have learned is that there is no need to "reinvent the wheel." This book is a practical, comprehensive guide that is beneficial for all entrepreneurs planning to operate as either a sole-tax practitioner or a tax business owner employing other tax preparers. Throughout this book, you will learn many best practices that will save you time and money, and help you grow a successful tax business.

Note: Purchasers of this guide who would like to also purchase the full set of four TPMs can request a credit for the price of this book to be used toward the purchase of the TPMs.

Chapter 1

Learning Tax Preparation and Obtaining Credentials

66 *Over and over again courts have said that there is nothing sinister in so arranging one's affairs so as to make taxes as low as possible. Everybody does so, rich or poor, and do right, for nobody owes any public duty to pay more taxes than the law demands. Taxes are enforced exactions, not voluntary contributions.* 99

- Justice Learned Hand,
U.S. Court of Appeals for the Second Circuit

Chapter 1 – Learning Tax Preparation & Obtaining Credentials

Your Purpose and Role as a Tax Preparer

Some people think being a tax preparer is a boring and tedious job that involves just working with numbers and dealing with confusing tax laws. In reality, working as a tax preparer is a very interesting and personally gratifying job. Our U.S. tax laws are currently designed to ensure that all taxpayers pay their fair share to help enable our federal government to operate and provide for our national security and the services and infrastructure we collectively use and need to maintain our quality of life.

As you learn more about the IRS tax code, you will realize that many tax laws that have been enacted by Congress over the years were designed to get U.S. citizens and businesses to behave in ways desired by our representatives who introduced the tax laws, or to provide financial assistance to those in need. Every tax law that is part of our massive tax code was logical to the representative(s) who introduced the tax law, but not necessarily logical to others. However, many tax laws are no longer logical to anyone because conditions today are different than when the tax law was enacted. Nevertheless, the United States, despite all of its shortcomings, is still the best place in the world to live. Our responsibility as U.S. citizens is to pay our fair share of income tax, and no more than that. Famous U.S. Court of Appeals Judge, Learned Hand, once said: "Over and over again courts have said that there is nothing sinister in so arranging one's affairs so as to make taxes as low as possible. Everybody does so, rich or poor, and do right, for nobody owes any public duty to pay more taxes than the law demands. Taxes are enforced exactions, not voluntary contributions." Our job as tax preparers is to make sure that our clients pay only their least legitimate tax; no more and no less.

As a tax preparer, you are helping your clients by making a dreaded task much easier for them, and, possibly even making the process a pleasant experience. You are providing your clients with the peace-of-mind in knowing that you will ensure they pay their least legitimate tax, as well as stand behind your work and be there for them should they hear from the IRS. You will develop relationships with your clients as they return year-after-year. Your clients will trust you with their personal, family, and financial information. They will  look forward to seeing you and you will look forward to serving them as their trusted confidant and advisor.

Chapter 1 – Learning Tax Preparation & Obtaining Credentials

Start with the Basics

Many options are available to learn income tax preparation. You might be planning to prepare only individual Form 1040 tax returns, more complex individual returns, small business corporations and partnerships, or all of the above. In any case, you must begin by learning the basics. Learning income tax is like learning math. You must have a solid foundation of basic tax knowledge before you can move on to more advanced tax subjects. United States income tax laws are extremely complex. No one can know all of the tax laws. When studying income tax and gaining experience over the years, you will come to understand that the more you learn, the more you realize how little you know. You will only retain the tax laws by preparing tax returns involving those laws. By applying what you learn in a tax course, you will internalize that knowledge. A good tax course will require you to complete tax return problems and prepare sample tax returns -- manually. Yes, the old pencil and paper method. If you prepare sample tax returns in the course using tax preparation software, you will not learn the tax laws because the tax software will make decisions for you.

Federal and State Education Requirements

Most taxpayers are unaware of the fact that there is currently no mandatory national licensing of tax preparers. Only three states require tax preparers to take a test and continue their education – California, Maryland, and Oregon. This means that there is no universal standard for tax preparers currently.

California and Oregon	If you plan to practice in California or Oregon, you must complete a Qualifying Course from an authorized provider such as The Income Tax School (ITS). The state Qualifying Course will include both federal and state curriculum. If you plan to practice in any other state, it is unlikely you will find a course that includes instruction in the tax laws of your state. However, you can learn the state tax laws while you are learning the federal laws by obtaining the state income tax instructions and preparing the state return for each federal return you prepare. Most state tax returns start with the Form 1040 results and may make additions and subtractions in income, deductions, exemptions, and tax credits to arrive at the state tax liability.
Maryland	Although a tax course is not required in Maryland, individual tax preparers are required to pass a Maryland Individual Tax Preparers examination, register for an IRS PTIN annually, register with Maryland and complete at least 16 hours of continuing professional education bi-annually.
	(Continued on next page)

Chapter 1 – Learning Tax Preparation & Obtaining Credentials

New York	If you think you will be paid to prepare at least one New York State tax return, or help to issue or administer a refund anticipation check for New York, you must register with New York State as a commercial tax return preparer and pay a $100 fee -- regardless of whether or not you live or work in New York. This is an annual registration. New York also has continuing education requirements for paid tax return preparers.

Over time, more states may enact some form of regulation or registration of tax preparers.

Voluntary IRS Regulations

The IRS does not currently require education for tax preparers to practice. However, the IRS does offer a voluntary education program, the Annual Filing Season Program (AFSP). This program provides important privileges and benefits not available to tax preparers who do not participate. The AFSP is described in detail later in this chapter.

Tax Education Options

Historically, many people who decide to become tax preparers have learned tax preparation by taking a tax course offered by one of the national tax firms. However, more recently, the national tax firms require that their students make a legal and binding commitment in writing to work for the tax firm if employment is offered. They will not admit someone to their tax course who does not meet their criteria to qualify for employment and make a commitment. Some people who plan to become self-employed as tax preparers will work for one of the national tax firms for a year or two to learn more about tax preparation and the tax business and then go out on their own. If you choose this option, you will likely be required to sign a non compete agreement that will keep you from soliciting and preparing tax returns for any of your clients from the company for about two years after you stop working there.

Today you have more options. Now many people have the choice to take a live course or an online course. A live course in tax preparation, other than those offered by national tax firms, may not be available in your community. The most likely option would be a community college or workforce development program, or a local provider of adult education that might be offered by your local government or a non-profit organization, or possibly the local state chapter of a tax professional association. However, you should make sure the course teaches practical application of tax preparation by requiring that tax return

Chapter 1 – Learning Tax Preparation & Obtaining Credentials

problems are prepared manually. Also, make sure that the tax course covers Form 1040 and all related schedules and statements. A live class typically takes about 45 hours of classroom instruction (e.g., sixteen 3-hour lessons) to cover all the necessary topics. This does not include homework reading and tax return practice assignments, which typically require about two hours for each hour of classroom instruction.

Advantages of Learning Tax Preparation Online

In our connected world, where most of us spend several hours a day online doing everything from shopping to banking, eLearning is a great way to get the education you need at your own pace and schedule. While some people may shy away from this method of learning, there are many advantages to eLearning that live instruction cannot offer. Below are advantages of learning online compared to classroom instruction.

- **Flexibility**

    If you only have an hour a day to get some learning time in, a live class probably won't work for you. If you prefer to work through your course early in the morning or late at night, more than likely, a live class won't be available at that time. With online courses, you can start anytime, and study at your own pace — 24/7, from anywhere with internet access.

- **Immediate Feedback**

    If you hate having to wait until the next class to find out how you did on a quiz or exam, online learning might be right up your alley. There's no waiting when it comes to eLearning. Quizzes, exams and homework assignments are automatically graded as soon as you complete them online. Some schools, such as ITS go a step further and provide instructional feedback to explain the right answers when wrong answers are chosen.

- **Convenience and Comfort**

    You don't have to leave your home to study for an online course. There is no getting up early to prepare for a morning class or staying out late for an evening class. No crowded classrooms or uncomfortable chairs that leave you with back pain at the end of the day. Sitting at a desk is optional – you can even study while relaxing in your bedroom or sitting in your favorite easy chair! Or you can head to your favorite coffee shop or community library to get in a few hours of study time. There is a long list of conveniences.

- **Resources**

  Aside from the course material, many online schools provide a student resource center with valuable information and FAQs, as well as a Student Forum for interaction with other students. Some schools, including ITS, also have a Career Center with links to job opportunities.

- **Responsive Instructor Support**

  With most traditional classrooms, if you need help from the instructor, you must schedule a time or come by during "office hours". At ITS, instructors are available by email to answer questions and generally reply within 24 hours during normal business hours. Phone support can also be arranged for more difficult topics. Students give ITS instructors top grades.

- **Cost Savings**

  There are also many savings to eLearning! You'll save money on gas and tolls by not incurring the expense to drive or take public transportation to a classroom location. Online tuition is also significantly lower than typical live classes. The ITS student text is provided online at no additional cost. So, it's not necessary to buy the hard copy of the text. However, a hard copy of the student text may be available for an affordable price. Most ITS students choose to purchase the hard copy of the text, which provides convenience and a future reference.

- **Online courses look great on your resume**

  With these great advantages, you can't go wrong with an eLearning option to meet your tax preparation education needs.

Chapter 1 – Learning Tax Preparation & Obtaining Credentials

Important Numbers You Will Need as a Tax Preparer

PTIN Number, For All Tax Preparers

PTIN stands for Preparer Tax Identification Number. This number is required by the IRS for anyone who prepares or assists in preparing federal tax returns for compensation.

Check out the IRS PTIN Application Checklist on the IRS website, https://www.irs.gov to find out more. You may apply and obtain a PTIN online before taking or completing a tax course.

EFIN Number, For Self-Employed Tax Preparers

Before you plan to electronically file tax returns as a self-employed tax preparer, you must also apply to become an authorized e-file provider with the IRS.

Once approved, you'll be given an IRS Electronic Filing Identification Number (EFIN) so you can e-file tax returns.

The Voluntary IRS Annual Filing Season Program (AFSP)

The voluntary IRS Annual Filing Season Program (AFSP) is intended to encourage non-credentialed tax return preparers to take continuing education (CE) courses to increase their knowledge and improve their filing season readiness. Participation requires 18 hours of CE, which includes a six (6) hour Annual Federal Tax Refresher (AFTR) course in basic tax filing issues and tax law updates, two (2) hours of ethics, as well as ten (10) hours of other federal tax law topics. If you are not an Enrolled Agent, an attorney, or a CPA, you should seriously consider participating in the voluntary IRS Annual Filing Season Program (AFSP).

The IRS launched the voluntary Annual Filing Season Program in 2015 as a way to "encourage continuing education (CE) and filing season readiness." According to an IRS release, 44,000 tax return preparers participated in the program in 2016. Here are some good reasons why you should consider the AFSP:

- **FREE Marketing to Taxpayers by the IRS**

  All tax return preparers who successfully complete the AFSP are listed on the IRS Federal Tax Return Preparers Directory, along with Enrolled Agents, CPAs and attorneys who have obtained an EFIN to prepare tax returns. This list is marketed by the IRS to taxpayers through a public education campaign.

  The campaign encourages taxpayers to select return preparers carefully and seek those with professional credentials or other select qualifications. This directory is provided by the IRS to help taxpayers determine who is qualified to prepare their taxes and is a practical tool for the millions of Americans who rely on the services of a paid return preparer.

- **Representing Your Clients**

  Annual Filing Season Program participants have limited representation rights. These rights give unenrolled tax preparers the ability to represent clients whose returns they prepared and signed, but only before revenue agents, customer service representatives, and similar IRS employees, including the Taxpayer Advocate Service. PTIN holders without an AFSP Record of Completion or other professional credential are only permitted to prepare tax returns. Think about that for a minute. If you cannot represent your client when they need you most, you could lose them to a competitor who can!

  An unenrolled return preparer is an individual other than an attorney, CPA, enrolled agent, enrolled retirement plan agent, or enrolled actuary who prepares and signs a taxpayer's return as the paid preparer, or who prepares a return but is not required (by the instructions to the return or regulations) to sign the return. (Attorneys, CPAs, and EAs continue with *unlimited* representation rights, and may represent their clients on any matters including audits, payment and/or collection issues, and appeals. To earn any of these three designations, you must pass a complex exam or series of exams and complete continuing education requirements each year.)

- **Promotion of Your Qualifications from the IRS**

  Upon completion of the IRS Annual Filing Season Program, you will receive a "Record of Completion." This provides you with a great way to promote your qualifications as a tax preparer. Completing the voluntary program will give you the ability to market yourself as a credentialed preparer. One way to promote that you have completed the program is by adding, "as seen on IRS.gov" to your email signature, business cards, or other promotional materials.

Chapter 1 – Learning Tax Preparation & Obtaining Credentials

- **You Set Yourself Apart**

  Taking the AFSP will allow you to prove that you are a qualified preparer. There are over 400,000 tax preparers, many of them choose not to complete the program. You can easily set yourself apart and have the means to show that you are qualified to prepare tax returns by completing the program, receiving your Record of Completion, and adding your name to the official IRS Directory.

- **The Education is Important**

  The program is a short refresher course that includes continuing education that you *should* be completing to better serve your clients. Why not get it done?

Things to Remember about the AFSP

- **Don't Miss the Deadline**

  The AFSP must be completed annually by December 31.

- **Be Sure to Sign the Circular 230 consent?**

  You must sign the Circular 230 consent – something you need to do in order to obtain your Record of Completion. It's a simple step that some people forget to do!

- **What is the Circular 230?**

  Circular 230, Regulations Governing Practice Before the Internal Revenue Service, contains rules governing attorneys, certified public accountants, enrolled agents, enrolled retirement plan agents, AFSP registered tax return preparers, and other persons representing taxpayers before the Internal Revenue Service.

- **Receive Your Record of Completion**

  The IRS Record of Completion is given once a tax preparer has completed the IRS Annual Filing Season Program (AFSP), set-up or renewed their PTIN, and signed the Circular 230 consent. Remember, the program was put in place to help reduce the number of unqualified preparers through education and testing. All tax return preparers who successfully complete the AFSP will be listed on the IRS Federal

Chapter 1 – Learning Tax Preparation & Obtaining Credentials

Tax Return Preparers Directory. The directory is there to help taxpayers determine who is qualified to prepare their taxes.

The Big Tax Preparer Myth

Many taxpayers with complex individual or small business tax returns think they need a Certified Public Accountant (CPA) to prepare their returns. However, tax is not accounting; it is law. Some CPAs specialize in tax but not all of them do. CPAs by definition are accountants and they typically do not learn the practical  application of preparing tax returns in accounting school. CPAs often learn practical income tax preparation by taking courses from income tax schools such as ITS, which is registered with the National Association of State Boards of Accountancy (NASBA) as a sponsor of Continuing Professional Education (CPE) for CPAs.

Tax Industry Credentials

There are several designations in the tax industry including the Certified Public Accountant (CPA), IRS Enrolled Agent (EA), and The Income Tax School's Chartered Tax Professional (CTP). All require testing and have continuing education requirements that tax professionals must meet in order to maintain their credentials.

The IRS Enrolled Agent (EA), considered the most significant professional credential in the tax preparation industry, is a designation awarded by the IRS to a person who has passed an intensive three-part exam administered for the IRS. This exam, also known as the IRS Special Enrollment Exam (SEE), must be passed to become an EA. The EA exam encompasses individual, corporation and partnership taxation, as well as IRS Due Diligence regulations. In comparison, the 4-part CPA Exam includes three parts of accounting and one-part income tax, primarily on corporate tax and tax theory. Some CPAs also become EAs. Becoming an EA provides many benefits and is a goal many tax preparers should aspire to attain.

Chapter 1 – Learning Tax Preparation & Obtaining Credentials

The Benefits of Becoming an IRS Enrolled Agent

Here are some of the many reasons to pursue your EA designation.

- **Unlimited Representation Rights**

    Unrolled Agents have unlimited representation rights; meaning they can represent their clients before the IRS on any matters including audits, payment/collection issues, and appeals. As IRS examinations are on the rise, and people are in need of representation for delinquent tax obligations or IRS collection activities, the need for Enrolled Agents has increased. Unenrolled  tax preparers without credentials are only permitted to represent a client whose tax return they have prepared and signed. And that is only if they have completed the IRS Annual Filing Season Program.

- **Prepare More Complicated Returns**

    As an EA, your earning potential is much higher because you have the knowledge to prepare more complicated tax returns. The credentials allow you to offer a wider range of services that include helping people with audits, representing clients at an IRS appeals office, preparing and filing documents on a client's behalf, corresponding directly with the IRS, attending hearings and conferences on behalf of your client, and providing written advice to third parties on the tax implications of business transactions.

- **IRS Examinations Are Up**

    The IRS has really started to increase the number of examinations they perform each season. This means that there is greater need for EAs as more people are being audited each year. Providing taxpayer representation services can also constitute a source of off-season revenue.

Chapter 1 – Learning Tax Preparation & Obtaining Credentials

- **Increase Your Credibility**

  Because the Enrolled Agent designation is the highest credential you can earn in this industry, you have more credibility as a tax preparer who has gone through a considerable amount of training and passed the Special Enrollment Examination (SEE).

- **Listing as an EA in Directories**

  Enrolled Agents are designated and listed as such on the IRS Federal Tax Return Preparers Directory. You can also join the National Association of Enrolled Agents (NAEA) http://www.naea.org, and be included in their searchable "Find Tax Experts Near You" directory of EAs, including specializations.

- **Be in Good Standing with the IRS**

  The IRS regulations on tax preparers are constantly changing. As an EA, you won't have to worry about future required credentials because you will already have them. As an EA, you do not have to take the IRS Annual Federal Tax Refresher Course to be listed in their National Database list of credentialed preparers, you are automatically included. Your only requirement is to complete continuing education.

About the IRS Special Enrollment Exam (SEE)

The IRS Special Enrollment Exam (SEE) is a three-part comprehensive IRS test that covers all aspects of federal taxation. The SEE also covers tax preparer responsibilities under IRS Circular 230. If you are getting ready to take the exam, thinking about taking the exam or in the midst of studying for the exam, here are some **study tips** to help you along the way.

1. Put together a study plan that covers all tax topics on the Special Enrollment Exam. This includes Individual Tax, Business Tax, Representation, and Practice and Procedures.

2. The exam is broken into three parts. You can study and test for each part one at a time and in any order you like. Once you pass one section, you have two years from that date to complete and pass the remaining two sections.

3. Do not cram. Start your studying early and pace yourself – cramming all of that information into a few massive study sessions will not help you retain the knowledge you need and may add stress and anxiety. Added anxiety never helps on test day, so make sure you take the time to prepare yourself for test day.

4. Find a study group. Meetup.com is a great place to search. You could also try looking in Google+ communities.

5. Study the old IRS Exam tests posted on the IRS website. They will help you get an idea for how the exam is structured, the topics that are covered and the way the questions are posed. Although these exams don't represent the current EA Exam – they can be a tremendous help. You can download old exams on the IRS website https://www.irs.gov/.

6. Don't underestimate the Representation, and Practice and Procedures sections. Read the entire Circular 230. There are sections in the test that are drawn from that document.

7. Go to the Thomson Prometric website: https://www.prometric.com/test-takers/search/irs, register, and download the recommended reading/study list.

8. Consider going through the ITS Chartered Tax Professional Program. If you are just getting started as a tax professional, then you might want to take some tax education classes.

9. Consider an Enrolled Agent exam review course, which is available through ITS. You can purchase the entire EA review, or you can purchase one part at a time. https://www.theincometaxschool.com/continuing-education/ea-review/

Chapter 1 – Learning Tax Preparation & Obtaining Credentials

The Perfect Pathway to Becoming an Enrolled Agent

If you are looking for a way to increase your knowledge in order to serve more taxpayers but aren't ready to take the SEE to become an EA, you might consider The Income Tax School's Chartered Tax Certificate Programs. These options are unique because they give you the opportunity to earn money as a tax professional while you study. This enables you to internalize the knowledge by applying what you learn, and in turn, will make you an even better tax preparer! You can begin preparing tax returns for the public after the Comprehensive Tax Course, which is the first course in any of the three Chartered Tax Certificate Programs.

- https://www.theincometaxschool.com/product/comprehensive-tax-course/

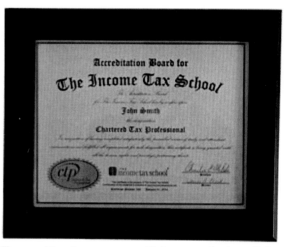

The ITS Chartered Tax Certificate Programs are the ideal pathway to becoming an EA. You can earn prestigious tax credentials such as the Chartered Tax Professional (CTP). It's possible to start with just the beginner, Comprehensive Tax Course, or a shorter certificate program, such as the Chartered Tax Advisor (CTA) or Chartered Tax Consultant (CTC), with the option to upgrade later. The CTP program provides the perfect pathway if you are considering preparing for the coveted IRS Enrolled Agent (EA) credential. It covers most of the topics on the SEE exam. With the knowledge from the CTP program, plus an EA Exam Review, you will be ready to sit for the SEE exam. Your clients will have more confidence in you, and you will stand out from your competitors, who lack credentials. A certificate of completion for your courses can be framed for you to display on your office wall. Graduates of the CTA, CTC, and CTP certificate programs are also provided with a framed certificate to make clients aware of the attainment of their professional designation.

There are so many tax preparers that simply "hang a shingle" and start preparing taxes with very little tax knowledge. Set yourself apart this tax season by going beyond the required PTIN with increased tax education and certificates to show for it.

Learn more about the pathway to becoming an Enrolled Agent:

- https://www.theincometaxschool.com/continuing-education/your-pathway-to-becoming-an-enrolled-agent/

Chapter 1 – Learning Tax Preparation & Obtaining Credentials

How to Succeed as an Enrolled Agent

Earning a credential is a significant accomplishment. Once you've earned a designation, the work is not over. Clients and employers will not just begin magically calling you. Here are 3 ways to leverage your new status to gain clients.

Put it on everything

After working so hard to earn that credential, and then maintaining that status through continuing your education each year, you will want to make sure everyone knows about it by adding your credential to things like:

- Business cards
- Email signature
- LinkedIn profile
- Hang your certificate in your office
- Flyers and marketing materials
- Your website

Educate Your Current and Potential Clients

Most people do not really know that there are different types of tax preparers and what those different types even mean. It's important that you communicate the difference and explain your qualifications. There are several ways you can do this:

- Explain what your status means on your website
- Add a line to your business card. For example, if you become an EA, add something like "EA, unlimited IRS representation rights"
- Explain the designation on your LinkedIn profile
- Include information about the designation on promotional materials

Important things to communicate would be the level of education you received, what type of representation rights you have and what it means for your clients, along with any ethical standards you're required to adhere to.

Market your services to people with more complicated forms

As a CTP or an EA (or both), your tax knowledge will go well beyond Form 1040EZ. While you don't want to turn anyone away, it's more lucrative to market your services to individual and small business taxpayers with more complicated tax situations. The more complicated the form, the more money you can charge. You will have a more successful tax season if you market your expertise to clients who really need your services rather than clients who are more likely to self-prepare and file using tax software.

There is a shortage of qualified tax preparers. Make your qualifications known and you will be sure to succeed. Many independent tax businesses are seeking experienced tax preparers who also meet their other employment criteria, such as having good people skills, a good attitude and work ethic, as well as the ability to instill confidence in their clients and to work effectively with other employees as a team player.

As Benjamin Franklin said, "In this world, nothing can be said to be certain except death and taxes." Therefore, there will always be a need for competent tax professionals.

Conclusion

Tax preparation is a very rewarding profession. Your role as a tax preparer is to ensure that your clients pay the least legitimate tax, while also making their tax preparation experience as pleasant as possible. Your clients also take comfort in knowing you will be available to help should the IRS contact them. You must decide what type(s) of taxpayers you will serve, and then obtain the appropriate level of education from a reputable source. There are many advantage to e-learning. To learn the tax law, you must prepare tax return assignments without the aid of tax software. Only California and Oregon require tax preparers to complete qualifying education. If you are not a CPA or attorney, you should consider earning a tax professional credential to obtain a major competitive advantage. The Enrolled Agent designation is the most significant credential in the tax industry. The Chartered Tax certificate programs from The Income Tax School provide an excellent pathway to become an EA, while earning a professional credential in the process. Unless you are a CPA or EA, participating in the voluntary IRS Annual Filing Season Program provides important benefits and should be given very serious consideration. To practice as a tax preparer, you will also need to apply to the IRS for a PTIN, and if you plan to be self-employed, you will need an EFIN to be able to e-file tax returns.

Chapter 2

Developing A Business Plan

"By failing to prepare, you are preparing to fail."

- Benjamin Franklin

Chapter 2 – Developing a Business Plan

Why a Business Plan?

Why should you, as an entrepreneur, spend many hours of your scarce time developing a written business plan? After all, you have a vision for your company and your plan is in your head.

One good reason is to ensure that someone else can pick up the ball and run with it if something happens to you. But even with you in the picture, you should develop a written business plan for the following reasons:

1. Putting your plan in writing causes you to think through every aspect of your business, thereby enabling you to identify and clarify obstacles and opportunities, determine areas in which you need professional help, set goals, and refine strategies and tactics.
2. It provides a clear action plan for you to follow.
3. Communicating your vision to your associates is essential for them to make meaningful contributions to the business.
4. Few lenders or investors will give you money unless you have a comprehensive written business plan.

Identify Your Mission and Commit to It

Why do you want to start your own business? Write down ALL the reasons – personal, professional, financial, and anything else you can think of. Keep these reasons handy to motivate you on tough days (and there will be plenty of tough days). These are your motivators.

Then, from your motivators, create your mission and vision for your business. Your mission should be your purpose. Why does your company exist? What does your business help you do for people? What do you want to create from your business? Your vision is how you carry out your mission. It will guide you in all aspects of how you will conduct business. For example, maybe collaboration is important to you. Write it into your vision of where the company will go in the future. Perhaps having the latest technology will play an important role. Maybe it has to do with how you relate to and treat your clients. Decide what is important to you about HOW you will do business and write it into your vision.

Chapter 2 – Developing a Business Plan

Finally, COMMIT. Commit to making your mission happen. Committing will strengthen your resolve to make it happen. Your vision and your motivators will provide the guidance to make it happen.

It must also be based on the utilization of what Peter Drucker, renowned author, and influential thinker on management, calls your company's "knowledge excellencies", or the special knowledge and expertise that makes your company successful. Your mission statement should reflect the following:

1. What your company does

2. Who your company does it for

3. Why and how your company does what is does

4. What value is provided by your company

Your mission statement should be succinct, simple, and easy to understand. A sample mission statement might read:

Mission

"To be the choice tax provider for small business owners, offering affordable and customized financial services with consistent quality and value."

Why Your Business Also Needs Guiding Principles

Your mission statement is not enough though. You need a set of standards that you can share with each new employee that will set the stage for how they conduct themselves as a representative of your company. These are what we call "Guiding Principles" that help build your company culture. They are your foundation. Your Guiding Principles help let employees know exactly what you expect. An example of some guiding principles includes:

1. Concern for People
2. Integrity
3. Personal Development
4. Excellence
5. Quality
6. Creativity
7. Productivity
8. Efficiency

Chapter 2 – Developing a Business Plan

9. Communication

10. Teamwork

11. Image

12. Community Service

Instilling strong guiding principles like the ones listed above will not only help guide your staff but will also differentiate your company from the competition. These principles are what will help set you apart, create a culture in your office, and can help you grow organically.

Writing Your Business Plan

If case you are wondering, you don't need a fancy degree or certification to create a business plan. But, you cannot delegate this project. As the business owner, you must be actively involved in the process. You are the one with the knowledge and vision necessary to develop a meaningful plan for your company. You should get input from key partners and management team members. It is also helpful to get objective input from others who are not as close to the business as you. There are many other resources like the Small Business Administration (SBA), your local Chamber of Commerce, among others.

As you write, be sure that your business plan is clear and concise. This will be key to investors and bankers, so they don't get lost or lose interest in your plan.

1. **Executive Summary**

   This summary should describe the founding purpose of your business (what you do, why, and what problem/market need you solve). Provide growth trends, historical financial statements, and future financial projections. Identify key suppliers and any strategic partners. Be sure to include the things that make you unique and the reasons why your business will be, or already is, successful. This is also where you would include any amount of money you are looking to raise. Don't forget a cover page to introduce your plan, which should include your contact information.

2. **A Company Overview**

   This section is a brief profile of your company, including where you are located, when the business was formed, and your business structure (form of legal entity). Be sure to include any history you may have, and all key milestones and achievements, with dates.

Chapter 2 – Developing a Business Plan

3. An Industry Analysis

A written analysis will help you clarify your company's situation and develop appropriate strategies. This should include information about the market you are in or will serve (including the size of the market), and current and future trends.

One very effective tool that can help you in this process is a "S.W.O.T." analysis. This will help you identify your company's Strengths, Weaknesses, Opportunities and Threats. The SWOT method can be viewed as a matrix as shown below. Strengths and weaknesses are usually internal factors. Opportunities and threats tend to be external factors. Obviously, we have more control over internal factors than external factors. Yet we must be aware of the external factors in order to develop effective strategies. A sample outline of a situational analysis for a tax preparation firm appears below. Strengths can usually be translated into opportunities. Opportunities to eliminate or counter weaknesses also exist. Weaknesses and threats can sometimes be turned into opportunities. Each item listed should be explained in writing for the benefit of all interested parties. Your SWOT analysis should be tailored to your unique situation. Use your imagination to expand on the opportunities listed in the following example.

Sample Tax Firm SWOT Analysis:

(INTERNAL)	(EXTERNAL)
STRENGTHS	**OPPORTUNITIES**
Experienced Associates Prime Office(s) Reputation/Image Income Tax School (continue)	Use Idle Resources During Off-Season (offices, computers, employees) Negotiate Joint Marketing Arrangements Expand Course & Seminar Offerings (continue)
WEAKNESSES	**THREATS**
Extreme Seasonality Undercapitalized Dependence on CEO (continue)	Tax Reform (e.g.: flat tax, tax simplification) Technology (enabling self-preparation) IRS Policies (e.g. tax preparer regulation) (continue)

Once you have developed your SWOT analysis, you can take it one step further and create a TOWS Matrix, which helps you develop strategies based on your SWOT factors. For example: Under weaknesses, weakness #2 is an inadequate training program. Under opportunities, your tax service has expansion potential.

Chapter 2 – Developing a Business Plan

So, combining that weakness with the opportunity, strategy #3 under weakness/opportunity strategies (the bottom righthand block) would be to operate an Income Tax School. Similarly, by combining two other different SWOT factors, you should be able to develop another strategy. This TOWS Matrix is a hypothetical example. You would need to create your own TOWS Matrix. We have included a TOWS Matrix template for you in the handout section of the control panel of this webinar system along with a copy of this PPT presentation.

Sample Tax Firm TOWS Matrix:

INTERNAL FACTORS / EXTERNAL FACTORS	STRENGTHS	WEAKNESSES
	Experienced Associates Prime Office(s) Reputation/Image Income Tax School	Extreme Seasonality Undercapitalized Dependence on CEO
OPPORTUNITIES	**S/O STRATEGIES**	**W/O STRATEGIES**
Use Idle Resources During Off-Season (offices, computers, employees) Negotiate Joint Marketing Arrangements Expand Course & Seminar Offerings	Offer live classes to recruit new preparers & grow business, have employees take advanced training to learn new skills so you can expand into new markets	Offer other services that are year-round, such as preparing ITIN forms, notary services, bookkeeping
THREATS	**S/T STRATEGIES**	**W/T STRATEGIES**
Tax Reform (e.g.: flat tax, tax simplification), Technology (enabling self-preparation) IRS Policies (e.g. tax preparer regulation)	Meet with clients in the off-season for year-end tax planning, Communicate more often with clients	Offer discount to clients who try to self-prepare & fail, Partner w/ company to offer self-prep on website

4. Customer Analysis

This is where you will include information about who your target market really is. This should include information about the needs of your target market and how you meet those needs. If possible, try to build profiles of your target market based on demographic information (age, location, gender, income level, education level, marital or family status, occupation, ethnic background) and psychographic information (personality, attitudes, values, interests/hobbies, lifestyles, behaviors). The more detailed you can be, the better!

Chapter 2 – Developing a Business Plan

5. Competitive Analysis

This section should include information about your competitors along with their strengths and weaknesses. Make sure you include your competitive advantages over your competition.... what you do better, why, and how it will make you more successful than your competition.

6. Marketing Plan

Here is where you will talk about your products and/or services, and how you plan to position yourself in the marketplace. For example, are you a high-end tax preparation firm, or are you a tax firm for the masses? You should include how you plan to market your products and/or services. Will you have a tax office storefront every 10 miles? Will you be exclusively online, or will you go to people's houses? How will people find out about you? What promotions will you run? And will you promote your business in the newspaper, through Yelp!, social media, direct mail, word of mouth, or some other way?

7. Operations Plan

This should contain the key things you need to do daily to become successful. Include future milestones you plan to accomplish over the next several years to meet your goals and become successful. Well-conceived and fully developed operating systems are essential to deliver competitive products and services. Such systems for a tax business include a policy & procedure manual, operating software (e.g.: tax preparation, accounting & client service), computer networking systems and management information systems, all employing up-to-date technology.

Delivery capability should also be described in detail. Who will manage and administer the business and what are their qualifications and credentials? How many people will be needed to perform the day-to-day operating tasks and what qualifications will be required? And how will these people be recruited? Facilities, including offices, workstations, work processing and administration areas must also be described. Finally, equipment, such as computers, furnishings, fixtures, signage, etc. should be addressed.

8. Management Team

Provide brief biographies of the management team in your business and include the key reasons why these people are qualified to implement your business plan. Also include any gaps and hiring needs you may have.

9. Financial Plan

Here you will explain how your company generates revenue. Capital requirements must be determined, and anticipated sources of funds identified. The first step is to define, in detail, the financial assumptions upon which your projected figures for revenue and expenses are based. Based on these assumptions, proforma financial statements (P&Ls and balance sheets) should be prepared for three to five years, and a monthly cash flow budget, including sources and uses of cash, should be prepared for at least one year.

Financial Controls should be defined, which should include the analysis of:

   a. variances from budgeted to actual results,
   b. financial statement (critical ratios), and
   c. financial reviews and audits

10. Appendix

This section can be used to include any additional information you may have. Financial statements, patent information, articles written about you, your employees, or the business, among other things.

Trade Names

If you operate under a trade name (a name other than your own legal name), you should consider the laws regarding trademarks and service marks. Many entrepreneurs have spent a great deal of time and money creating awareness of a

Chapter 2 – Developing a Business Plan

trade name only to learn too late that someone else has the prior legal right to use that name. You can hire a service to conduct a search to be sure the name you are considering is not already being used. A trademark service or a trademark and patent attorney can assist with your application to the US Patent and Trademark Office, although it is not difficult to do it yourself.

Here are two quick reasons why you might want to operate your business under a trade name instead of your own name:

1. Consider the fact that future generations of your family may be unwilling or unable to run your business.

2. A family name can make it more difficult to sell when you are ready to retire or move onto your next venture.

Spreading Out Seasonality and Diversifying Your Business

As a seasonal business threatened with radical legislative and technological changes, you must also be thinking about diversifying to ensure future survival and prosperity. Fortunately, many opportunities exist to add complimentary services and/or products to your tax practice. However, you must not neglect your core business or fail to recognize and exploit new opportunities in the tax preparation industry resulting from new industry trends. In choosing new opportunities, you should find no shortage of ideas, only a shortage of resources necessary to capitalize on available opportunities. You will especially want to find opportunities to flatten out the seasonality of your revenue. The key is to identify potential services and products that would complement your business and utilize your knowledge excellencies and available resources, including idle employees, tax office locations, equipment, etc. Then, you must prioritize these ideas in order of feasibility and potential for success.

Your Short-term Plan

While you are developing your business plan, you must still run your business and generate revenue and profits. Therefore, you should simultaneously develop and implement a short-term (6-18 month) action plan. You should prioritize the opportunities identified through your SWOT analysis/TOWS Matrix and decide, given available resources, which goals can realistically be accomplished during the current and subsequent year. However, unless essential for survival, you should not pursue short-term goals that are not consistent with your long-range strategies.

Implementation of Your Plan

The biggest mistake entrepreneurs make in business planning is to fail to implement their plans. If the plan is well conceived, it should be put into action. To ensure that this happens, an action plan must be developed. Time frames should be established to implement each element of the business plan. An "activity timetable" and monthly cash flow budget constitute the implementation tools that must be properly used to ensure success. Remember the sage advice of the adage: "plan your work and work your plan".

Tracking What Works and What Doesn't Work

Systems should be developed to monitor the success of the plan and determine if modifications are necessary. Such systems include methods of measuring and evaluating results and obtaining feedback from clients and employees. Too often marketing campaigns are blindly repeated year-after-year without any idea as to whether they have worked. Don't fall into that trap. Set up a procedure to track the sources of all new clients and to learn the reasons prior clients don't return. Your associates should be provided with incentives to be concerned about the growth of your practice. You should also conduct surveys of your clients and prospective clients to determine whether their needs and wants are being satisfied. Using a unique code for different marketing efforts and tracking how new clients found you are simple ways to find out what is working for you.

Analysis of Results

Evaluation of financial results might include a break-even analysis of each campaign. A market share analysis (before and after) would serve to document marketing success. Client satisfaction surveys will help in evaluating the quality of products and services. Input from associates, perhaps through an advisory board, could provide valuable insight to help improve quality and efficiency.

Establish an Advisory Board to Grow Your Company

"No man is an island; entire of himself…" This famous line written in 1624 by English poet John Donne is still sage advice for anyone, especially an entrepreneur. If you're satisfied being an independent contractor compensated directly in proportion to your personal services rendered, you won't need a board. But if you want to build a company that will still have market value when you are no longer in the picture, you'll need the advice and help of seasoned business experts with skills and knowledge you lack. No one is competent in every area of expertise needed to succeed in business. The most successful

Chapter 2 – Developing a Business Plan

entrepreneurs recognize their limitations and bring in people with complementary strengths to counter their weaknesses.

Start-up companies often have a severe handicap. They are usually too risky to attract private investors and the high caliber board of directors needed to ensure their success. "Angels" know they are prime targets for unscrupulous people who would like to reach into their deep pockets. They are also averse to unnecessary risk and usually prefer to minimize their exposure through syndication with other "angels" and professionals whose judgement they respect. Signing onto a formal board of directors of an unproven company about which they know little is just not prudent. So how can you as a struggling entrepreneur get these key people to buy into your company? Start by identifying several key people who have the resources, contacts, and expertise to help ensure the success of your business and meet your criteria for advisors. Your solution may be an executive advisory board, or maybe just one or two sophisticated advisors who have achieved the level of success to which you aspire.

Chapter 2 – Developing a Business Plan

Example of Advisory Board Membership Criteria	Responsibilities

1. Caliber of major corporation top executive with track record of exceptional achievement & success
2. Experience & expertise in one or more of the following areas of critical importance to Your Company's development
   a. Entrepreneurial Management
   b. Corporate finance & accounting
   c. Marketing
   d. Sales & promotional
   e. Computer systems & MIS
   f. Commercial & investment banking
   g. Corporate & securities law
3. Key strengths & circle of contacts should complement & not closely duplicate those of other advisors
4. Open-minded, innovative, willing to voice & defend ideas, & a team player
	1. Attend meetings regularly
	2. Learn about company & industry
	3. Promote Your Company:
	   a. Refer clients when appropriate
	   b. Be alert to business opportunities
	   c. Provide advice in all key areas of decision making

Incentives for Advisors	**Support**
1. Stock option, no cash remuneration 2. Reimbursement of any authorized expenses incurred 3. Opportunity for future board of director's seat with pay & additional stock options 4. Insight into future investment opportunities in your company 5. Possible sale of professional services to your company 6. Interaction with a group of top business leaders 7. Being part of the development of a future Fortune 500 company	1. Meeting agenda, prior meeting minutes, financial statement & other pertinent information to be provided one week prior to each meeting 2. Reminder memo & phone call prior to meeting date 3. Thank you notes after meetings & updates throughout the year

A highly accomplished group of 4-6 professionals and entrepreneurs could collectively provide the expertise and experience needed to complement you as the business owner. Funding is by no means the most significant contribution of an advisory board. Far more valuable than money is the expert guidance an elite group can provide for you to develop the strategies and tactics to achieve impressive growth.

Chapter 2 – Developing a Business Plan

The doors that can be opened by such high-profile advocates can also provide your company with an invaluable competitive advantage. A strong advisory board can work wonders for a start-up company.

Conclusion

Developing a business plan is no small task but it is a project that is well worth your effort. The process will enable you to clarify your vision as an entrepreneur and think through all of the strategies, tactics and action steps you should be taking to start and grow your tax business and ensure your success. As with any major project, planning is not so ominous when broken down into smaller tasks that can be completed one step at a time. Management guru, Peter Drucker, said: "To lead you must anticipate the future and see what others cannot." Your business plan can help you position your business to survive in the near-term and prosper well into the future. The fastest way to finish something is to start. So, what are you waiting for?

Chapter 3

Risk Management

Some risks that are thought to be unknown, are not unknown. With some foresight and critical thought, some risks that at first glance may seem unforeseen, can in fact be foreseen. Armed with the right set of tools, procedures, knowledge and insight, light can be shed on variables that lead to risk, allowing us to manage them.

- Daniel Wagner

Chapter 3 – Risk Management

Maintaining adequate business insurance is essential. A basic or traditional business insurance package includes the first four items listed below. However, you should seriously consider adding other optional insurance coverage for additional protection.

- **Workers' Compensation Insurance**

  This insurance is required by law to cover medical, rehabilitation and lost wages for employees who are injured on the job, as well as liability in the event an injured employee sues your business.

- **General Liability Insurance**

  Comprehensive coverage is necessary to insure against accident or injury that may occur on your premises. Be sure to study your policy and be aware of all exclusions that apply.

- **Auto Insurance**

  If you have a vehicle that is owned by your business, you will need insurance coverage in the name of your business. Consider increasing your deductible to keep the cost down, assuming you could afford to pay the deductible in the event of an accident caused by you. A minimum of $1 million of liability coverage is recommended, as a lawsuit could result in severe financial hardship or even bankruptcy.

- **Property & Casualty Insurance**

  You should buy replacement cost insurance that would be adequate to replace your furniture, equipment, and facilities in today's cost rather than what you originally paid for those assets. Also, consider including a provision that would adjust your coverage for inflation.

In addition to the traditional insurance package listed above, you should also consider the following optional insurance items below:

Chapter 3 – Risk Management

- **Umbrella Liability Insurance**

  This insurance protects you when accidents happen, and your current liability insurance policies aren't able to cover all the expenses. Basically, it picks up where your business auto liability, general liability or other liability coverage stops, giving you additional coverage against bodily injury and/or property damage. It's a good safety net to have!

- **Employee Practices Liability Insurance**

  This optional Worker's Compensation coverage will insure you for claims arising from illegal employee behavior such as sexual harassment and discrimination.

- **Errors and Omissions Liability Insurance**

  Errors and omissions (E&O) liability insurance covers professionals for errors and oversights that occur when providing services such as tax preparation. Tax businesses should seriously consider this type of insurance that protects in the event of a claim made against your firm due to an error or omission caused by you or an employee. It typically covers the costs of legal defense, judgments, and settlements. This protection is vital as a tax preparer since you are dealing with other peoples' financial information and there is the risk of making a mistake or overlooking something. It is a very good idea for all tax preparers to have this type of insurance. If you are a member of a tax professional association such as the National Association of Tax Professionals (NATP) or the National Association of Enrolled Agents (NAEA), the association may arrange for an insurance agency to offer E&O insurance at discounted rates for members.

- **Business Interruption Insurance**

  In the event of a casualty that causes your business to be shut down, this coverage would provide for you to be compensated for the loss of income during the time that your business was unable to be in operation.

Chapter 3 – Risk Management

- **Business Overhead Insurance**

  This coverage would pay the cost of business expenses such as rent, employee salaries, debt payments, if you as the owner become disabled and unable to generate revenue.

- **Life Insurance**

  Life insurance should be considered for you to provide for your family's needs in the event of your death. Term life insurance should be considered to keep the cost affordable.

- **Key Person Insurance**

  The business would be the beneficiary of this type of life insurance to cover the potential death of you or a key executive of your business. Coverage should be adequate to hire a replacement for you if you are the sole owner, or to pay for the purchase of your partner's stock in the company if such an obligation would be created by the event of the death of you or the key person.

- **Disability Insurance**

  If you or a key executive becomes disabled, this insurance would replace the wages lost due to the inability to work. Usually a disability policy provides for payment of 60% of the wages during the period you are unable to work. Be sure to consider that if you pay for this insurance directly, the disability benefits would be non-taxable, but if the company pays the premiums, the benefits would be taxable. Therefore, it may be advisable for the company to pay you a higher wage so you could afford to pay the premiums personally.

- **Data Breach Insurance**

  Our digital age has resulted in additional risks for which we must seriously consider insurance. The greatest risk we face is a Data Breach that could lead to the theft of your clients' identities.

Chapter 3 – Risk Management

Why You Really Need a Data Breach Policy

If you were to ask an insurance agent whether your business needed data breach insurance, they would ask if your company collects any of the following types of information.

- Social Security Numbers
- Banking/Financial Information
- Credit Cards/Debit Cards/Other Payment Cards
- Health Information & Medical Records

Because you are in the tax industry, the answer to all of those is yes. As a tax business owner, you should make sure you are protected in the event of a data breach.

A data breach could be a catastrophe, easily resulting in your business being shut down by the IRS or being sued, and even potential bankruptcy. IBM recently estimated that the average data breach costs $4 million. In recent years, the number of U.S. data breaches have hit all-time records. Because of the increased risk, data breach insurance is something tax business owners should seriously consider.

A good data breach policy does three key things:

1. Takes protective measures to guard against the loss of sensitive consumer information
2. Reacts swiftly and comprehensively to a data breach when it occurs
3. Covers the incident response costs, which can include legal services, forensic investigations, notification mailings to impacted individuals, call center support, credit monitoring, and fraud remediation expenses

Data breaches can happen even if you are doing all the right things, which is why getting coverage is crucial. Here are some of the most common ways a data breach can happen.

- Criminals obtain access to account information from lost or stolen laptops, backup drives or smartphones
- Criminals obtain access to stored documents left unsecured on your premises
- Criminals hack into your database
- Criminals con employees into divulging passwords and login credentials

Chapter 3 – Risk Management

In addition to data breach insurance, you should also make sure you have the following security controls in place.

- Anti-Virus Software

- Password-protected computers, laptops, and other mobile devices

- Secured wireless connectivity for laptops and other mobile devices

- A Firewall

- Data stored on laptops, back-up tapes, or other portable media is encrypted

- Annual training for employees concerning data security and the handling of personal information

You should also be training staff on cybersecurity best practices. There are a lot of fraudsters out there with phishing scams that target internal staff – especially in the tax industry. For example, one of the popular phishing scams targets tax preparers via email. The email appears to be a notification from your tax software provider and warns that your account has been locked. It prompts you to enter your login credentials in order to "unlock your account". But what it's really doing is collecting login information that can be used to gain access to your client's information. This is why it's so important to train and educate staff on how data breaches happen and what to do to prevent them.

Due to today's unprecedented threats of data breach, it has become crucial that you take extra precautions to guard your information. That means staying on top of the latest scams, employing cybersecurity protections, and getting data breach insurance.

Know the Scams

As a professional in the industry, it's important to stay on-top of the phishing and malware scams that are out there. It's also important to relay information to employees and clients as a proactive way to fight identity theft.

IRS Security Campaigns

The IRS regularly sends out email notices as new scams come to light. You can sign-up to receive alerts on the IRS website. To help educate taxpayers and tax preparers, the IRS has six awareness campaigns:

Chapter 3 – Risk Management

1. **Working Virtually: Protecting Tax Data at Home and at Work**

   Working Virtually: Protecting Tax Data at Home and at Work is a Security Summit awareness campaign to highlight security actions key to protecting tax professionals as they respond to COVID-19 while working remotely from their office and clients.

   https://www.irs.gov/newsroom/working-virtually-protecting-tax-data-at-home-and-at-work

2. **Tax Security 2.0**

   The "Taxes-Security-Together" Checklist is a Security Summit awareness campaign to call on tax professionals nationwide to take time to review their current security practices, enhance safeguards where necessary and take steps to protect their businesses from global cybercriminal syndicates prowling the Internet. https://www.irs.gov/newsroom/tax-security-2-0

3. **Protect Your Clients; Protect Yourself: Security 101**

   Protect Your Clients; Protect Yourself: Tax Security 101 is a Security Summit awareness campaign intended to provide tax professionals with the basic information they need to better protect taxpayer data and to help prevent the filing of fraudulent tax returns. https://www.irs.gov/newsroom/protect-your-clients-protect-yourself-tax-security-101

4. **Don't Take the Bait**

   The Don't Take the Bait awareness series is focused on the need for tax professionals to increase their computer security and be cautious of spear phishing scams. Tax professionals must remember that they have a legal requirement under federal law to protect taxpayer information. See

also: Continuing Education Credit for Qualified Data Security Courses.
https://www.irs.gov/e-file-providers/dont-take-the-bait

5. **Protect Your Clients; Protect Yourself**

   Every tax professional in the United States, whether a member of a major accounting firm or an owner of a one-person storefront, is a potential target for highly sophisticated, well-funded and technologically adept cybercriminals around the world. https://www.irs.gov/tax-professionals/protect-your-clients-protect-yourself

6. **Taxes-Security-Together**

   We are asking you, taxpayers, tax professionals and businesses, to join with us to create an even stronger partnership. Our "Taxes-Security-Together" awareness campaign is an effort to better inform you about the actions you can take to protect your sensitive data. https://www.irs.gov/individuals/taxes-security-together

These campaigns contain important safeguarding tips for taxpayers and tax preparers that you should be aware of. Here are four resources to read up on:

1. **Identity Theft Central**

   https://www.irs.gov/identity-theft-central

2. **Tax Scams/Consumer Alerts**

   https://www.irs.gov/newsroom/tax-scams-consumer-alerts

3. **Publication 4557, Safeguarding Taxpayer Data: A Guide for Your Business**

   https://www.irs.gov/pub/irs-pdf/p4557.pdf

4. **Data Theft Information for Tax Professional**

   https://www.irs.gov/individuals/data-theft-information-for-tax-professionals

IRS Safeguards

The IRS has made big strides in identifying and implementing additional taxpayer safeguards. The main emphasis is on authentication of legitimate tax filers, information sharing, and cybersecurity. Safeguards you may see include:

Chapter 3 – Risk Management

- New data elements will be collected by the IRS to help improve authentication of the taxpayer and identify possible identity theft scams
- Several "Work Groups" were formed in various industries to help identify and safeguard information. Those groups are:

  - Authentication Work Group: Tasked with identifying ways to strengthening authentication practices, including new ways to validate taxpayers and return information.
  - Financial Services Work Group: Tasked with examining ways to prevent criminals from potentially accessing tax-time financial products, deposit accounts, and pre-paid debit cards.
  - Information Sharing Work Group: Tasked with identifying opportunities to improve the collective capabilities for detecting and preventing Identity theft tax refund fraud.
  - Strategic Threat Assessment and Response (STAR) Work Group: Tasked with taking a holistic look at the entire tax ecosystem, identifying points of vulnerability (threats/risks), developing a strategy to mitigate or prevent threats.
  - Communication and Taxpayer Awareness Work Group: Tasked with increasing awareness among individuals, businesses, and tax professionals on the need to protect sensitive tax and financial information.
  - Tax Professional Work Group: Tasked with examining how new requirements will affect tax preparers who use professional software and how preparers can help prevent identity theft tax refund fraud.

The IRS sends out Alerts and Fact Sheets throughout the tax season warning taxpayers and tax preparers of popular and new scams. Be sure you are on their email list to receive these notices. Below is an example of one of these IRS notices.

Chapter 3 – Risk Management

IRS Fact Sheet
Identity Theft Information for Tax Professionals
FS-2017-4, March 2017

Tax professionals play a critical role in assisting clients, both individuals and businesses, who are victims of tax-related identity theft. The IRS, state tax agencies and the tax industry are working to prevent and detect identity theft as well as reduce the time it takes to resolve these cases.

What is tax-related identity theft?

Tax-related identity theft occurs when someone uses a Social Security number (SSN) — either a client's, a spouse's, or dependent's — to file a tax return claiming a fraudulent refund. Thieves may also use a stolen Employer Identification Number (EIN) from a business client to create false Forms W-2 to support refund fraud schemes.

How to know if a client is a victim of tax-related identity theft

Tax professionals may be unaware a client is a victim of identity theft until they attempt to file the tax return and it is rejected as a duplicate return. Other indicators include receiving a notice regarding:

- More than one tax return filed using the client's SSN

- A balance due, refund offset, or collection action taken for a year in which no return was filed

- IRS or state records indicate the client received wages from an unknown employer

- An amended tax return, fictitious employees or about a defunct, closed or dormant business (for business clients)

Did someone file a tax return or W-2 using a client's SSN?

If a client's SSN has been compromised, whether from a data breach, computer hack or stolen wallet, and they have reason to believe they are at risk for tax-related identity theft, tax pros should take these steps:

- If the client received an IRS or state notice, respond immediately.

- Complete IRS Form 14039, Identity Theft Affidavit, if directed to do so by the IRS or if the client's e-file return rejects because of a duplicate SSN and there are no other errors (example: transposed numbers). Fax or mail to the IRS according to the instructions.

Chapter 3 – Risk Management

- Follow identity theft reporting procedures provided on the client's state revenue agency website.

- To inquire about specific client's return information, preparers must have a power of attorney on file and must authenticate their identity with the IRS or state customer service representative.

What can preparers do if a client is a victim of identity theft?

The Federal Trade Commission, the lead federal agency on general identity theft issues, has recommended steps identity theft victims should take to protect their credit. See https://www.identitytheft.gov/ for general recommendations for clients. Other steps include:

- For identity theft victims who previously contacted IRS and **have not achieved a resolution**, contact IRS for specialized assistance at 800-908-4490. Contact state revenue agencies per the website's instructions.

- Clients should continue to file returns and pay taxes, even if it must be done by paper.

How can preparers protect clients' sensitive information?

- When providing clients with copies of their tax returns, preparers can redact or mark out the Social Security numbers and bank account information for client protection.

- The IRS, state tax agencies and the tax industry launched an ongoing awareness campaign for taxpayers called Taxes. Security. Together. A similar awareness effort is directed at tax professionals, Protect Your Clients; Protect Yourself.

- Be aware that tax preparation businesses can become a target for criminals. Follow IRS security guidelines in Publication 4557, Safeguarding Taxpayer Data, for protecting taxpayer information.

Related Resources:

- Publication 5199 Tax Preparer Guide to Identity Theft

- Publication 5027 Identity Theft Information for Taxpayers

- Publication 4600 Safeguarding Taxpayer Information

Conclusion

Certain types of insurance policies are essential for any business to have. You should also consider other types of optional insurance to protect your, your family and your business from events that could be catastrophic. Risk management is critical to make sure you are adequately insured and have policies and procedures in place to comply with the IRS privacy rules and to prevent security breaches.

Chapter 4

Getting Started As A Tax Business Owner

The secret of getting ahead is getting started.

- Mark Twain

Chapter 4 – Getting Started as a Tax Business Owner

It's the age-old dilemma: How are you supposed to start your own tax business (a full-time job itself) while holding down another job already? It's hard to take that leap of faith knowing that if you leave your current job, you may struggle to pay your bills until your business starts bringing in enough income.

It's also hard sometimes to find the time and energy to do the responsible things while also following your passion. Here are some tips and warnings that will help give you some direction and much-needed focus. They can help spark the motivation and practical organization you need to make progress towards owning your own successful tax business.

Get Serious About Time Management

Since time and energy are going to be your two most precious resources as you ramp up your own business, you'll need to get serious about how you manage both.

Sleep

What is the minimum amount of sleep you need to function well? Some people must have a full eight hours of sleep. Are you one of them? Or, could you scale it back to seven, maybe six and a half, or even six hours, to maximize your waking hours and devote a little extra time to your new business? Do NOT skip sleep. However, figure out what your magic minimum amount of sleep is so you can still rest your body and your brain and gain an extra hour or so for the extra work of starting a business. Then, and this is very important, stick to that schedule. Don't get four hours of sleep one night only to crash and sleep for ten the next night. Then you will have gained nothing. Find the right schedule for you and stick to it.

Give Your Most Productive Hours to Your New Business.

You may have come across a popular saying, "Give your passion project the best part of your day." If you're a night owl, stay up late and spend time building your business. If you come home from work wiped out, go to bed early and then get up early so you're fresh and ready to devote quality time to your business road map and actions. Find the schedule that works best for you, so you can go at your project with a fresh, alert, motivated mind.

Evaluate Your Current Time Commitments

Make a list of what you're already committed to doing. How much time do you devote to each? Are you able to shift any time away from these activities and apply them to your new business activities?

Chapter 4 – Getting Started as a Tax Business Owner

4 Things to be Mindful of

As motivated as you may feel about having an action plan for getting your new business started, remember the importance of balance, and keep these four points in mind.

1. Don't let starting your business interfere with your current, income-generating job. Not only will you put your job and income at risk before you're ready to leave them behind – it's disrespectful and unethical.

2. Remind yourself that the sacrifices you make now will pay off in the future when you have more free time and more income stability.

3. Limit contact with people who are negative about your new endeavor.

4. Limiting contact with negative people doesn't mean avoiding honest feedback. Find people who can really challenge your ideas and give you honest, objective observations. Friends and family are great, but if they're afraid of hurting your feelings, they may not tell you what they're really thinking. Seek out objective critiques to make sure you're not way off base with any of your goals or your strategy.

Key Considerations if You Want to Open a Tax Business

Self-employment can be very gratifying and rewarding. Just be sure that you have considered as many of the pros and cons as you can think of before you jump in. If you like to work nine-to-five and collect a regular paycheck, you may want to rethink starting a business. It requires real commitment, and without a boss you need to be highly motivated and self-directed. The main reasons most people become an entrepreneur are to have *freedom* to control their own destiny and realize rewards for their hard work. However, the price of owning your own business is working long hours and taking risks. If you think tax business ownership is for you, here are some factors to consider to get your tax business up and running.

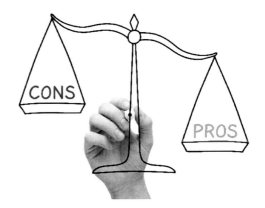

Buying a Tax Franchise

The easiest way to start a tax business may be to purchase a tax franchise. However, the cost of the initial franchise fee and the ongoing royalty (see example on the next page) may be prohibitive for many aspiring tax business owners.

Chapter 4 – Getting Started as a Tax Business Owner

Cost of a Jackson Hewitt franchise

The financial requirement is **$50,000** (Liquid Cash) and the initial Jackson-Hewitt franchise fee is **$15,000-$25,000**, with a total investment ranging **from $43,130-$110,255**, respectively. There is also an ongoing royalty fee of up to 15% with a franchise agreement that lasts 10 years and is renewable.

Jackson Hewitt Tax Service® Franchise Cost & Opportunities
Source: https://www.franchisehelp.com/franchises/jackson-hewitt-tax-service/

The key benefits of owning a tax franchise are:

1. Instant name recognition
2. Access to a proven operating system
3. Training & support
4. Tax preparation software

© 2009 Ted Goff

"This is the part of the contract that says what a nice person you are and how much we like you."

Given these resources, your chances of succeeding are greater than starting your own tax business from scratch. You might also be able to obtain bank financing to cover your start-up costs. But you would need to build your tax business revenue to a level that would generate enough profit, after paying ongoing royalties and servicing debt, to pay yourself a reasonable income. This would not be an easy feat.

There are negatives of owning a tax franchise in addition to the high expense and perpetual royalties described above. You will have the rights to a single office location unless you can afford to buy multiple franchises, assuming they are available in the locations you desire. Therefore, your ability to expand may be very limited. Your flexibility to innovate will also be limited as you will be required to strictly adhere to the franchise operating system.

Chapter 4 – Getting Started as a Tax Business Owner

Becoming an Independent Tax Business Owner

Becoming an Independent Tax Business Owner is as easy as getting a business license, buying tax software, obtaining a PTIN through the IRS website, setting up your office, and developing a plan to get clients to ensure a profitable business.

Independent tax business ownership has some appealing benefits:

- Lower startup costs

- Higher profit margins

- Greater flexibility to innovate

- Opportunity to expand

- Being in control of your own destiny

Availability of Resources

Being an independent tax business owner doesn't mean that you must start totally from scratch. You don't have to "reinvent the wheel." There are many resources available for you to get started. In fact, almost everything that would be provided to you as a franchise owner is available from other sources. The following are some of your options.

Tax Preparation as a Part-Time Business

Tax preparation does not have to be a full-time business, at least not initially. Also, tax preparation could be started as a business to be combined with a related or complementary business. Many people who start businesses do so on a part-time basis initially, so they don't have to give up their full-time job, which is their main source of income. This is especially true for a seasonal business. In this case, tax preparation is a "side hustle", and is often a great way to test the waters!

The term side hustle is a phrase that refers to making extra money on the side. A side hustle could be a way to extra money while pursuing your real passion, or a way to delve into a new passion by pursuing it on the side. Either way you look at it, tax preparation fits the bill as a side hustle and, in some cases, a complimentary service to other careers such as financial planning. It can be a great way to get started in the tax preparation business. So, if you can't seem to make up your mind about whether to buy into a franchise or start your own tax business, consider trying tax preparation as a side hustle for a while and see how it goes. It may help you decide the right path for you.

Chapter 4 – Getting Started as a Tax Business Owner

Examples of people who might consider taxes as a side hustle:

- **Stay at Home Parents**
    - Tax preparation allows you the flexibility to work from home during the hours that you choose. It's the perfect side hustle for parents of young children looking to earn money while keeping their most important job (being a parent) at the forefront. Tax season occurs during a time when your children are in school and you are free when they are out of school during the summer months.

- **Travelers**
    - Want to travel the world? You are in luck! Tax preparation is a very seasonal business. So, you can work hard January through April, during tax season, and spend the rest of the year traveling!

- **Early Retirees**
    - Retirees looking for a way to earn extra cash without committing to a schedule could take up tax preparation. It allows for summer free time with the grandkids and the flexibility to work when you want.

- **Professionals**
    - Tax preparation can be a great complimentary add-on service for professionals who are already in the financial industry. Financial Advisors, Accountants, Lawyers, and even Realtors can add some additional income by making tax preparation their side hustle.

- **Entrepreneurs/Startups/Wantrepreneurs**
  If you're interested in owning a business and pursuing your passion of becoming an entrepreneur, but still need cash flow while you "test the waters," tax preparation can be a great option. Due to its seasonality, you will have time off to plan and also to meet personal obligations, such as taking your family on a vacation.

Chapter 4 – Getting Started as a Tax Business Owner

Legal Forms of Organizing Your Business

You will need to decide which one of the following options will be best way for you to organize your business.

- **Sole-Proprietor**
  - If you operate as a sole proprietor, you can be personally liable for all debt and other obligations of your business if your business is sued or becomes insolvent. Creditors would then be able to go after both your business and your personal assets, such as your house. Your business income and expenses would be reported on Schedule C of your personal Form 1040.

- **Limited Liability Company (LLC)**
  - Your best option may be to form a Limited Liability Company (LLC) to limit your liability to the assets of your business. An LLC may also realize lower tax liability than that of a C-Corporation if you sell your business. Your business income and expenses would be reported on a separate tax return. However, the net income or loss would be reported on your personal tax return (Form 1040) and the tax returns of any other shareholder. A loss would reduce your personal taxable income and a profit would be taxed at your personal tax rate.

- **C-Corporation**
  If you legally organize your business as a "C-Corporation," the cost of this option would likely be greater than any other alternative, and if you sell your business, you may pay higher taxes on the gain. In the event that your business fails, your liability would be limited to the assets of the business. However, an LLC will provide the same protection for less cost. Any net income of the business would be taxed at the C-Corporate tax rate and any loss could be carried back or forward.

- **Partnership**
  If two or more individuals have ownership interest in your business and you are

not legally organized as a C-corporation or an LLC, you are legally considered a partnership. As a partnership, you and your partners have the same liability issues as those of a sole proprietorship. You could also be liable for obligations of your partner(s). The net income or loss would be reported on the personal tax returns (Form 1040) of each of the partners.

Other important considerations

As a sole proprietor or partnership, if you or any partner dies, the assets of the business would go to the heirs, which could jeopardize the continued existence of the business. With an LLC or a C-Corporation, the business would continue to exist perpetually with the same business licenses, bank accounts, trade name and other business elements. There is also a perception of greater stability and prestige associated with an LLC or corporation.

Regardless of which form of business organization you choose, you will still be liable if you personally guarantee a contract, such as a lease. Also, if the officers of a corporation do not follow the rules or do something illegal, they can be held responsible for their negligence or improper actions. As a corporation, you must maintain separate business bank accounts, file annual reports and meet other requirements of the law.

These are not all of the considerations, and you might be wise to consult with an attorney and, possibly, a financial planner for advice. You should also consider taking advantage of free or low-cost consulting services, seminars and events available from your local Small Business Development Center (SBDC) and Chamber of Commerce.

The IRS has some great information on their website:

- **Starting a Business**

  https://www.irs.gov/businesses/small-businesses-self-employed/starting-a-business

- **Checklist for Starting a Business**

  https://www.irs.gov/businesses/small-businesses-self-employed/checklist-for-starting-a-business

- **State Links**

  https://www.irs.gov/businesses/small-businesses-self-employed/state-government-websites

Chapter 4 – Getting Started as a Tax Business Owner

- **Publications and Forms for the Self-Employed**

  https://www.irs.gov/businesses/small-businesses-self-employed/publications-and-forms-for-the-self-employed

The U.S. Small Business Administration also has some great information on their website:

- **How to Start a Business**
  https://www.sba.gov/starting-business/how-start-business

Bank Financing

Banks make money by charging a reasonable interest rate to lend money without taking risk. Obtaining a bank loan for your start-up tax business will not be feasible unless you can provide adequate collateral and clearly demonstrate that your business will generate the cash flow necessary to make your loan payments. Even then, the bank will probably require a loan guarantee from a government agency such as the Small Business Administration (SBA). Even with collateral and an SBA loan guarantee, most banks will shy away from providing financing for a start-up service business.

There are lenders that fill the void left by traditional banks. One such non-bank lender I am familiar with is Virginia Commercial Finance (VCF). John McCauley, CEO of VCF provides an excellent explanation of the criteria used by lenders in considering the credit-worthiness of a prospective borrower. Below is the link to an excellent article by John McCauley on how to obtain a working capital loan.

- https://www.linkedin.com/pulse/how-your-collateral-can-provide-you-more-working-capital-mccauley

Other Resources

When you are ready to start your business, seek out your local Small Business Development Center (SBDC). You might also read the suggestions on how to build your tax business available on The Income Tax School website at the link below.

- http://www.theincometaxschool.com/build-your-tax-business

Conclusion

Starting your own tax business is a major commitment that should not be taken lightly. To succeed as an entrepreneur, you must be willing to work hard, be self-directed and take risks. Buying a franchise is an option that can increase your chances of being successful as a business owner. However, the cost of a franchise is out of reach for most people, and there are constraints that may be undesirable. Fortunately, you don't have to

Chapter 4 – Getting Started as a Tax Business Owner

"reinvent the wheel." All of the resources you will need as a tax business owner are available from providers such as The Income Tax School and tax professional associations. If you truly have the passion to be an entrepreneur, as well as drive and perseverance, you will succeed!

Chapter 5

Establishing Your Tax Office

If you don't build your dream, someone else will hire you to help them build theirs.

- Dhirubhai Ambani, founder
Reliance Industries

Chapter 5 – Establishing Your Tax Office

Where should you locate your tax preparation business? This decision may depend on how you plan to position your business in the market, what you can afford initially, and your future plans for growth. If you plan to be a sole-proprietor or if your financial resources are extremely limited, operating as a home-based business may be your best option, at least to start. Whether you operate in your home, or in a professional office, it is important to project a professional image and provide privacy and a high level of security. A major advantage of operating in your home is the low overhead that allows you to charge lower fees and still generate the same or better profit margins than tax firms operating in a professional office or a storefront. Below are some considerations pertaining to these options.

Home-Based Office

If you operate in your home, ideally, you should use a private office, or a room repurposed as a private office. Some home-based tax preparers have a separate entrance to their tax office. It may even be feasible to have exterior signage. It is essential for you to research all of the ordinances governing your residence and make sure you do not violate any regulations pertaining to operating a business in your home. Some tax preparers have  their residence in a commercially-zoned area where they can convert the front of their residence into a professional office with exterior signage and a separate entrance, while also living in the another part of the same house.

Your clients expect their personal information to be held in strict confidence. In addition, you must conform to all of the privacy and security regulations of the IRS, that are discussed in other chapters in this book. You must have a locking file cabinet and/or locking desk drawers to keep your client files and documents secure. Whenever you are away from your office, even to go to the bathroom, the drawer(s) with your client files must be locked.

Office furnishings should include a desk, file cabinet and comfortable chairs for you and your clients. Your office should have a door that can be closed for privacy. Adequate lighting is also important. Essentially, your office environment must be conducive to conducting a private interview. If you expect additional clients to arrive at your home office before you have finished your current client interview, you will need a comfortable reception area for them to wait in. Unless a member of your household will always be available to greet clients, your outside entrance door should have an intercom, ideally with a camera, that is connected to your private office.

Chapter 5 – Establishing Your Tax Office

Office equipment will be the same whether you operate in a home office, a professional office building, or a storefront office. If feasible, you should have a separate telephone service for your business. You will also need internet service that is adequate to e-File your clients' tax returns.

Your home office may be permanent, or possibly, only temporary until you are able to grow your tax business to a level of revenue and profitability where you can afford to move into a professional office building or a storefront office. You may be able to save a fair amount of money by purchasing used or refurbished office furniture and equipment.

Brick and Mortar Business

Moving your tax preparation service from your home office to a separate business location is a major step that requires careful planning and preparation. You will be adding considerable overhead expenses to your business. These costs can only be justified by your ability to generate substantially more revenue at your new business location than the extra costs you will incur. You need to be confident that the benefits will outweigh the costs.

One way to cover some of the added costs is to increase your prices assuming they are lower that your main competitors and you feel confident that the vast majority of your clients will still use your services and not go to a competitor or decide to prepare their own returns. When you move to a business office, you can no longer compete solely on price. However, the new location should also result in more clients due to a more professional atmosphere, greater visibility and, possibly a more convenient location.

Your basic options are:

1. A professional office building or condo
2. A retail storefront
3. An "Executive Suites" office

Chapter 5 – Establishing Your Tax Office

Professional Office Building

This option would be more effective for an "executive tax service" catering primarily or exclusively to clients with more complex tax situations such as:

1. Executives

2. Professionals (doctors, lawyers, chiropractors, etc.)

3. Small business owners

4. Financially independent seniors

These four client segments have in common more complex tax situations and the lack of interest or ability to prepare their own tax returns. You will be competing with independent CPAs, small CPA firms and upper-end tax professionals. Your office should provide a professional business environment, privacy, convenience of location, easy access and ample free parking. Your occupancy cost will likely be less than a storefront office. However, you will not likely enjoy the benefits of signage, and high traffic and visibility afforded by a prime retail storefront location.

Executive Suites Office

This is a great alternative to leasing your own private office in a professional office building. There are several very appealing advantages to an executive suites office. The benefits include:

1. Fast Setup – you can start your business very quickly with this type of office space.

2. Reception Area with a receptionist who answers the phones and greets clients for all business tenants.

3. Private Office(s) for your tax service

4. Furniture available for you to rent at an affordable rate (usually you have the option of providing your own furniture)

5. Telephone Extension for your business with a phone number assigned to your business (or your previously used business phone number)

6. Conference Room available to all tenants by reservation

7. Equipment shared by tenants including copiers, scanner, fax, postage meter, etc.

8. Break Room where tenants can have lunch or a snack (coffee may be provided and vending machines are usually available)

9. Networking Opportunities with other professionals in the building

Chapter 5 – Establishing Your Tax Office

A major benefit with an executive suites office is that you have the option of renting your office on a seasonal basis for just 4 months (January through April), thereby reducing your office rent to just one-third of the cost of a professional office building lease. Your office occupancy and operating cost is further reduced through the sharing of common areas, equipment, services and a common receptionist. If you lease a private office on a seasonal basis, you may still be able to use the Executive Suites services during the off-season at a fraction of the cost, and will always have a professional receptionist answering your phone!

Virtual Tax Service

You may also consider operating a "virtual tax service" with no physical office to serve clients in person. Given existing technology and computer systems that are available to anyone, clients can be served remotely. In fact, many tax preparation clients are served remotely by tax firms who have established relationships with clients who have since moved to other cities, states and even foreign countries. The challenge for establishing a virtual tax service is recruiting new clients remotely. With an easy-to-follow, secure website and some testimonials from friends and family who have used your service, you could be well on your way to a successful operation. A virtual tax business can be a very profitable business model.

Having a virtual tax office will make it possible for you to:

- Operate leaner and more efficiently to reduce costs and increase profit margins

- Be more responsive to clients with cloud-based software you can access from anywhere (rather than having to "get back to your desk")

- Eliminate some of the day-to-day office tasks that can be either automated with tax practice management software or that can be streamlined with cloud-based software and software-as-a-service (SaaS)

- Attract new customers who appreciate how up-to-date and secure your virtual office is and how easy you are to work with as a result

Even if you decide to have a physical office space later, or you already have a physical office space, setting up your office with the technology to offer your services virtually is likely to improve communication with your clients and broaden your clientbase.

BONUS: You and any staff you hire will also have more flexibility to work from anywhere and as needed. Imagine if your tax preparer can answer the phone and set appointments from a mobile phone while taking his or her kids to soccer practice! So many people look for and really value flexibility in their jobs. You may be able to attract better employees (and earn their loyalty) by being able to offer the flexibility and work-life balance that a

Chapter 5 – Establishing Your Tax Office

virtual tax office has the potential to provide. You also aren't limited by geography. You could hire the most talented people from anywhere in the world!

Retail Storefront Office

A storefront is usually best if you want to build a high-volume mass-market tax business. There are many considerations in site-selection and leasing a retail storefront office. Such considerations are covered in great detail in our Tax Business Expansion Guide. Key benefits of a retail storefront office are signange, traffic, and visibility which should result in attracting more clients then you would in a professional office building. The added cost of a prime retail storefront office should reduce the marketing expense you will need to incur to attract new clients.

If your operating plan calls for a retail storefront office to compete directly with the national mass market tax firms such as H&R Block, Jackson Hewitt and Liberty Tax Service, the decision process is more complex and the occupancy costs are greater. This book will not cover the myriad of details involved in retail storefront office site-selection and leasing. Those details are covered in the ITS Tax Office Expansion Guide. Below is an overview of the considerations.

Storefront Office Site-selection

Tax office site selection is a critical decision processes that can make the difference between success and failure. When planning to open or relocate a tax office, the target community of taxpayers for that office must be large enough so that you can reasonably attain the required market share you need to be successful in that area. Once that has been determined, the specific office location is the next crucial decision.

A retail storefront with high visibility will usually be necessary for a successful mass-market tax service. Site selection involves many key considerations such as type of shopping center or office building, population and demographics of drawing area, traffic, visibility, parking, access, etc. Below is a checklist of considerations in selecting a site.

Chapter 5 – Establishing Your Tax Office

Site Selection Checklist

- ☐ Population
- ☐ Drawing Area
- ☐ Socio-Economic Profile
- ☐ Barriers-Natural/Psychological
- ☐ Future Trends
- ☐ Competitors Nearby
- ☐ Distance from Your Nearest Office
- ☐ Traffic Flow
- ☐ Access
- ☐ Visibility
- ☐ Sign Privileges
- ☐ Parking
- ☐ Image/Appearance
- ☐ Anchor Tenants
- ☐ Other Tenants/Vacancies
- ☐ Type of Shopping Center
- ☐ Tenant's Responsibilities
- ☐ Automatic Renewal
- ☐ Other Considerations

Storefront Office Leasing

Once a desirable office is identified, lease negotiation is the next major challenge. There are many pitfalls in negotiating a lease, and hiring a lawyer to help is not necessarily the best approach. Economic considerations include rent and pass-through charges, security deposit, up-fitting cost, rent abatement, cost of utilities, repairs & maintenance, signage cost and any other expenses the tenant must pay. Occupancy considerations include permitted use, sign privileges, hours of operation required, tenant rules & regulations, and other factors. Legal considerations include the lease term, options to renew, default provisions and the ability to cure, notice required, venue, casualty provisions, personal guarantee, right to sub-rent and assignment rights. There are many leasing pitfalls; and there are strategies to counter these land mines.

There are different types and characteristics of landlords and you should understand what the typical goals are of the landlord type with which you are dealing. Landlord types include:

Chapter 5 – Establishing Your Tax Office

- Individual Owner/Investor
- Individual Owner/Co-tenant
- Limited Partnership/Corporation
- Property Development Company
- Investment Trust Company

In addition, you must also consider if you will be negotiating directly with the landlord or through a broker.

Signing a lease for an office is a decision that will greatly impact your tax business. A good choice can dramatically improve your success, but a mistake could be disastrous. You must not take this chore lightly or rush through the process. Information and knowledge are power, and to be on equal footing with the landlord, or more likely the landlord's leasing agent, you must educate yourself in the rules of the leasing game and obtain as much information about the property, the landlord and the local market conditions as possible. Much of the information should have been obtained during your site selection. Additional information needed to negotiate a lease might include the following (partial list):

Storefront Leasing Checklist

- ☐ History of the Premises
- ☐ Lease Term & Options
- ☐ Use of the Premises
- ☐ Base Rent & Payment Terms
- ☐ Pass-through Charges
- ☐ Security Deposit
- ☐ Utilities Expense
- ☐ Insurance
- ☐ Landlord Improvements to Premises
- ☐ Free Rent
- ☐ Sign Privileges
- ☐ Sub-renting Privileges
- ☐ Parking Privileges
- ☐ Default Provision
- ☐ Casualty Provision
- ☐ Lease Assignment Option
- ☐ Personal Guarantee
- ☐ Landlord's Responsibilities

Chapter 5 – Establishing Your Tax Office

- ☐ Tenant's Responsibilities
- ☐ Damage, Destruction, and Condemnation
- ☐ "Escape" Clause
- ☐ Shopping Center Rules
- ☐ Automatic Renewal
- ☐ Other Considerations

Conclusion

You must decide if you will operate your office from your home, develop a virtual tax service, rent an office in a professional office building or Executive Suites, or lease a storefront office. Many new tax business owners start by operating from their homes and later move to a professional office or a storefront office. An "Executive Suites" office is a very attractive option. Locating and leasing a retail storefront office is a complex process and you should consider investing in the ITS Tax Business Expansion Guide for insight into the process of site selection and lease negotiation.

Chapter 6

Tax Office Operating Systems

Organize around business functions, not people. Build systems within each business function. Let systems run the business and people run the systems. People come and go but the systems remain constant.

- Michael Gerber
E-Myth Revisited

Chapter 6 – Tax Office Operating Systems

Systematic Operating Methods

The foundation of an efficient and effective workplace is the structure, discipline and consistency provided by well-conceived systematic operating methods. World-class companies like Disney, McDonald's and Ritz Carleton all have well defined operating methods.

Systematic operating methods constitute a key element of the franchising system provided by all national tax firms. To operate your tax business professionally, you also need to employ proven best practices. Systematic operating methods will also ensure continued growth and profitability of your tax business. As small business management guru, Michael Gerber, said, to succeed as a small business owner you need to "operate on your business and not in your business." Making this transition can be a daunting task. The first step is to have a written policy and procedure manual.

Why a Policy and Procedure Manual is Important

A policies and procedures (P&P) manual is critical to ensure that employees understand what is expected of them and know how they should handle the myriad of duties and responsibilities in the day-to-day operations of the business. Implementing systematic methods of operating your business is very important if your tax firm employs or plans to employ more than a couple of people, and it is essential in operating more than one office effectively. As more employees are added, communication and management becomes more complex. Tax preparers and other tax office employees can no longer turn to the tax business owner whenever they have a question about how a particular situation should be handled. Yet, the owner wants things to be done his or her way. Below is a summary of the key elements of a tax office P&P manual.

Tax Office Policies and Procedures

Employees need standard answers to scores of questions such as:

- How should the telephone be answered?
- How should client problems be resolved?
- How should tax returns be priced?

Chapter 6 – Tax Office Operating Systems

- How are tax returns prepared, checked, processed and e-filed?
- How are IRS Due Diligence requirements met?
- How are payments and bank deposits handled?
- How are daily results reported?
- How are tax preparers paid?

The list goes on and on. Best tax business practices have been tried, tested, refined and proven over many years. Systematic operating methods of operating your business should be documented in writing in a "Policies & Procedures Manual." Your "P&P Manual" will be a reference guide for tax preparers and other tax office employees, and will also serve as an essential training tool.

No Need to "Reinvent the Wheel"

Fortunately, spending many hours creating your own P&P manual, or purchasing an expensive franchise is not the only way to obtain systematic operating methods. There is no need to "reinvent the wheel." A policy and procedure manual, or tax office operations manual, is available for a relatively modest cost from other sources, including The Income Tax School.

Learn more about the Tax Office Operations Manual available at The Income Tax School.

- https://www.theincometaxschool.com/product/tax-office-operations-manual/

In addition to the routine "nuts & bolts" of preparing tax returns, ensuring IRS due diligence and operating a tax office, other critical issues must be considered in developing tax service policies and procedures such as the following:

Tools to Do the Job

Employee costs constitute the greatest expense in most service businesses. Not giving your employees adequate tools to do the job is "penny wise and pound foolish." Not having everything necessary to prepare tax returns efficiently will increase your employee cost and create employee frustration that will probably result in client dissatisfaction. Employing cutting edge technology can greatly improve efficiency and employee morale. Be sure to provide all of the little things that make employees' jobs easier. Something as basic as not having scotch tape or a stapler or staples can create frustration. Providing adequate tools and supplies to do the job will increase employee productivity and satisfaction, and also result in better client service and satisfaction.

Chapter 6 – Tax Office Operating Systems

Tax Season Equipment & Supplies

When purchasing is put off until the last minute, the result is often inferior quality, higher costs and late delivery. The first step is to take inventory of all existing equipment and supplies to determine shortages and avoid ordering excess items. Price quotes for each item should be obtained from several suppliers and purchase decisions should be based on value for the quality desired. For some supplies, it might be cost-effective to order enough for two years if the incremental cost per additional unit would result in a much lower price per unit. Your tax preparers should be provided with forms to take inventory of all office supplies and equipment and to request additional items when needed.

Choosing Tax Preparation Software for Your Business

There are quite a few high-quality tax preparation software products for tax professionals from which you can choose. Your tax software vendor or service bureau (a tax software reseller) can also be a great resource to help you achieve tax business success. When choosing the tax software that will best suit your needs, you should consider the types of returns you and/or your staff will be preparing and what you can afford. The following are some key considerations.

1. **How many tax returns do you expect to prepare?**

   If you will only prepare a small number of returns, it will probably be less expensive to choose a pay-per-return option. For example, TaxWise has a pay-per-return option for tax preparers who will prepare a small amount of returns. This package allows you to access the full Federal and State 1040 as well as business and specialty forms. It also gives you access to secure e-filing and offers customer service and support. Other tax software vendors also offer pay-per-return options.

2. **What types of returns will you be preparing?**
   - If you plan to only prepare Form 1040 and 1040A returns, and local state returns, then an expensive high-end software product would be overkill. Look for a low-cost software product that has positive reviews. There are many options to choose from.
   - If you plan to prepare complex individual and business returns (such as corporations and partnerships), and more complex returns (including estates and trusts), then a high-end software application such as Intuit's Lacerte may be needed.

Chapter 6 – Tax Office Operating Systems

- If you plan on preparing returns for multiple states, then you will need tax software that includes availability of software for every state you may need.

3. Could a cloud-based tax software option be a good choice?

If you are looking for an option that will help you save money, consider cloud-based software. Cloud-based tax software is less sophisticated but saves money and time by eliminating the need to do time-consuming installations and updates. Intuit Tax Online is a great choice.

4. What level of technical software support will you need?

Make sure you research the level of support that comes with each software package. Different vendors have different options, so be sure to read carefully and go with a package that suits your needs. Often a "Service Bureau" (value-added reseller) will provide better support than the tax software vendor.

Compare Tax Software Options

Once you answer the questions above, it's important to also compare your tax software options so you make the best choice for you and your business. Several organizations put out an annual survey comparing different software vendors. Check out our blog for a recent update on comparisons:

- https://www.theincometaxschool.com/blog/tax-preparation-software-for-independent-tax-business-owners/

Bank Products for Independent Tax Business Owners

If you plan to offer tax preparation services to your clients, you should consider offering refund advance checks, or other bank products. These services are not limited to the big national chains and can be made available to you by contacting the same banks they use.

Tax Office Set-up

Everything that will be needed for a tax office to operate efficiently should be in place before the start of tax season. Exterior signage should be cleaned and illuminated. Windows should be cleaned and all interior fix-up and cleaning should be completed before opening day. A good practice is to prepare and complete a pre-season checklist of all necessary tax office equipment, fixtures and supplies, cleaning, and set-up tasks.

Chapter 6 – Tax Office Operating Systems

Tax preparers should start the tax season in a clean, professional environment and have everything they need to provide professional service.

Ways to Make Your Tax Office More Inviting

Think about the last time you sat in a reception area. Notice it's not called a "waiting room." What was it like? Was it bright and welcoming? Were there things to do? When clients come to have their taxes prepared, you want the entire experience to be pleasant – this includes time sitting in your reception area. While it's true that no one likes to wait, making your clients more comfortable will help the wait not feel so long and enhance the overall experience.

Here are some ways you can make your office more inviting and help ensure your clients' experience is positive.

1. **A friendly face that greets them immediately**

   First impressions are lasting ones. For a tax business, first impressions happen when a potential client calls or when they walk through the door. Think about your office. What does a person walking through the

   door see when they arrive? Do they see a clean, professional looking environment or a mess of paperwork? What experience do they have when they step foot into your office for the first time? Are they welcomed and cared for or neglected and ignored?

   Here are some things to consider ensuring clients have a great first impression, of you, your office, and the job you did for them. Do you have a receptionist or a desk that faces the front door? No one wants to stand around wondering if anyone is going to immerge from a cubicle to greet them. Make sure there is someone in sight to immediately acknowledge all clients coming in the door. Consider installing windows in private tax offices and a bell on the door so tax preparers can see and hear clients entering the office. This is to ensure everyone knows when someone walks through the door.

Chapter 6 – Tax Office Operating Systems

2. Answer all phone calls by the third ring

Everyone in your office should be held responsible for answering the phones. Tax preparers can and should help answer the phones, especially when the call is from a local number. If the phones are not answered, your clients will think there is no one there, and you will lose business.

3. Cleanliness

Make a plan to clean the office before clients start coming in and keep it clean throughout the season. Keeping your reception area and all tax offices clean and uncluttered is essential to maintain a professional office image. Also, be sure to keep your restrooms clean and well supplied.

4. Up-to-date magazines

It's nice to offer guests magazines to read while they are waiting but no one wants to read last year's news. Make it a point to update your magazines throughout the season.

5. Offer beverages

Coffee is always a nice touch – whether it's a carafe up front or one of those single cup machines. Consider offering regular and decaf coffee, tea or even apple cider to guests when they arrive. You can also offer water or sodas. There doesn't have to be a drink  area up front, it can be offered to clients upon arrival, but a drink station up front is nice so that clients can help themselves.

Chapter 6 – Tax Office Operating Systems

6. Snacks

Want to really go the extra mile? Offer snacks to guests. It just adds an extra level of customer service. Plus, you never know who skipped lunch and will be unbelievably grateful for the snack!

7. TV

Television is always a great distraction for people waiting – especially if they have children with them.

8. Kid toys

Speaking of children... it's not uncommon for parents to have the kids with them when they come in. If you're a parent you know, sometimes it's just unavoidable. Having toys available for children to play with while they are in the office makes the experience much more pleasant because they have something to do.

9. Offer a Drop Off Service

If clients have items they need to drop off and they don't have questions, why make them wait for their preparer to either finish up with a client or phone call? Make it convenient for your clients by offering a drop off service – either through a receptionist or a secure box at the front of your office with instructions on how to leave documents safely and securely. This makes it easy for clients to get their paperwork in whenever they have time. You may even want to consider an after-hours secure drop off for items to be received when the office is closed.

10. Provide Private Offices for Client Interviews

A private office is appealing to clients; however, tax office space limitations often make it impractical. In this case, semi-private workstations with partitions are sufficient. Clients are divulging confidential information about their finances and personal details such as employment status, possibly divorce, etc. A desk area that is equipped with at least privacy partitions to prevent someone nearby from overhearing a personal conversation is important to your clients.

11. Make Client Tax Interviews Professional, Friendly and Thorough

Your clients expect and deserve much more than just a correct tax return. That is a given. Clients will only choose you over other options if you provide a positive experience and added value. Making the experience positive and adding value requires making a good first impression, showing genuine concern for the client, being very friendly and courteous, and making the client aware of what you have done to minimize their taxes. You should always end the interview with questions and comments such as:

- "Have I answered all of your questions satisfactorily?"
- "Is there anything else I can assist you with today?"
- "Please refer your friends and family to us, we would love to help them."
- "We look forward to seeing you again next year."

You should aim to be known not only for accurate tax returns, but also for your great service, prompt responses, positive attitudes, and professional environment. Your clients have lots of options, and they chose you. Make sure that you keep them happy, keep them coming back, and keep them referring new clients to you!

12. Efficiency

Your clients can tell if your tax office is not functioning efficiently, possibly because your computers and software systems are obsolete, or your tax preparers do not have the tools and research resources needed to do their jobs efficiently. You should provide your employees with a comprehensive equipment and supply checklist and a requisition form for them to request any missing items. Using a Customer Relationship Management (CRM) software system to manage client data can also add a greater level of professionalism to your tax service.

13. Music

Music is great for ambiance and adds a level of privacy by covering up the noise of conversations, phone calls, etc.

14. Ambiance

Adding artwork to your office walls is also a nice touch. You might consider prints of local landmarks as a source of artwork that would be appealing to most of your clients. You want your tax office to feel established and put together.

Maintaining a Professional Office Image is Everyone's Responsibility

It takes a team to accomplish a successful tax season. Office managers should hold the entire team or staff responsible for keeping office and workstations clean, organized, and uncluttered. Here are some reminders to give to your team to ensure everyone is pitching in.

- Always pick up paper or trash that may be lying on the floor or litter that may be outside the storefront.
- If the entrance doormat is dirty, get the vacuum and vacuum the mat.
- If the entrance door glass is smudged, clean it.
- Don't forget to clean up in the Break Room.
- After using the conference room, put the chairs back in place and clear the table.
- If there is something in need of repair or there is a maintenance issue, email the person in charge.

Hearing "It's not my job" is not helpful. All these responsibilities are part of everyone's job. Pitching in as a team will ensure that you present a professional image and promote a clean and healthy environment for your clients and employees.

Benefits of Adopting Systematic Operation Methods

Implementing systematic operating methods will ensure that your tax office runs smoothly and that your tax preparers work efficiently and professionally. A tax office that runs smoothly with tax preparers who work efficiently and professionally will make a very favorable impression on your clients. Equally, or possibly more importantly, your tax preparers and other employees will feel good about working in a tax office where they know exactly what to do and how to do it. They will also appreciate having all of the tools,

Chapter 6 – Tax Office Operating Systems

supplies and support necessary to do their jobs. If employee morale is high, they will provide more professional service to the clients they serve, resulting in a more positive experience for the clients.

Conclusion

There is no need to "reinvent the wheel." Adopting proven systematic operating methods will enable you, as an independent tax business owner, to be on a level playing field with the national tax firms. In fact, you will have a big advantage because you can make key decisions wisely as a motivated business owner. You will also have greater flexibility to make changes quickly. The result will be increased efficiency and a more profitable tax business with the potential to grow.

Chapter 7

Buying A Tax Practice

"A pessimist sees the difficulty in every opportunity. An optimist sees the opportunity in every difficulty."

- Winston Churchill
British Prime Minister

Chapter 7 – Buying a Tax Practice

The fastest way to grow your tax business may be to acquire one or more other local tax practices. This chapter will explore that option and provide a sample acquisition strategy.

Aging Tax Practitioner Population

Many tax preparers practicing in the tax industry today are elderly. This is a reflection, in part, of the demographics of the U.S. People who comprise our "Baby Boom" bulge are already retirement age and many tax professionals are included in that demographic profile. Baby Boomers are people who were born after World War II, approximately between the years 1946 to 1964. The youngest Baby Boomers are now in their mid-50's, with the oldest in their mid-70's.

Target Tax Practices

A sole tax practitioner who is ready to retire or who must give up his or her practice due to health issues will typically have a difficult time finding a buyer unless the tax practice is very large. Most of these tax practices consist of only the number of tax returns that the sole tax practitioner can personally prepare, or wishes to prepare, primarily during the tax season. Depending upon the complexity of the average tax return, this number may range from 50 to 300, generating revenue of between $25,000 and $100,000. You might also find the opportunity to acquire a much larger tax practice, possibly as much as $500,000 or more. A larger tax business will most likely be sold through a business broker. Adding this much revenue at one time to your tax business through an acquisition could constitute significant growth for your tax business. Smaller tax practices are easier for you to acquire because a business broker will not usually be involved. The sole practitioner may be more interested in making sure that his or her clients will be well taken care of than getting top dollar for the sale of the tax practice.

> *Disclaimer: All examples and sample legal documents are being provided for illustration purposes only. The author of this book is not an attorney and is not qualified to provide legal advice. Before making any legal decisions, you should consult with a qualified attorney who is familiar with the laws of the state in which you operate and/or make an agreement to purchase a tax practice.*

Valuation and Payment Terms

The average value of a tax business is one times revenue. The value could be as low as approximately .75 or as high as 1.25 times revenue depending upon the profitability,

Chapter 7 – Buying a Tax Practice

reflected by the average charge, overhead expenses, and client retention rate of the business. The key to a successful acquisition is to ensure that you will have a positive cash flow during the time period that you are paying for the business. We recommend that you pay a percentage of the revenue for the seller's tax returns that are prepared by you during the acquisition period, which should typically be from 3 to 5 years. The percentage of revenue should be no more than the following, which all add up to 1 x revenue:

- 3 Years – 33.33%

- 4 Years – 25%

- 5 Years – 20%

Research and Due Diligence

Before you ever make the decision to buy a business or someone's client base, you should always do your research and due diligence. This will ensure you are making the best buying decision. It's also the best way for you to assess the value of the business and any risks associated with the purchase. The seller will probably have you sign a non-disclosure agreement before giving you access to key information.

Purchase of Practice Agreement

Exhibit A, following the conclusion of this chapter is an example of a basic agreement to purchase a tax practice, including a Non-Compete, Non-Solicitation Agreement.

Notifying Seller's Clients

The seller's clients should be notified before the start of tax season of the transfer of their tax records to the buyer. This should be done by first having the seller mail a personalized letter to each of his or her clients. It is then recommended that the buyer host an open house to introduce the seller's clients to the buyer and the buyer's tax professionals who will provide tax preparation services for the clients of the seller. Below is a sample letter to notify the seller's clients, along with a sample open house invitation.

Letter to Seller's Clients

On the next page is a sample letter from the seller to the seller's clients. Note that this seller's fees were lower than those of the buyer. Therefore, the letter indicates that there will be an increase in fees. The seller's clients may realize that they have been getting a good deal and the increase may come as no surprise. If they are not willing to accept a gradual increase to your fair fees, then they should make other arrangements.

Chapter 7 – Buying a Tax Practice

Seller's Tax Service Letterhead

_____, 20____

Dear (client),

We have enjoyed the privilege of providing income tax preparation services for you in the past, and we appreciate you placing your confidence and trust in us. We have decided to phase out our tax preparation business and move toward retirement. However, we want to make sure that your need for affordable professional tax services will continue to be met in the future. Therefore, we have arranged for a highly reputable locally-based firm, _____Buyer_____, to continue to provide you with the level of tax preparation services to which you have been accustomed.

____Buyer_____ (www.buyertax.com) was founded in _____in _____ and has been recognized as a valued corporate citizen. Among the many awards received by __Buyer__ is the ____Key Award_____. _Buyer's_ founder, __Founder/ CEO___, has more than ____ years of experience and is widely recognized as a leader in the tax preparation industry and in the local community. __Buyer__ provides a Triple Guarantee of Accuracy, Year-Round Service and Satisfaction or you pay no fee.

__Founder___ has assured us that, while their fees are higher than the fees we have charged (due to greater overhead costs) they will not increase your fee this year by more than 20% for the same return that we prepared for you last year.

For your convenience, __Buyer__ will serve you this tax season in their __Local__ office in the _____ Center. The office will be open weekdays from 9:00 a.m. to 8:00 p.m., Saturdays from 9:00 a.m. to 5:00 p.m. and Sundays from 1:00 to 5:00 p.m.

Appointments may be scheduled by calling the office at (888) 555-1234.

We have greatly enjoyed serving you in the past and believe that you will find the service of the tax professionals at _Buyer__ to be of true value in the future.

Sincerely,

(Seller's Signature)

Chapter 7 – Buying a Tax Practice

Open House Invitation

On the next page is a sample open house invitation sent from the buyer to the seller's clients. In this case, the buyer organized and handled all aspects of the open house and paid for all the expenses. It's recommended that the seller and his or her spouse attend the open house, along with the buyer's president, vice-president, division manager(s) and senior tax preparers, including any EAs and CPAs. This makes for a nice event to meet the seller's clients and celebrate the seller's retirement. The event can be held at your office or public meeting space. The open house should not be a condition of the sale, but the sellers would be very appreciative that you would take the time and incur the expense to host an open house in honor of the seller's retirement.

Open House

You are cordially invited to an Open House in honor
of the retirement of John Smith, CPA.

Please join in the celebration! Also, please take this opportunity
to meet our Director of Operations, Jane Smith, EA, and other
experienced tax professionals at Buyer's Tax, who are ready to provide
you with the personal service you have experienced in the past.

Tuesday, November XX, 20XX
From 3:00 p.m. until 7:00 p.m.
Food & drinks will be provided.
Hosted by

Buyer's Tax, Inc.

Your Address
City, State Zip Code

R.S.V.P. 888.555.1234
info@buyerstax.com

Chapter 7 – Buying a Tax Practice

Employing the Seller

Some sellers may be interested in continuing to work part time, possibly only preparing the tax returns of their favorite long-term clients. If this is the seller's desire, it is a perfectly acceptable option. You could employ the seller under the same terms that you employ other tax preparers with comparable experience and credentials. If the seller were not preparing those returns, you would have paid one of your employees to prepare them. If you still have a positive cash flow, this arrangement is fine. You will need to consider the workstation arrangement. For example, you could schedule the seller to work 2 days per week and schedule another part-time employee to work the other 3 or 4 days using the same workstation.

Transferring the Client Files

If the seller has been using the same tax preparation software as you, that is a plus! If not, hopefully your tax software will have the option to import the files from the seller's tax software. If transferring the files is not possible, you might consider making an adjustment in the purchase price to cover the cost of inputting the clients' tax return data into your tax software. Even if you don't make such an adjustment in the purchase price, you will still have a positive cash flow based on the valuations and payment terms recommended in this chapter.

Conclusion

Buying a local tax practice can provide the opportunity for you to increase your tax business to ensure growth. Buying two or more tax practices would be even better. Before you agree to the purchase, you should learn about the seller's tax practice. You should purchase the assets only (not the company, just the client files) and not assume any prior liabilities that may arise from errors made by the seller. By paying only a percentage (not more than 1/3) of the revenue realized from clients that have their returns prepared by you, you will be assured of a positive cash flow throughout the term of the purchase. Be sure to execute the appropriate legal agreements after seeking the advice of a qualified local attorney. You should also have the seller mail a letter to his or her clients (at the seller's expense). You should host an open house (at the buyer's expense) at your office so the clients will become familiar with your office and can meet you and your employees.

Chapter 7 – Buying a Tax Practice

EXHIBIT A
Tax Practice Purchase Agreement and Non-compete, Non-solicitation Agreement

Tax Practice Purchase Agreement

Your Tax Firm ("Buyer") has agreed to purchase a tax practice from XYX Tax Firm ("Seller") and Seller has agreed to sell the tax practice of Seller to Buyer. The practice consists of approximately ____income tax preparation clients of Seller ("Clients"). Buyer agrees to purchase the assets specified only and not the legal entity. ("Assets"). The agreed purchase price of the assets is 25% of the total revenue realized by Buyer from the Clients during the calendar years of 20__, 20__, 20__ and 20__. Buyer will provide an accounting to Seller of the Clients served and the revenue received for each of these years. Payments will be made no later than 30 days after the end of each calendar quarter.

Seller warrants that he/she has delivered all client files and computer tax data for the Clients to Buyer and that he/she has completed all client work for the (immediately prior) tax year as well as any corrections discovered during the due diligence process. Seller agrees to sign the non-compete, non-solicitation and confidentiality agreement included as Exhibit 1 to this purchase agreement.

Buyer agrees to make all payments required under this agreement as described above. Buyer will immediately provide year-round service to the Clients along with the Buyer's Guarantee.

Buyer will not be liable for any damages incurred by Clients resulting from errors made by Seller in serving Clients of Seller, including but not limited to the reimbursement to Clients of any IRS, State or other interest or penalties pertaining to services provided by Seller.

Agreed and Accepted: _____ day of

Buyer's Tax Firm

BY _____
Buyer

_____
Seller

Chapter 7 – Buying a Tax Practice

EXHIBIT 1
Non-Compete, Non-Solicitation Agreement - Page 1

THIS NON-COMPETE, NON-SOLICITATION AGREEMENT ("Agreement") is made on___, 20__, between Your Tax Firm ("Buyer") and You and Seller's Tax Firm ("Seller"). In consideration of the mutual covenant of the Sale of Assets Agreement entered into on_____, 20___. between Buyer and Seller and the mutual covenants herein contained, Buyer and Seller agree as follows:

1. **Conflicting Employment**. Seller agrees that, for a period of (2) years from the date of your Sale of Assets Agreement with Buyer, you will not, directly or indirectly, on behalf of yourself or other person, business or entity, provide or assist in providing to any former income tax preparation customer of you or Seller or any customer of Buyer, any tax preparation services substantially similar to those provided by Seller, or (2) solicit or assist in soliciting any customer of Buyer for the purpose of providing any tax preparation services substantially similar to those provided by you. Seller agrees that all tax returns prepared by you shall be processed through Buyer in all respects. The only exceptions are (1) returns prepared for Seller's immediate family members (defined as spouse, parents, children, brothers and sisters).

2. **Non-Competition; Non-Solicitation of Customers.** As consideration for the purchase of assets from Seller, Seller covenants and agrees that for a period of two (2) years from the date of Seller's Sale of Assets Agreement with Buyer, regardless of the reason therefor, Seller shall not, directly or indirectly (whether alone or as a partner or in joint venture with another person or entity, or as an officer, director, shareholder, employee, consultant or agent of any corporation or other entity or as a trustee of any trust:

(1) provide or assist in providing to any customer of Seller any tax preparation services substantially similar to those provided by you through Seller or

(2) solicit or assist in soliciting any customer of Buyer who was serviced by you or Seller for the purpose of providing any tax preparation services substantially similar to those provided by you through Seller. For purposes of this Agreement, "customer" shall mean any person, business or entity serviced by you or Seller on the last date of your self-employment or within the two (2) years prior to your last date of self-employment or employment with Seller.

3. **Remedies.** Seller has had an opportunity to have this document reviewed by independent counsel. Seller has carefully read and considered the provisions of this Agreement and, having done so, agrees that the restrictions set forth therein are fair and reasonable and are reasonably required for the protection of the interests of Buyer, its officers, directors and other employees. In the event that, notwithstanding the foregoing, any of the provisions of this Agreement shall be held by a court to be invalid or unenforceable, the remaining provisions hereof are independent and shall nevertheless continue to be valid and enforceable as though the invalid or unenforceable parts had not been included therein. In the event that any provisions of paragraphs 1 or 2 shall be declared by a court to exceed the maximum duration and scope permitted by the substantive law under which such restrictions are interpreted, the parties agree that the court may modify the duration and scope of the restrictions herein as it deems reasonable. Seller acknowledges compliance with this Agreement is necessary to protect the business and goodwill of Buyer and that a breach will result in irreparable harm and continuing damage to Buyer, for which money

EXHIBIT 1
Non-Compete, Non-Solicitation Agreement – Page 2

damages would not provide adequate relief. Consequently, Seller agrees that, in the event Seller breaches or threatens to breach this Agreement, Buyer shall be entitled to both a preliminary and/or permanent injunction in order to prevent the continuation of such harm. Seller agrees that such injunction shall be available without the posting of any bond or other security by Buyer. If Seller violates a covenant and as a consequence Buyer seeks injunctive relief from a court, such injunctive relief may be applied prospectively to include the duration of the covenant unexpired at the time of the first breach, notwithstanding that the covenant may have otherwise expired at the time a lawsuit is filed or the time the relief is granted. In addition, Buyer shall be entitled to money damages in an amount of 150% of the fees realized by Seller or Buyer from any customer lost by Buyer as a result of Seller's breach of this Agreement for the most recent year the customer was served by Buyer.

The liquidated damages set forth herein have been included because damages would be difficult to calculate and this is a reasonable approximation of the damages Buyer would suffer as a result of a breach of this Agreement, particularly given the repeat nature of Buyer's business. Seller expressly waives any defense as to the validity of the liquidated damages provision on the grounds that such damages are void as penalties or are not reasonably related to actual damages. The liquidated damages provision shall not prohibit Buyer from pursuing any other remedy, including by way of example only injunctive relief. Seller acknowledges and agrees that all remedies are cumulative. Seller agrees to pay reasonable attorney's fees and costs incurred by Buyer in enforcement of this Agreement.

4. **Applicable law; Forum.** This Agreement shall be governed by and construed in accordance with the laws of the ____(Name of State)____, exclusive of its conflict of law provisions. The parties further agree that any legal action or proceeding seeking the interpretation or enforcement of this Agreement or any provision thereof, or seeking the resolution of any disputes or controversies arising from or relating to this Agreement, shall be instituted exclusively in the Circuit Court for the _____ Name of County _____ or the United States District Court, Name of District . For the purposes of this Agreement, Seller acknowledges and submits to the personal and subject matter jurisdiction of the Circuit Court for the County of _____, and the United States District Court, Name of District and Division .

5. **Miscellaneous.** This Agreement contains the entire understanding between the parties and supersedes all prior written or oral agreements or understandings between them. No amendment to this Agreement shall be valid unless in writing and signed by the parties. Any failure by Buyer to exercise any right under this Agreement shall not be construed as a waiver of the right to exercise the same or any other right at any time. Seller's covenants, obligations and agreements hereunder shall survive the termination of any employment or contractor status with Seller and the termination of this Agreement, regardless of the reason therefore. This Agreement shall be executed in multiple copies and each executed copy shall constitute an original, but the copies shall be deemed one and the same instrument. Section headings are used for convenience of reference only and shall not affect the meaning of any provision of this Agreement.

IN WITNESS WHEREOF, the parties have executed this Agreement on the date first above written.

BY _____
Buyer

_____
Seller

Chapter 8

Marketing Planning

"Strategy is not the consequence of planning, but the opposite: it's the starting point."

- Henry Mintzberg

Chapter 8 - Marketing Planning

Your tax season marketing budget should be determined, and a plan should be completely formulated 4-6 weeks prior to tax season. In some cases, maybe even further out than that to ensure placement of advertisements when and where you want them, and to lock in sponsorships during key months, such as January and February. This will ensure that marketing strategies and tactics are budgeted and well thought out and will allow time for refinement as tax season approaches. The plan can then be implemented in a timely manner during tax season.

The marketing plan should consider the topics listed below that will be discussed in detail in the following six chapters:

1. Pricing Your Services

2. Mass Media Advertising

3. Digital Marketing

4. Your Website

5. Social Media Marketing

6. Neighborhood Marketing

Hiring a Marketing Consultant

To help you develop and implement your marketing plan, you might consider engaging a professional marketing consultant. Be wary, however, as some people who present themselves as consultants lack the qualifications to be of real value. You should determine the credentials and experience of any consultant you are considering. You should also ask for customer references of other small business owners of companies that are of comparable size to your business. You will not likely be able to afford a full-service marketing agency. If a marketing agency does offer you a good deal, you might wind up with their lowest level people. There might also be free or low-cost options available for small businesses in your community. You should check with your local Chamber of Commerce or Small Business Development Center (SBDC). Also, the Small Business Administration (SBA) might provide a volunteer "SCORE Business Mentor."

Strategies and Tactics

To develop a marketing plan, it is helpful to understand the difference between strategies and tactics. A strategy is a broad method of attaining a goal. For example, if your goal is to attain a 5% share of tax returns in your local market, a strategy could be a mass media advertising campaign, and tactics might be to run commercials on selected network TV and radio stations that offer commercials in the best day-parts and with the most efficient pricing.

Establish Your Marketing Budget

Established businesses might allocate 5-10% of their projected revenue for marketing. However, a new business would probably need to spend a much greater percentage because start-up revenue will not be as high as an established business. Your challenge is to determine how much revenue is being generated by each of your marketing expenditures. Sometimes it is not possible to determine the revenue realized from a marketing initiative, but it may still be necessary to spend the money. Nevertheless, there are usually other ways to measure the results. There are some costs you must incur, such as the cost of creating a professional website and professional literature. One philosophy is to continue to spend money on any marketing tactic that generates as much as you are spending (or more). You may need to spend more than you originally budgeted to take advantage of opportunities. Even if a tactic is a break-even proposition, you will benefit from the lifetime value of the new clients. In the chapters ahead, you will be provided with many very effective strategies and tactics that will not break your modest budget as a small business owner.

Identify Your Target Clients

You should decide whether you want to be a mass market tax preparer or if you will specialize in preparing tax returns for certain segments of taxpayers. One option is to serve lower-income taxpayers who are seeking to obtain some money immediately and have the tax preparer's fees paid from the expected refund. At the other extreme, you could specialize in serving high-income taxpayers, including complexities such as sole-proprietor business income, rental properties, K-1  distributions, stock transactions, etc. Or you could focus on serving one or more taxpayer niches, such as doctors, police officers, U.S. expatriates, or even Mary Kay consultants. The marketing strategies and tactics that you use will be determined by the type(s) of taxpayers you plan to serve.

Conduct Market Research

Effective marketing planning requires that you obtain information about your prospective clients, the competition, the industry, and the environment. By knowing your market, you should be able to create marketing programs that produce better results.

Determine Your Competitive Positioning

Determining what makes you different and better than your key competitors is essential. This characteristic is referred to by marketing experts as a "Unique Selling Proposition" or USP. For example, your USP might be that you are a retired U.S. Army Colonel who specializes in preparing tax returns for military personnel. Or maybe you operate a tax service that caters to taxpayers with more complex tax returns and you employ only IRS Enrolled Agents. Or, perhaps you cater to low-income taxpayers and charge lower fees than any of your local competitors.

Chapter 8 - Marketing Planning

Learn about Key Competitors

Once you decide how you will position your tax business, you should learn as much as possible about your direct competitors. This information will help you to determine how to differentiate yourself and become the best alternative, or maybe the only option if you have a niche market! In the next chapter, Pricing Your Services, we discuss the tactic of using "Secret Shoppers" to learn about your competitor's pricing. Your shoppers can also obtain a great deal of additional information about your competitors. This information will help you to determine how you can stand out from your competitors.

Develop an Action Plan

Most independent tax business owners must work on multiple strategies and tactics to succeed. All the options described by the following six chapters should be given serious consideration. Once you decide on your marketing strategies, you should develop a timetable of all actions that must be implemented to realize your marketing goals.

Conduct Test Marketing

Experimenting with new advertising methods is a good idea if you can test the water before making a major financial commitment. Advertising sales reps can make a very convincing case for the advertisements they are selling. They will show you statistics and tell you how well their advertising has worked for others. Don't believe it until it works for you. The only way to find out if something is as good as it seems is to test it on a limited basis. If the advertising generates more than it costs, you should consider buying more of it. If not, either drop it, or try another variation of your test. A failure does not always prove that the medium is faulty; it could mean that your message was flawed.

Evaluate Your Marketing Campaign Results

Too often marketing campaigns are blindly repeated year-after-year without any idea as to whether they have worked. Don't fall into that trap. Set up a procedure to track the sources of all new customers and to learn the reasons previous customers do not return. You should also conduct surveys of your clients and prospective clients to determine whether their needs and wants are being satisfied.

> **TIP:** Be sure to include a different tracking code for each advertisement you run. Then, keep a record of how many new clients come in with each type of code, along with the revenue received for each of those clients. This will help you evaluate whether certain marketing efforts are working.

TIP: Ask new clients how they heard about you when they come in, especially if they don't mention a special offer or have a coupon with them. Keep track of this information as well.

TIP: You should not stop marketing after tax season.

Conclusion

You should develop a marketing plan well in advance of the beginning of the tax season. Decide the types of taxpayers you will serve and their characteristics. Also learn about your competitors and determine how you will be different and better than them. Incorporate the strategies and tactics in the following chapters that will enable you to meet your marketing goals. Develop an action plan to implement your marketing tactics on a timely basis. Front-load your marketing campaign and test any paid advertising on a small scale before spending a lot of money. Set a budget but be flexible; if you are generating enough revenue to cover your cost, spending more makes sense. Be sure to evaluate the results of your marketing initiatives to ensure you are not wasting your money.

Chapter 9

Pricing Your Services

"The buyer is entitled to a bargain. The seller is entitled to a profit. So, there is a fine margin in between where the price is right."

- Conrad Hilton

Chapter 9 – Pricing Your Services

The cost of preparing any tax return can vary dramatically among different tax practitioners. IRS law prohibits tax preparers from basing their fees on the amount of tax refund realized by the client. Many tax practitioners charge by the hour, others operate from a standard schedule of charges, and some simply charge "what the traffic will bear." Higher levels of tax expertise typically command higher fees.

Determining Your Fees

If you operate a home-based tax business, you will not have a lot of overhead. Therefore, you would be able to charge a lower fee than if you operate in a storefront. Lower fees can help you gain market share. However, be careful not to price your services too low. If your services are a lot lower than the general market price in your area, clients may become concerned that you are not as competent as the other tax professionals. In addition, your profit margin will be lower and the value of your business will be less. Also, if you move into a storefront or a professional office in the future, your fees must be adequate to cover your new overhead expenses. It is easy to lower fees in the future, but much harder to increase fees. However, if your fees are too high, you may attract fewer clients and your revenue could be less. In academic marketing jargon, this dilemma is called "price elasticity." Your challenge is to determine the fees that would enable you to generate the greatest revenue and profit. In any event, your fees should probably be at least comparable and probably somewhat lower than the fees charged by the national tax firms.

Check Out the Competition

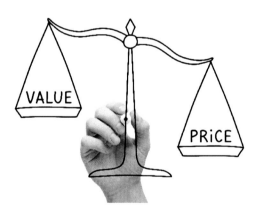

You need to know the value of your service and understand the local market. Obviously, when setting your fees, you must be competitive. Therefore, it is important for you to find out the fees charged by your local key competitors. Calling the main competitors in your area for a price quote based on a scenario will give you an idea as to whether or not you are pricing your services competitively. If they will not provide a price quote or estimate by phone, you could recruit a friend or relative to "shop" your main competitor(s) in person, posing as a potential client. Obtaining national average pricing can also help. National tax preparer price surveys are conducted annually by some of the accounting and tax professional associations, such as the National Association of Tax Professionals https://www.natptax.com.

Chapter 9 – Pricing Your Services

Pricing Policies

Your clients could be charged fees based on the time it takes to prepare their returns, i.e., an hourly rate assigned to each preparer based upon their experience, expertise and productivity. Another method is to charge based on the tax schedules and statements required to prepare your clients' tax returns. Typically, the national tax firms use the latter method upon which to base their fees.

Charging by the Forms

The fairest pricing method may be to base your fees on the complexity of the income tax return, determined by the schedules and statements required. You simply charge a base price for the type of return you are preparing…1040EZ, 1040A, 1040, etc. and then charge for additional schedules and statements, etc. You can also charge for the following:

- Additional line entries
- Compiling tax information
- State tax returns; local and foreign
- E-filing
- Bank products
- Amended returns
- Taxpayer representation: audit, offer in compromise
- Copies of tax returns

- Non-individual returns: 1065, 1120, 1041

If you employ other tax preparers, charging by the forms is also more equitable because some tax preparers are slower or less efficient than others.

For example, a newer preparer may need more time to research a tax situation he or she has not yet encountered. Therefore, charging a standard hourly rate would be unfair to your client. Your client should not pay a higher fee if a less efficient or less experienced tax preparer takes longer to prepare his or her tax return. In addition, establishing different hourly rates for each one of your tax preparers based on their efficiency, and increasing their rates as they become more productive would be difficult and very subjective.

TIP: One example is to charge a base fee for Form 1040, plus additional fees for each statement and schedule required, with extra charges for multiple items, such as W-2s, interest and dividends and stock sales. An hourly rate could be charged for bookkeeping or "compiling tax information." A separate schedule of charges could be used for non-individual returns such as corporations and partnerships. An example of a Schedule of Charges is included in the Tax Office Operations Manual available for purchase through The Income Tax School.

- https://www.theincometaxschool.com/product/tax-office-operations-manual/

Chapter 9 – Pricing Your Services

Pricing by the Hour

If you are a sole practitioner, it might be appropriate to charge by the hour. You may not want to do this unless you will be preparing complicated returns. Charging by the hour would also make it difficult for you to compare your fees with national averages published in surveys by professional associations. Many basic tax returns will take less than an hour to complete and you could run the risk of charging inappropriately. However, you could establish a minimum charge. Remember the client is paying for your knowledge, experience, and credentials, and not just for the time it takes to compile the tax return.

Quoting Fees in Advance

Charging by the schedules and statements required makes it more feasible for you to quote the fee in advance that will apply regardless of how long it may take for you or another tax preparer to complete the return. If a client's tax return is complicated, you may have difficulty quoting an exact price before conducting a thorough interview. However, you should be able to conduct a short phone interview to provide a rough estimate of the probable fee. A telephone interview form should be used for this purpose. If a fee is quoted in advance, the prospective client should be advised that the fee was based on the schedules and statements required based on the information provided by the taxpayer. If something new comes up during the interview requiring additional forms to be completed, an additional fee would be charged. The completed interview form should remain on file until the potential client comes in for service in case there is a change in the information provided, which could affect the price quoted over the phone.

Most people who inquire about price simply want a "ball park figure" to determine whether the cost will be reasonable and affordable. You should welcome questions about pricing and disclose as much as possible about the basis for your fees in advance. If you deliver value-added services at no additional cost, such as assistance in the event of an audit, a tax-planning session, a state tax return, etc., you should mention them. The bottom line is that people are afraid of the unknown. If you can tell a prospective client what you would charge up front you have eliminated that concern.

Chapter 9 – Pricing Your Services

Sample Rates for a Home-based Tax Business

Personal Income Tax Preparation - Federal and State - Price List	
1040EZ, 1040A Short Form - includes 1 state	$75
1040 Long Form - includes 1 state	$150
1040X - Amended Federal Return	$100

Additional Schedules/Forms Necessary to be Filed with 1040A or 1040	
Schedule B	$10 to $75 per form
Electronic Filing	FREE
Non-resident State	$40 per state
Schedule E	$40 per page
Schedule C	$50 to $200 per form
Schedules A, D, F, 8863, 8812	$5 to $20 per form
Earned Income Tax Credit qualification analysis	$5 per form
Other schedules or Forms	to be discussed
Hourly rate (applies only in unusual, complicated, and lengthy matters):	$75 to $150 per hour

Business Income Tax Preparation - Price List	
Tax preparation: active entities Corporations, Partnerships, or Trusts Includes 1 domicile state tax return	$300-$500
Tax preparation: inactive entities Corporations, Partnerships, or Trusts Includes 1 domicile state tax return	$300-$500
Schedule, worksheets or attachments	$25-$50 each
Interviews, consulting, and analysis invoiced at *standard hourly rates for complex, or lengthy issues only	$75 to $150 per hour
Foreign, or non-resident state	$50-$100 each

Chapter 9 – Pricing Your Services

Sample Rates for a Brick and Mortar Tax Business

Personal Income Tax Preparation - Federal and State - Price List	
1040EZ, includes 1 state	$75
1040A includes 1 state	$186
1040 Long Form - includes 1 state	$186
1040X - Amended Federal Return	$100

Additional Schedules/Forms Necessary to be Filed with 1040A or 1040	
Schedule B	$39 + $4 for each entry
Electronic Filing	FREE
Non-resident State	$55
Schedule E	$33 + $27 for each property
Schedule C	$70 + additional cost for each schedule or form completed for Schedule C
Schedules A	$60 + additional cost for each schedule or form completed for Schedule A
Schedule D	$45 +4 for each entry
Schedule F	$75 + additional cost for each schedule or form completed for Schedule F
8863	$40
8812	$30
Earned Income Tax Credit qualification analysis	$45 + the cost of additional EIC forms and Schedules needed for due diligence
Other Schedules or Forms	
Hourly rate (applies only in unusual, complicated, and lengthy matters):	$100-$150

Business Income Tax Preparation - Price List	
Tax preparation: active entities Corporations, Partnerships, or Trusts Includes 1 domicile state tax return	$300 + additional forms and schedules
Tax preparation: inactive entities Corporations, Partnerships, or Trusts Includes 1 domicile state tax return	$300 + additional forms and schedules
Schedule, worksheets or attachments	$10-$75 each
Interviews, consulting, and analysis invoiced at *standard hourly rates for complex, or lengthy issues only	$100-$150
Foreign, or non-resident state	$55

Chapter 9 – Pricing Your Services

Invoices

You should prepare an invoice or bill for every client including the date of service, fees and method of payment. This feature is available in most computerized tax programs. Don't forget to maintain a copy of each invoice for your own accounting and tax records. Providing your written guarantee with your invoice is also a good practice as it adds perceived value and can be deemed as the terms of a legal agreement.

Accepting Payments

You'll need to decide what types of payment you are willing to accept. Due to the proliferation of credit cards, fewer people carry cash and personal checks with them.

PayPal or Merchant Account

You will probably want to accept credit and debit cards as soon as possible. You can get merchant services through a bank or you can simply sign on with PayPal. Paypal is an online payment service that allows you to send and receive money over the Internet and it can be added to your website. You should investigate both options and decide which is best for your business. Fees will vary.

Credit Cards

Some people may not be able to afford to pay for your services when payment is due and will need to pay with a credit card (or a debit or stored value card). Others may want to pay with a credit card merely because it provides additional benefits such as airline mileage points or cash back rewards. Your business banker should be able to provide you with the capability to accept credit cards. You could also shop for better rates. Keep in mind that you will be charged fees for credit card purchases, and this should be factored into your pricing.

Checks

It's a good business practice to accept personal and business checks from your clients. It is important to make paying for your services as convenient as possible. Unfortunately, there is some risk involved with accepting checks and you should be prepared for that situation.

You should develop and post your check acceptance policy. Some suggestions include:

- The check must be preprinted with the person's name, business name and correct address.
- Starter checks should not be accepted.

Chapter 9 – Pricing Your Services

- Require clients to have a phone number on the check. The physical address on the check must match their mailing address – no P.O. Boxes. (You should have the mailing address from the tax return.)

- A driver's license number or state I.D. number along with the state of issue and expiration date should be on the check. (You can write it on there.)

- You might decide not to accept checks from new clients. However, you may want to allow exceptions when you perceive there would be little risk.

Some clients will have checks that don't have a phone number, street address, and ID information preprinted on them. In that case, the information can be written on the check by you or the client. You should validate the information by viewing a driver's license, etc.

You should also have a return check policy such as - *Any returned checks will be assessed a service fee of $XX.00* based on fees charged by your bank and the additional time needed to deal with a returned check). Be sure to post the returned check fee as part of your check acceptance policy where clients can see it. Also, be sure to deposit checks daily to ensure the client still has money in their bank account to cover the check.

Your business banker will probably be able to provide you with the capability to have checks approved instantly by using a check processing machine. However, you must consider the cost of any necessary equipment.

Cash

Good old cash is always acceptable, but cash is becoming rarer these days, except for low-income taxpayers who may not qualify for a credit card or bank account. Be sure to put all cash into the bank daily so that you don't spend it, lose it or have it stolen. You should always keep your personal and business affairs separate.

Offering a Satisfaction Guarantee

Offering a satisfaction guarantee is a very good thing for your business. A satisfaction guarantee might read as follows: "If you are not pleased with the service you receive in the preparation of your tax return(s) and you choose to neither file them nor allow us to redo them, we will refund your fee in full." The number of clients that decide not to accept a tax return prepared by a reputable tax firm is insignificant; probably less than one-tenth of 1 percent. This is a very small price to pay to be able to tell prospective clients "if you are not happy with

the fee we charge for the return we prepare, you will not have to accept the return and you will owe us nothing."

If you have employees who are compensated based entirely or in part by the fees realized for the returns they prepare, a satisfaction guarantee will incentivize your employees to satisfy your clients. If a client is not satisfied and you are unable to rectify the situation, you will need to honor your guarantee. Employees who are paid commissions should only be credited with revenue that you actually collect for returns that they prepare.

Unfortunately, you may have to refund some client fees but it is vital that you keep your promises to your clients. The manner in which you handle client complaints and honor your guarantee can be the difference between retaining and losing a client over an honest mistake. In addition, your reputation is at stake.

Be sure to communicate the benefits of your guarantee to your clients and prospects. The guarantee adds value to your service and can differentiate your practice from competitors. When there are no strings attached, and clients are afforded a "way out" if they are not satisfied, the decision to have their tax return prepared by you is much easier. Your policy should clearly state what the guarantee will provide to the client. Your clients are paying for your tax services, and your guarantee is an important part of that product.

One method to try to keep that client, is to honor your guarantee and offer to prepare their tax return for free, or at a discount of 50%, the following year. The cost of free preparation next year is a small price to pay to retain a client. The lifetime value of each client is substantial. In addition, if you lose the client, he/she will most likely tell several other people about the negative experience.

Additional Guarantees

- **Accuracy**

  You should offer a "Guarantee of Accuracy" or you pay all fees incurred due to your error. This accuracy guarantee is nothing more than stating that you will pay for any monetary damages incurred by your client for which you would be legally responsibility. Also, in the event of a legal dispute, your guarantee could, conceivably, be viewed as a contract that would limit your liability to the damages stated by the guarantee.

Chapter 9 – Pricing Your Services

- **Year-Round Service**

  Being available year-round to assist clients also super important. It is essential to be available to your clients at any time throughout the year to help them, at no additional cost, should they have a tax problem or a tax question. This commitment should include helping your clients if they receive a letter from the IRS or state taxation department. You should also consider agreeing to help with an IRS audit at no additional charge, provided that the audit can be resolved by mail. However, it is recommended to charge fees to help the client with an office audit (requiring one of your employees to go to the office of the IRS or other taxing agency). You should also charge fees for taxpayer representation services requiring an Enrolled Agent, CPA or attorney. These type of audits and representation can take up much more of your time.

Conclusion

You must decide whether you will base your fees on the time it takes to prepare tax returns, or the schedules and statements required. However, tasks other than actual tax return preparation may require establishing a time charge for those items. The fees you can charge to attract the largest number of clients to generate the greatest revenue and profits will be affected by:

1. the expenses to provide your services
2. the price your prospective clients are willing to pay
3. the fees your competitors charge

Prospective clients who call your office seeking a price quote may dismiss you as an option if you refuse to give them some idea as to what you would charge to prepare their tax returns. You should be prepared to accept credit cards, in addition to cash for your services. Having a policy pertaining to accepting personal checks is also advisable. Offering a Satisfaction Guarantee can result in much more revenue than it might cost. A written Accuracy Guarantee is also advisable, and being available to your clients year-round is very important.

Chapter 10

Mass Media Advertising

A good advertisement is one which sells the product without drawing attention to itself.

- David Ogilvy

Chapter 10 – Mass Media Advertising

John Wanamaker (1838-1922) was a very successful United States entrepreneur and a pioneer in marketing. He opened one of the first and most successful US department store chains, which eventually was merged into Macy's. Wanamaker coined the phrase "Half the money I spend on advertising is wasted; the trouble is I don't know which half." Most advertisers are faced with the same challenge today.

Mass Media

Mass media is marketing communication that reaches a large, broad audience. A mass media strategy can be used to create awareness and name recognition among all taxpayers, and is many times more effective in selling to lower and middle-income taxpayers. Upwardly mobile, executive-level, and small business taxpayers are less likely to be influenced by mass media advertising, like a television commercial. At least not with the quality of a television commercial that an independent tax business owner can afford to have produced and attain adequate reach and frequency. Mass media advertising can be written, broadcast, or spoken through television, radio, movies, newspapers, magazines, direct mail, and more! Digital marketing can also be used for mass media advertising, and it will be covered in Chapter 11.

TIP: Target your advertising to be more effective and efficient to pre-qualified prospects. Tailor the ad message so you are not wasting advertising dollars on audience members who are not prospective clients,

Segmenting Your Targeted Clients

Mass media advertising is effective in creating awareness, name recognition, and differentiating your firm from the competition. However, it is difficult to effectively sell with mass marketing because tax preparation service is not a commodity. Although some taxpayers with more simple tax returns seem to treat it as one, the pool of taxpayers is made up of people having widely varying tax situations and needs. It's

important to determine the needs and wants of each group and develop strategies to meet those needs and market to that client segment effectively.

Chapter 10 – Mass Media Advertising

Low-income taxpayers usually qualify for Earned Income Tax Credit (EITC) and, many times, are prospective Refund Advance clients. A Refund Advance is a no-interest loan that is repaid with the taxpayer's refund. It is only available early January through the end of February of each year. The primary needs of these clients are speed of refund, price, and convenience, in that order.

The middle-income group are by far the largest client segment and constitute the mainstay of traditional mass-market tax firms. These taxpayers are concerned about price, speed of refund, and convenience, in that order. They are also concerned about knowledge and professionalism of the tax preparer, year-round service, and the tax firm's stability and willingness to stand behind its work. They tend to be loyal if they receive true value and are treated with courtesy and respect.

Upwardly mobile taxpayers are professional white-collar workers, such as line-managers, teachers, engineers, nurses, medical technicians, computer programmers, etc. They generally have college degrees. Upwardly mobile taxpayers are somewhat less concerned about speed of refund and price. Knowledge and professionalism of the tax preparer, convenience, year-round service, and the tax firm's stability and willingness to stand behind its work are all very important. They may need tax planning advice and assistance with tax questions during the off-season. They will remain loyal if they receive personal service, preferably from the same tax professional year after year.

Executive level taxpayers are the high-income segment – the tip of the pyramid. Although small in numbers, they are the most lucrative clients and the ones most in need of professional tax assistance. They include middle managers, attorneys, college professors, and small business owners. Executive level clients often have complex returns, but not always. They are the least price-sensitive of all clients, and often the most demanding. They expect a private office interview with an expert, sophisticated tax professional who will be available year-round to help them with tax planning, estimates, and tax questions. Executive level clients are willing to pay extra for special service.

TIP: Television and radio advertising are least expensive in the first quarter of the year. So, you will have more buying power at the beginning of the tax season. In addition, you are dealing with a diminishing market, meaning that every day that goes by during tax season, more taxpayers have filed. So, it's better to load your advertising dollars in the beginning of the tax season if you are doing mass media advertising. But keep in mind that different types of taxpayers file at different points during the tax season.

Chapter 10 – Mass Media Advertising

After defining your client segments, you should determine strategies and tactics to market effectively to each group. Your advertising media selection should be based on reaching your target market(s) as efficiently and cost-effectively as possible. Ad creation should appeal to the needs and wants of your target prospects.

TIP: Recruit and train tax preparers that are bilingual and then advertise that you have bilingual preparers. This will allow you to market to an entirely new set of demographics that you may not have been able to tap into before.

Network Television

The five network TV stations, ABC, CBS, NBC, FOX, and the CW, are typically the main vehicles used for mass media TV advertising. However, cable TV can also be used for mass media advertising. Tax season will be the most important time period for you to utilize TV advertising. TV is perceived as being extremely expensive and there is some justification for that perception. The cost of a professionally produced TV commercial can be astronomical, but it doesn't have to be. An effective TV commercial can be professionally produced for as little as $1,000, but you will need to shop very carefully for the right advertising professional and/or production house.

TIP: Consider using two 15-second spots as bookends (2 different commercials in the same commercial break), instead of one 30-second commercial. This will help you if you have more than one message to deliver. This will also help to increase the frequency of the message being delivered.

Media Buying

Buying media is a specialized skill, which requires knowledge of your target clients' behavior, the media, and the criteria used to measure the value of TV and radio programming. A broadcast station sales rep's advice can be very helpful, but never let a media sales rep talk you into buying a package. Instead of relying on the sales rep, you could hire a professional media buyer at no cost to you since the station pays the media buyer's commission. It is important for you to learn about the key factors applicable to the tax industry when buying media. Some of the most important considerations are…

- Your efficiency goal is to get the lowest cost-per-thousand ("CPM") for adults 18 and over, which would include all taxpayers.

- Your commercial should, ideally, reach 100% of the audience with an average frequency of at least five times.

Chapter 10 – Mass Media Advertising

- Schedule varying run times and programs. Your sales rep should be able to identify the most efficient programs and/or run times.

- You should require that all stations quote from the most recent rating services stats (e.g. Nielson).

- Compress the intensity of your campaign at the start of tax season, allowing less frequent or no running spots later on in the season.

- Ask for proposals from each of the four network TV stations. Tough negotiating is part of the game. It's not unusual for a station to be asked to resubmit 3-4 times before it tells you that's the bottom line.

Cable TV

While network TV is most effective for reaching the mass-market, cable TV is best used to reach a target market. Cable TV can zero in on specific demographic consumer profiles. Cost per thousand on cable is more expensive than network, but the value of being able to target to your desired market can make it more efficient.

Radio Advertising

Radio can be used much like network TV due to its ability to reach the mass-market. The cost efficiency of radio is not as great as network TV. However, radio commercial production costs are lower, and radio can be used effectively with a smaller budget. Using radio and network TV simultaneously will increase frequency and can produce synergistic results. As with TV, it usually pays to hire a professional to produce your radio commercial.

Radio is higher priced, up to twice as much as TV. However, radio is more targeted, and it can complement and reinforce TV. Radio can be a very effective vehicle to reach specific client segments from fast refund clients to executive level taxpayers. Radio can be used to target particular ethnic groups, or taxpayers with specific levels of income.

TIP: Consider sponsoring the local metro traffic report can get your name and a brief message aired on several radio stations during drive time with great frequency at a modest cost.

Chapter 10 – Mass Media Advertising

Besides increasing reach and frequency, double the information can be provided by radio commercials. Since mass-market radio is passive, the best day parts are drive times (rush hour/lunch hour) when listeners in their cars are a captive audience.

Note: Network TV and radio mass-media advertising may only be cost-effective if you have office locations convenient to most viewers or listeners in the TV or radio Designated Marketing Area (DMA).

Print

Newspaper can still be effective in rural markets and as a targeted advertising medium. Your local community newspaper might be well read. If you can get your local newspaper to trade an article for an ad, that could be an effective tactic. The condition for you to buy an ad would be for the newspaper to publish an article about you and your tax firm.

While newspaper is often ineffective as a mass-marketing vehicle (at least in larger markets), it can be used effectively to reach certain target markets.

Types of newspapers and how to use them efficiently:

- **Daily News**

  If you have offices throughout the daily newspaper's circulation coverage area, the daily newspaper should be much more efficient than local weekly newspapers. However, many daily newspapers (in response to competition from local weekly newspapers) have introduced local supplements that are distributed only to subscribers in local areas. These local supplements (usually published weekly) are often considerably more cost effective than local weeklies. Daily newspaper advertising rates are rarely negotiable or commissionable to an agency.

- **Weekly News**

  In such a community, the weekly newspaper will probably be widely read and could be an efficient vehicle to reach the local market. In larger markets, local community weeklies are usually not as widely read because most people read the daily newspaper. Yet a community weekly newspaper can be efficient if your only office is in that same community.

- **Weekly Special Interest**

  Many weekly newspapers are targeted to specific audiences such as senior citizens, business owners, young singles, college students, homemakers, ethnic groups, etc. Special interest newspapers can be effective vehicles to target to specific taxpayer segments, provided that your ad is customized to appeal to the target reader.

- **Shopper**

  These newspapers usually contain only ads and no editorial content. Shoppers can be the most efficient of all newspapers for budget tax preparation and fast refund services. Many taxpayers seeking short form tax preparation and fast refund services are the types who are looking for a bargain.

- **Newspaper Classified**

  Classified ads are inexpensive, but usually are not effective to advertise tax services. Classified display (display ads run in the classified section) are much more visible, but also costlier.

Many newspapers nationwide have reduced staffing in recent years as subscriber and advertising dollars have moved away from print media toward online content. Many newspapers have seen growth in their audience for digital content.

Like special interest newspapers, magazines and newsletters can reach targeted audiences, but require customized ads. National magazines usually publish regional editions, but these regions are usually too far-reaching for most tax services. Each publication must be evaluated separately. A well-designed display ad in a local magazine targeted to small business owners could generate lucrative business tax returns and accounting work.

TIP: A group tax discount coupon published in a major employer's employee newsletter could result in new business.

Chapter 10 – Mass Media Advertising

Mass Mailing

The most cost-effective form of mass mailing, in terms of cost per recipient, may be a coupon pack such as Val-Pak and coupon books such as Reach Magazine. However, your message is diluted by being one of a couple dozen advertisers that each get a quick glance – especially if you're not the only tax service advertising in the mailing.

Postcards are the most cost-efficient form of solo direct mail. The cost of designing and printing postcards is significantly less than that of a brochure or even a letter (which adds the cost of an envelope). A postcard with a hard-hitting headline, strong copy, and good graphic design can be very professional looking and effective.

TIP: Testing on a small scale is always advisable before committing to a major direct mail campaign, or any major advertising campaign.

If you are targeting upwardly mobile or executive level prospects, a letter in a #10 envelope might be the most effective format. The more personal you can make the letter the better. You could sign each letter individually in blue ink so it is obvious that your signature is not printed or photocopied. Customized form letters can be used to appeal to taxpayers with special needs. You can write them yourself or purchase sample letters from tax professional suppliers.

Almost any list can be purchased for a moderate cost from list brokers or trade and professional associations, such as newlyweds, ministers, military personnel, police officers, outside sales reps, doctors, etc. You can send targeted letters to individuals with certain life changes including new home buyers, newly retired, newborn baby, recently married, etc. Alternatively, you can use your business's events to target appropriate clients, like sending letters to residents in your business neighborhood, or thanking existing clients for their referrals, etc.

TIP: Consider mailing gift certificates for free tax preparation services to recent high school graduates. This offer is designed to introduce young taxpayers to the tax firm with the hope of establishing a life-long relationship. Variations of this idea include mailing to college seniors, offering discounts instead of free tax returns, and offering free electronic filing for self-prepared returns.

Outdoor Advertising

Billboards can be rented for as short as one month, and they are usually sold in lots of at least a dozen. The cost per thousand (CPM) for billboard readers can approach the efficiency of network TV. However, the impact of a billboard is not comparable to that of

Chapter 10 – Mass Media Advertising

a TV commercial. The reader will only glance at it from a passing vehicle for one to three seconds. Therefore, the headline must be very concise, ideally just three or four words or less. The illustration must be attention getting and should clearly convey your message and the benefits to be realized.

Outdoor advertising can also be used to direct clients to your office if a strategically located billboard facing the main flow of traffic toward your office is available. A directional billboard would be especially beneficial if your office has poor sign exposure.

Mass-Transit Advertising

Mass-transit advertising includes signs on commuter buses and trains and at bus and train stations. Outdoor advertising can also be purchased for a short time period to coincide with and reinforce an advertising flight on TV.

Signs inside buses and trains (and at stations) are different than billboards in that they can contain much more information. They can also be outfitted with add-ons such as tear-off coupons or reply postcards containing your literature. This direct response feature makes precise measurement of the ad campaign's effectiveness feasible.

Cinema Advertising

Cinema Advertising can be an effective way to reach new clients. Trivia and advertisements run 15-20 minutes before the movies begin and the audience is a very captive one. Offering free movie tickets with paid tax preparation is a great way to expand your client base. Tickets can usually be purchased at a discounted rate in larger quantities. This vehicle is especially effective if your office is located in the same center or immediate vicinity of the cinema.

Telemarketing

There's no reason why a telemarketing campaign can't work for tax preparers. The key is to purchase or compile a calling list of likely prospects, develop an effective script, and have a skilled telemarketer make the calls. A positive approach might be to offer free tax information and a special introductory discount if the prospect decides to have you prepare his taxes.

Chapter 10 – Mass Media Advertising

Internet Marketing

Technically, the Internet is a mass-market medium. It's an essential marketing vehicle for all tax professionals. The Internet constitutes a market too big for any entrepreneur to ignore. By effectively using the Internet, a local tax professional can create a regional, national, or even worldwide presence, and an image to rival the giant tax preparation firms. Considering the plethora of ways to market your tax business using the internet, the best practices will be covered in the following chapters.

Conclusion

Mass media advertising is a very cost-effective strategy to reach all taxpayers with sufficient frequency to convey your message, but only if you have offices that are conveniently located to serve all, or at least most, of the viewers in the Designated Market Area (DMA). However, you must consider the fact that about 50% of all taxpayers prepare their own tax returns. A self-preparer is not likely to seek professional help unless the taxpayer or the family experiences a significant event that would result in tax complications beyond the taxpayer's knowledge base. Most of the other 50% of taxpayers who already have a relationship with a tax professional they use every year are very unlikely to change tax preparers. Even if they are not completely satisfied, changing is not easy for them, especially because their tax preparer is familiar with their tax situation and has copies of their tax records. Only a small percentage of these taxpayers would be dissatisfied enough with the service they received or the price they paid, or possibly due to an error that was made, to consider changing their tax preparer. Therefore, we can reasonably assume that only about 10% of all taxpayers may be receptive to hiring a professional tax preparer or switching to a new tax preparer. The problem with mass media advertising is that you are paying to reach 100% of all taxpayers, when only an estimated 10% might be interested. Consequently, you are paying to reach 90% of the taxpayers who are not your prospects. This fact makes mass media advertising a very expensive option for tax preparers. Targeted advertising and niche marketing are the most cost-effective strategies for most tax professionals. These marketing tactics will be covered in the following chapters.

Chapter 11

Digital Marketing

"As you've noticed, people don't want to be sold. What people do want is news and information about the things they care about."

- Larry Weber

Chapter 11 – Digital Marketing

What is Digital Marketing?

The term "Digital Marketing" is used by marketing managers, marketing consultants, operations managers, and many others. But what does the term mean? Digital marketing encompasses all your online marketing efforts. Digital Marketing is a very broad strategy that includes a variety of different marketing channels such as the following:

- Your Website
- Email Marketing
- Pay-Per-Click Advertising (PPC)
- Search Engine Optimization (SEO)
- Display Advertising
- Social Media Marketing (SMM) – such as Twitter, Facebook, Google+
- Professional Networks - LinkedIn
- Content Marketing – such as blogs, whitepapers, ebooks
- Affiliate Marketing
- Video Marketing – such as YouTube, Vimeo
- Podcasting
- Photo Sharing – such as Flickr, Instagram
- Online Public Relations
- Mobile Phone Marketing – such as text messaging/Short Message Service (SMS) and picture messaging/Multimedia Messaging Service (MMS)
- …and much more!

Deciding which channels to focus your efforts on depends on your goals as a business and the kind of clients you are targeting. Not all digital marketing tools will be applicable or work for your tax business. The business and marketing landscape has changed throughout the years and will continue to change. It is important to grow with the vast opportunities provided by the Internet. In this chapter, we will discuss which channels and techniques will work best for your tax business.

Chapter 11 – Digital Marketing

Your Website

A website is more essential than a business card today and will reflect the image you present to your clients and prospects. This is one type of marketing where the people are seeking you out and want more information about your company. Your clients are looking for information and your content is the key to whether or not they will visit your website again. If you can be seen as "the source" for tax-related information, you will be in demand when the need arises for assistance. You do not have to be an expert or spend a lot of money to have a presence on the web. It is easier and a lot less expensive than you might think.

> **TIP:** One user-friendly website builder that is powerful yet simple for easily creating professional business websites without any programming skills or additional software is https://www.wix.com.

Chapter 12 will discuss in further detail how to optimize your website.

Social Media

Your social media pages will be the second, if not the first, place that your clients will use to discover you and seek more information. Building an online presence is extremely valuable and one of the best ways to gain exposure and compete with national tax firms. It's important to have a couple of well-managed social media channels. For a tax office, you should look at Facebook, LinkedIn, and Twitter, which offer a means to reach many new, potential clients.

Chapter 13 will discuss in further detail how you should be using social media for your business.

Search Engine Optimization (SEO)

You may have heard of the term SEO before, but many people don't really understand what it means. The search engines (like Google, Yahoo, Bing) have "spiders" that "crawl" the Internet looking for the most relevant content for whatever is being searched. When someone finds your website naturally by using keywords and phrases, it is called an organic search. You did not pay for that person to click on your site at that specific moment. The best websites spend a lot of time working on organic or natural optimization.

According to Search Engine Journal, https://www.searchenginejournal.com/seo-guide/ranking-signals, the top 7 ranking signals for websites are:

113

Chapter 11 – Digital Marketing

1. Publishing high-quality content
2. Making your site mobile-friendly
3. Creating a secure website (HTTPS)
4. Improving your user experience
5. Optimizing your page speed
6. Mastering your on-page optimization (SEO)
7. Earning relevant and authoritative backlinks

Your Website's Content

You can optimize your website by adding relevant high-quality content that you wish to be recognized for. The first step is to determine what people that are interested in your product or service are searching for online. Once you know what keywords or phrases are being used to search for the product or service you offer, you can choose the ones that are most relevant to your business and start adding them to your website.

Mobile-friendly Website

Having a mobile friendly website is very important and is now considered the norm. But as we all know, things are changing rapidly. Google now gives a better SEO ranking to websites that are primarily meant for mobile optimization, meaning desktop viewing is given less weight than before. Make sure you don't rush the launch of your mobile website version before it is completely finished and flawless. Having errors on a running mobile website will end up having more consequences in the long run.

Creating a Secure Website

Some Internet browsers now flag websites that are not HTTPS as "not secure". If this happens to you, it could keep people from ever visiting your website. HTTPS establishes an encrypted link between the user's browser and your website. This added level of security protects the integrity of your website and lets your clients know they are visiting a secure site. It's extremely important that your website it secure. Users need to feel confident that they can click through your website safely and place an order or share information on your website securely. If you have a client portal for clients to share information, you will need to use HTTPS.

Improving Your User's Experience

If your website is hard to follow or doesn't flow well, you run the risk of people leaving and not coming back. You don't need a complicated website. The simpler the better! It helps to make a list of the top things you truly need on your website and then consider what type of additional content could be added to keep visitors coming back. A blog is often a great way to add fresh content on a regular basis without adding information all over your

Chapter 11 – Digital Marketing

website. People can go to one place for up-to-date information. Also, if you have any pop-ups, be sure they do not cover all of the main content on the page.

Optimizing Your Page Speed

To help your pages load faster, you should use smaller file sizes for anything housed on your website, reduce or eliminate the number of redirects you have, remove any irrelevant code, among other things.

Mastering On-page Optimization

Search engine optimization, or SEO, are super important here. You need to find the best pages to use certain relevant keywords. Write quality content about key topics that are important to what you do. Be sure to include a title and description for the search engines to find each page. Using a main heading (H1) and at least one subheading (H2) on webpages can boost your SEO rankings. Add relevant inbound and outbound links whenever possible. Add images, videos, and infographics whenever possible to break up your text. Have a few exact-match anchor text links. This is when you use text links on your website with an exact keyword(s) that you want to rank for and nothing else. **You should only have a few of these on your website, as too many can penalize you.**

Quality Links

Quality internal and external links are also important if you want a high-ranking website. Once you create content that is in demand and relevant to your audience, you can promote that content through various online channels, which will allow trusted users in the industry to share and link your content. The search engines will then consider your content more relevant.

> **TIP:** Be careful not to hire someone who says they can get you a bunch of back links very quickly. Quality back links take time to build because they are valid and credible. That's why the search engines like them so much!

Pay-Per-Click Advertising (PPC)

Pay-per-click is an online advertising channel where you as the advertiser are charged by a host whenever your web ad is clicked. While other fee structures exist, like cost-per-impression (CPI), PPC is the most common way of billing online ads. There are different types of online ads that use the PPC method. Below are the most important two types; Search Engine Marketing and Display Advertising.

Search Engine Marketing (SEM)

Search Engine Marketing is one of the most common ways to use PPC advertising. Basically, when someone searches on Google, Yahoo, BING, or another search engine, they put in one or more keywords and then they get results based on those search terms.

Chapter 11 – Digital Marketing

At the top and side of these search engines, the user will see "sponsored links" with a short description that is sort of a sales pitch with a link for more information. When you click on one of these sponsored links, it will take you to their website and the company will pay a small fee each time this happens. Based on the keywords and message you choose; you can reach a broad market or a much more targeted market. When using Google AdWords, you have control over your budget. You decide the average amount you want to spend each day. On the days when your ad is more popular, AdWords will allow up to 20% more of your average daily budget so you won't miss out on those valuable clicks. But don't worry, they lower your maximum budget on other days so that, over the course of a month, your overall spending will average out to the limit you've set (assuming your campaign runs for a full month).

To create successful ad campaigns, you will need to:

- Define you marketing goals (visit your website, make an appointment, call your business, etc.)
- Determine what types of ads you will run
- Refine the geographical location you want your ads to show
- Set a smart budget
- Segment your ad groups properly
- Write effective content
- Take advantage of optional ad extensions
- Fine tune your keywords to be relevant to what is being searched

AdWords calculates a score, called Ad Rank, for every ad in the auction. Ad Rank determines your ad position and whether your ads are eligible to show at all. The ad with the highest Ad Rank gets to show in the top position, and so on. Your Ad Rank has six main factors:

- Your bid – What you set as your maximum budget for the ad.
- The quality of your ads and landing page – How relevant your ad and website are to the search.
- Ad rank thresholds – a minimum threshold that an ad must achieve to even appear.

Chapter 11 – Digital Marketing

- The competitiveness of an auction – the higher-ranking ad usually wins but paying a higher cost per click could allow a lower ranking ad to win the auction.

- The content of the person's search – their content, location, time of search, what device they're searching on, and more.

- The expected impact from your ad extensions and other ad formats – Utilization of the ad extensions.

TIP: Consider hiring an expert to setup or manage your Google Adwords account. Google Partners is Google's program for advertising agencies, digital marketing professionals, and other online consultants who manage AdWords accounts. Each Google Partner is required to attain a certified badge that shows they have demonstrated AdWords skill and expertise, met AdWords spend requirements, delivered agency and client revenue growth, and sustained and grown client base. Use the Google Partner Search online: https://www.google.com/partners

Display Advertising

Display advertising is advertising on other websites, using images, audio, and video content. Banners on high-traffic websites tend to be very expensive and rarely generate enough revenue to cover their cost. Remember that the Internet is a worldwide medium. Websites that are targeted to universal audiences are not likely to be cost-effective advertising vehicles for a local firm. However, many websites are targeted to local communities, and an increasing number of universal sites have special sections with content targeted to local communities (e.g. Yahoo, Bing, Google). Many local daily newspapers and TV stations and have developed websites to provide additional advertising opportunities for local businesses. Opportunities also exist to advertise on the websites of local non-profit organizations, including civic and business groups. Trade associations, such as the National Association of Tax Professionals (NATP), National Association of Enrolled Agents (NAEA), and the National Society of Accountants (NSA), provide opportunities for their members to be listed on their websites. Local business associations, such as the Chamber of Commerce and Better Business Bureau, also provide opportunities for their members to have exposure on their websites. The most cost-effective way to advertise on the Internet may be to negotiate reciprocal links with appropriate high-traffic, reputable and relevant websites to your own website.

Chapter 11 – Digital Marketing

Online Reviews – Learn to Love Them!

How many stars does your company business page have on Facebook? How about your local BBB page? Online reviews are everywhere, and they are worth looking into.

Are you asking your clients to review your business? You should!
Did you know that *91 percent of people regularly or occasionally read online reviews, and 84 percent trust online reviews as much as a personal recommendation?*

Online reviews are the best way to judge a company's trustworthiness and service beyond asking a friend. You need to know what your online reviews say about you. You need to know your score across the web. It's important to know what potential customers are reading about you online. It could be great things, but it could also be turning people off.

Here are some of the most common places for reviews – places you should have accounts with and be checking on a regular basis.

Google Reviews

Every business with an address has a free Google Business page. Do you have yours claimed? This page also houses Google reviews that users can leave about your business. Want to check yours? Just search your business in Google and look on the right-hand side of the search results. There you will find your listing and any reviews clients have left. If you've claimed your business page, you should get an email notification when someone leaves a review.

Nearly half of US adults said they've Googled someone before doing business with them.

- 45% said they have found something in an online search that made them decide *not* to do business with the person.

- 56% have found something that solidified their decision to do business with the person.

Yelp!

Love it or hate it, Yelp is a popular place for people to leave reviews. Yelp is a local-search service powered by crowd-sourced review forum. You can look up any local business on Yelp, check out its offerings (if the business has completed its Yelp profile), and then read or leave reviews. It doesn't matter if you're on Yelp or not, people can still leave reviews about your business. Might as well claim your business account and stay on top of it.

Here are 2 stats from Yelp! that will make you want to pay attention:

- Every one star increase in a Yelp! rating means a 5 to 9% increase in revenue.

- 82% of Yelp users said they typically visit Yelp! because they intend to buy a product or service.

Better Business Bureau

The Better Business Bureau has been around since the 1900s! Their goal was to correct advertising abuses. In response to marketplace demands, BBBs quickly expanded to monitor business performance and provide consumers with vital information to avoid the pitfalls in the marketplace. Every region has its own BBB Chapter where business owners can become BBB Accredited.

The BBB also handles consumer complaints and allows consumers to rate businesses on its website. As a business, it's advantageous of you to not only go through the accreditation process but to keep up with your ratings and reviews.

Facebook

If you have a Facebook page, you have a place for people to leave reviews. Lots of Facebook users check out Facebook reviews to see what others are saying. Be sure to take a look at yours!

LinkedIn

Since we're talking about reviews, it's worth mentioning that people can leave recommendations for you on your personal LinkedIn profile. Just another great place you can shine.

How to Handle a Bad Review

Bad reviews happen. Sometimes they're completely fabricated, sometimes they're the result of an unfortunate miscommunication, and sometimes you just flat out messed up. Unfortunately, most platforms that handle reviews do not allow the reviews to be deleted unless they include profanity or hate speech.

The best way to handle a negative review is to respond diplomatically (without picking a fight), and ask that the person contacts you offline so that the issue can be resolved. If you messed up, apologize. If the person is being unreasonable, take the conversation offline. The worst thing you can do is hash out a disagreement in a long comment chain for the world to see. What people *do* want to see is that you addressed the problem and attempted to solve it.

TIP: Don't just respond to the negative reviews. A simple thank you for a positive review can go a long way!

Online reviews are important to watch and address when they come in. Knowing what people are saying about you online can go a long way. As they say, "Feedback is the breakfast of champions."

Conclusion

Digital Marketing has become a way-of-life for businesses today. Most independent tax business owners will need expert help to meet this challenge. Fortunately, education, assistance and support are provided to independent tax professionals by tax software developers, tax industry vendors, and tax professional associations. Independent tax professionals will be challenged to remain competitive with the national tax firms, and to keep in step with the rapidly changing tax industry environment. Independent tax business owners need to work cooperatively to meet this challenge. And, don't neglect the task of monitoring your reviews and developing positive ones.

Chapter 12

Your Website

Websites promote you 24/7: No employee will do that.

- Paul Cookson

Chapter 12 – Your Website

As mentioned earlier, your website is more important than your business card today. If you don't have one, potential clients looking for you on the Internet won't find you there and will likely end up going to one of your competitors. The main goal of your website is to create conversions… or new clients!

Start with a Basic Website

If you're just starting your business, your website may be fairly basic, but a basic website is better than none at all! You can create a professional looking website that is easy for visitors to navigate simply.

The top pages you need to include on your website are:

- **Home**

    This is your home page where you should provide a very summary of who you are and what you offer. This page needs to be interesting and engaging as it's your first impression with a potential client.

- **About Us**

    This is a good place to tell your story. People love a good story! Include your picture and a short bio about yourself. If you have employees, be sure to include their pictures and information, too. You want people to connect with you and your business! This is also a great place to include information about your company's philosophy and/or mission statement. You can also include links to additional pages with articles, information about awards you or your company may have received, and press releases about your company and key employees.

- **Services**

    Here is where you should explain all the services you offer. If you have a lot of offerings, consider categorizing them, and even link to additional pages if it's a lot of information. You don't want to overwhelm your reader with too much information on one page. Don't forget to list the benefits and value-added services you offer that make you different and better than your competitors!

Chapter 12 – Your Website

- **Products**

  If you have products, you can list them here, along with any features and benefits. For example, you may have refund products such as a Refund Transfer.

- **Frequently Asked Questions (FAQs)**

  This is the place where you can answer questions that you hear a lot. Questions like…How much do you charge? Do I need to make an appointment? How long will my appointment take? What should I bring to my appointment? What should I do if I get an IRS letter? Your goal here is to encourage visitors to call you and/or schedule an appointment. Make sure that all information is up-to-date. To help facilitate this, it may be wise to have a section where people that have visited your site can email you to inform you of any errors they may catch. Be sure to ask and answer questions as positively as possible, while being as honest and realistic at the same time. You can always add more questions to this list.

- **Contact Us**

  This section is very important. The last thing you want is someone who has a question and no way to get in touch with you. Include your phone number, fax number, address, and e-mail address. A hyperlink to send an e-mail right from your site is also helpful. It's also a good idea to have your email and phone number in the header or footer of every page for quick access.

- **Locations**

  If you have more than one location, you may also need a locations page. It's helpful to include directions and/or landmarks to help find locations faster. Linking your office addresses to maps and directions is a great way to show clients where you are located, and it helps them get accurate directions.

- **Privacy Policy**

  Because you are dealing with such personal information, you should include your privacy policy. This should include information you collect, how you collect it, how

Chapter 12 – Your Website

it's used, etc. If you don't have a policy, you can create one fairly quickly. Be sure to follow all IRS guidelines for tax professionals and tax businesses.

- **Other Helpful Pages**

  - Tax Tips to Help Clients Save on Taxes
  - Calendar of Events: This helps clients stay up-to-date on filing deadlines
  - Special Offers: These may help increase business. Have a new client discount offer or coupons available for clients to print.

TIP: Considering creating your website in WordPress. This is a free Open Source system, which allows you to create an e-commerce website including a blog and, if needed, a shopping cart. Then, you can easily make content changes yourself without paying a web developer for every single change you have.

Once you have all the basics on your website, you can consider adding a few bells and whistles. Remember that you are a professional service business. You don't want to your website to be too busy or flashy. Some great additions for your tax business are:

- Client organizers
- Client portal with secure file sharing
- Calculators
- Testimonials/Reviews

- Online appointment scheduling
- Online credit card payments
- Online tax service
- A Blog

TIP: Several of the larger tax software companies offer an online tax service that you can add to your website very easily and then you can share in the revenue! This is a great way to compete with the national chains and alternatives to your service.

Many of these add-ons can be obtained from tax industry vendors at affordable prices. You should also consider adding a resource page with free articles along with archived monthly client e-newsletters. Your website is a never-ending, work-in-process that must not be neglected because of constant changes in tax laws and the needs of your clients and prospects.

Be sure to continuously add fresh content, such as new whitepapers, articles and news releases, in addition to product offerings or special. Also be sure to keep up with your content and delete anything that is not current. Make sure your content is valuable to clients and prospects and include compelling calls-to-action.

Chapter 12 – Your Website

Being Mobile Friendly

A mobile-friendly website is essential for your business. Think about how many times you use your phone daily to search for a nearby business that has a service you require. What if the website you pull up is hard to read or navigate? Chances are good, you will leave that website to find an easier one in just seconds.

Mobile users are looking for a quick, mobile-friendly experience with all the information they seek literally at their fingertips. It's important to take into account the increasing use of smartphones or tablets in finding local businesses and to make sure you design a mobile website that makes it as easy as possible for the consumer to choose your local business. Google, Yahoo!, Bing, and other search engines will even give a better SEO ranking to websites that are primarily optimized for mobile.

> **TIP:** You can use this link to test your website to see how it looks to mobile viewers:
>
> - https://www.google.com/webmasters/tools/mobile-friendly/

Communication Tools

Live Chat

Live chat has become very popular on websites. For a low monthly fee, you can have a live chat feature added to your website. This enables you to have a real-time, online private discussion typed simultaneously with someone visiting your website. This is a great way for someone to ask a quick question without having to pick up the phone. It also lets website visitors feel a little more in control of the conversation and allows them to remain anonymous if they prefer. While this can be a great tool, be careful not to get too detailed in answering tax questions on a live chat. You may not have all the information necessary to give the best answer. Therefore, it's best to keep your Q/A fairly basic and broader in nature.

Client Reviews

Potential clients love to hear feedback from real clients when they are in the process of deciding whether to become a client themselves. It enhances your credibility and helps potential clients feel confident that they are making the right decision by choosing you. Although, making reviews an automated process does add to the legitimacy of them.

Chapter 12 – Your Website

Don't worry, you'll get a chance to look over each client's comments before they go live on your website. And that's important, because sometimes there is bad language or it's really just spam. It's important to post *all* of your valid reviews – good and bad. If you receive a negative review, you should include a sincere reply and make every effort to make it right. Keep in mind, complaints should be seen as opportunities to win back clients. You never know when you might change an unhappy client into a raving fan! Responding to a message from an unhappy customer gives you a chance you may not have had otherwise had to respond to him and others with the same concern.

TIP: Review plug ins are available for your website if you use WordPress. There are also third-party services available; or you can add testimonials to your website manually. You should also consider other sources for reviews that were mentioned in the previous chapter, such as Google, Yelp!, Facebook, among others.

Contact Forms

Contact forms are another great way for customers to contact your business without having to pick up the phone. These forms can be set up to send any inquiries straight to your inbox. The forms can be customized to ask for certain information and can even include captcha forms to avoid bots. Contact forms are preferred overusing your business email on your website because bots will scan your website and send spam emails to the address listed on your site. Contact forms are also a great way to collect contact information for leads. These are easy to create with a WordPress plugin.

Secure File-Sharing

This is a way to share any size file through a secure website. You can pay a fee to have it added to your website or you can pay for a membership at websites like https://www.sharefile.com and http://www.dropbox.com. This is extremely useful in the tax industry because of all the confidential information that needs to be shared between each client and your business. It will also save you and your clients time from dropping off missing documents.

TIP: One option is CCH's iFirm® Client Portal, which can be easily added to your website and allows customers and tax preparers to share information and documents securely, and even sign important documents virtually.

- https://taxna.wolterskluwer.com/firm-management-and-workflow/ifirm/portal

Chapter 12 – Your Website

A Blog on Your Website

Even though you may not see yourself as a writer, you are an expert in the field of tax preparation. Many of the top tax preparation firms are blogging and there are benefits to doing it. Here are a few reasons why blogging is good:

- **Blogging Increases SEO**

  Good blogs are updated regularly, which provides fresh content to your website. Once a week is sufficient, and search engines give websites with fresh content and/or a blog higher rating than those without one.

- **It Helps Potential Clients Find You**

  Depending on your content, you may have potential clients searching online for exactly what you are writing about. Now they will find you and view you as an expert in that field.

- **Visitors Stay on Your Website Longer**

  More content gives visitors another reason to stay on your website, and in turn, helps them become clients.

- **A Blog Helps Visitors Get to Know You and What You Have to Offer**

  A blog is more of a conversation. So, readers get to see more of your personality.

- **You Can Showcase Your Tax Knowledge**

  It's another way to differentiate yourself from the competition and show readers that you are an expert in your field.

What Should You Blog About?

You can use frequently asked questions to help you get started. Also, think about what's currently going on in the tax industry and the struggles your real-life clients are having related to tax, and let those be your launching pad. You can also ask your clients what

Chapter 12 – Your Website

they want to know more about. Be sure that you are truly providing added value for your clients and not just promoting your business.

Consider Being a Guest Blogger on Someone Else's Website

Content marketing has become an important part of marketing for every business. Beyond sharing your expertise on your own blog or creating whitepapers for download, there's another great option – that could help get you in front of fresh eyeballs. It's called guest blogging. Guest blogging is just what it sounds like. Creating original content for someone else's website or blog.

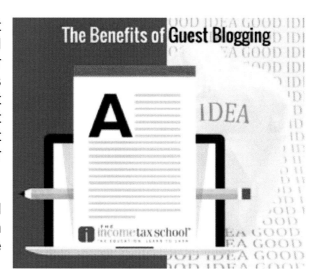

Guest blogging can be a great way to extend your reach and get your name or business in front of a different audience. It also has the following advantages:

- Shows off your expertise
- Offers insight into your industry that another audience may not be aware of
- Allows you to link back to your website (this can help increase your SEO)
- Is a way to promote your business and services
- Adds credibility to your voice, and can be used as a promotional tool (as seen on X website)

Choosing Who to Blog For

You don't want to write for just anybody. The partnership should benefit both you and the blog you're writing for. Look for websites and blogs with high readership – the last thing you want to do is spend time crafting a blog post that no one will see. You should also make sure that the information you offer is of value to the readers in the publication. Here are some ideas:

- Blogs or websites that cover the tax industry
- Companies in your area that offer complimentary services (banks, financial institutions, etc.)
- Local business associations
- Major online publications that cover tax topics
- Local news publications

Chapter 12 – Your Website

- Organizations whose members could benefit from tax tips
- A niche market that you serve

What You Should Write About

Think about the audience and what they would find valuable. Overall, topics should offer insight and advice that readers could learn from or use in their own situations.

- Tax industry news that might affect them
- Tax tips
- Bookkeeping and payroll tips
- Tips on choosing the right tax preparer

To find possible places to guest blog, reach out with an email, introduce yourself, and offer up some topics and a timeline. If they have an editorial calendar, they'll appreciate the early planning and you may just land on their calendar.

Your Domain Name

An important decision you will need to make is choosing your domain name. This is your website address on the Internet. You want to pick something that is easy to remember, easy to spell, and not too long. Your email addresses can match your domain to make things unified. Be sure to pick something relevant to your business and the industry.

Hosting

Hosting is the service of keeping your website live on the Internet and readily accessible at all times to anyone and everyone. In a perfect world, you want to host your website on a dedicated server that will never be offline. There are different types of hosting available.

Chapter 12 – Your Website

- **Shared Web Hosting**

  This is one server that is being shared between many customers and/or websites. This is less expensive, but it *can* slow down your website if other sites on the server are really busy. It can also be a less flexible option if you have specific needs.

- **A Website Builder**

  If you go through a site builder website to create your website, they will usually host your website for you. The cost is low and they make things very easy, but as you grow you may have issues if you want to become an ecommerce website or if you want to have more custom items on your website.

- **Cloud Hosting**

  This is sort of in between shared and dedicated hosting. Services are provided through multiple connected servers. This reduces the chances of downtime, provides more bandwidth and additional resources as needed.

- **Dedicated Hosting**

  This is when you have your own dedicated server where all its resources are meant for just your website. This is more expensive, but it gives you flexibility, full control, and more.

Most companies choose shared web hosting to provide this service. Hosting should include a secure place for your website to reside, maintenance and security updates, increased bandwidth as needed, alerts when the server (the computer system where your website is kept electronically) goes down, and more. If significant downtimes occur, you may be able to get a refund. If they are regular downtime occurrences, it's time to choose a new host.

Website Maintenance Issues

A website is like a car. It runs fine and then suddenly a tire goes flat. Broken links are examples of website flat tires. If you click on a link and it doesn't take you where it should, that's a broken link. Sometimes, the code has to be fixed because something else changed within a website and inadvertently affected the link; but sometimes broken links occur for no apparent reason. Be sure to check the website often to make sure everything is working properly. Keep your web designer, webmaster, or other person maintaining the website informed so that problems can be fixed right away. Other than a server going

Chapter 12 – Your Website

down, nothing turns off visitors faster than broken links. Broken links also hurt your website ranking.

If your website does go down, notify the host immediately. It's likely you won't know about it until you get a complaint. If your website is down, your e-mail may also be down.

Responding quickly is essential, especially since you may not know how long your site has been offline. At the very least, you should ask for an estimate of how long it will be before the website is up again, so you can share that information by e-mail with customers who will appreciate your concern for their satisfaction.

Search Engine Optimization (SEO)

As covered in Chapter 11 – Digital Marketing, SEO is important because it helps others find your website. The process has become complicated by the number of search engines available, how they accept information, and how often. The best way to handle search engine optimization is to hire an expert for the job. Your designer may handle search engine optimization, or you may have to go elsewhere for that service. However, your designer will need to know what keywords you will be using so they can be added to the text within your website. Refer to Chapter 11 – Digital Marketing, to learn how to optimize your website for SEO.

Ways to Increase Conversions on Your Website

Your website is a major marketing tool that, if set-up properly can produce calls, walk-ins, appointments, newsletter sign-ups, or really anything your business needs. Setting up a website is only the first step. Getting it to convert visitors into clients or newsletter subscribers is your next challenge.

So, what specifically, is a website conversion? A conversion rate equals the percentage of website visitors who take a specific action on your website. It could be contacting you for an appointment, signing up for your email newsletter, learning more about your services, reading your blog, downloading a whitepaper, etc. Whatever you aim to be the action goal for website visitors to take, is your "conversion". Here are some easy ways to increase conversions on your website and drive more traffic this coming tax season.

Clear Calls to Action

Do customers know what to do or where to go when they get to your website? One of the easiest ways to increase conversions is to guide visitors where you want them to go with

Chapter 12 – Your Website

clear calls to action. That could mean a pop-up that prompts them to enter their email address, a big bold contact form button that catches their attention, or other design features that draw attention to your calls to action. Make sure any action you want a visitor to take is clearly stated and that your calls to action are "above the fold" ...before you need to scroll down.

Easy Navigation

If website visitors don't know where to find the information they need, they will not likely convert to customers. Your website should be easy to navigate with clear categories and sub-categories that have accurate navigation titles. Visitors need to have a general idea of what they are going to find on a page before they click on it.

Building Trust and Confidence

Website visitors need to feel confident that you are an expert in your field and that you can prepare their tax returns accurately. There are many ways you can do this from your website. Here are some examples.

- Provide social proof with customer testimonials.

- Offer a money back guarantee.

- Include trust seals on your website (for example from the Better Business Bureau or other local organizations that show credentials).

- Show your expertise with free downloads and valuable information.

Explainer Video

If you want a quick way to deliver your message, an explainer video is an excellent feature to add to your website. If you have a lot of information to convey, it easier to digest in video format than in written format. Video content is a great compliment to the rest of the content on your website. There are lots of different formats you could go with. Your website is an important part of your marketing and should always be a work in progress. These five tips should help you start gaining more conversions this upcoming season.

Legal Considerations

A final cost you should consider is legal consultation. Your website should have a legal disclaimer to protect yourself from liabilities associated with providing information, products, and services over the Internet. This subject is easy to research by clicking on existing legal links on similar websites and is a good starting point to create your own. When your disclaimer is drawn up, have it reviewed by your lawyer to ensure you are protecting yourself as much as possible from legal complications. Security of the website is most closely tied to legal issues. If you are accepting credit card payments or requesting personal information, make sure that your systems are designed and maintained

Chapter 12 – Your Website

securely; and have the disclaimers in place to ensure both customer confidence and your own protection. Trademark infringements should be avoided. If in doubt, you should consult a qualified trademark and patent attorney.

Conclusion

Your website should not merely be an electronic brochure; it must also be a tool to serve your clients more effectively and a distribution channel for your tax and financial services. Building a website is only the first step; your website must be regularly maintained, and continuously updated and enhanced. Bringing traffic to your website will be a never-ending challenge, requiring regular search engine optimization and the regular addition of new content and features to your site.

Chapter 13

Social Media Marketing

Content is fire, Social Media is Gasoline.

- Jay Baer

Chapter 13 – Social Media Marketing

It is estimated that the average person spends nearly two hours on social media every day. That's a lot of screen time your business could be capitalizing on! As social media channels become more prevalent, screen time is only going to increase. It is even taking over some of our TV time! It's crucial for your business to have a presence on social media. Not only does it increase your exposure, it makes you more competitive with national firms, and your social media presence is expected among consumers.

Managing Your Social Media Marketing

Social media can be a very cost-effective method to attract new clients. However, keeping up with everything you should be doing to capitalize on this important opportunity can be very time-consuming. In addition, it's hard to know how best to leverage social media and break through the noise. If you or one of your employees is social media savvy, you could manage your social media marketing in-house. If not, or if no one has the time to do it properly in-house, you might consider hiring a social medial marketing professional on a contract basis. The benefits of hiring an independent contractor, if you can find the right person, are well worth the investment. Just like you may tell your small

business clients that it does not pay for them to be doing their own bookkeeping, it may not pay for you to do your own social media marketing. However, even if you hire an expert social media marketer like Ashley Ray, Owner of Be Emergent, you should educate yourself on social media so you have an understanding of what that person should be doing for your tax business.

It's important to have a couple of well-managed social media channels. For a tax office, you should look at Facebook, LinkedIn and Twitter, which offer a means to reach many new, potential clients.

Connecting through Social Media

Facebook

With over 1.7 billion daily users, it's hard to ignore the importance of Facebook. The most important thing to remember about this channel is that consistency and engagement are crucial. Facebook uses an algorithm to determine what content it serves up to each user. This means that everyone who likes your company Facebook page won't necessarily see every post. It all depends on how engaged they are with your content.

Facebook Best Practices

- Post daily to keep your audience engaged
- Consider these questions before posting:
    - Would my audience find this valuable?
    - Would I share it?
- Use a mix of images (like infographics, pics, quotes), video, and links.
- It's ok to post blog posts more than once on Facebook, just make sure you spread them out.
- Highlight your staff and show off your company culture. This adds more personality to your page and can help your audience connect to you.
- Go Live! Facebook Live is a great way to mix it up. Live videos get more reach than other types of posts.
- Share content from referral partners or complimentary local businesses and be sure to tag them to increase your reach.

Metrics

Facebook Insights is a great place to go for metrics. Metrics you should be looking for:

- Likes
- Engagement
- Reach
- Referral traffic to website (you can find that metric in Google Analytics)

Chapter 13 – Social Media Marketing

LinkedIn

LinkedIn is a social media platform specifically designed for networking that tax professionals (actually, all professionals) should be utilizing daily. Think of LinkedIn as an extension of your networking. This isn't a platform for catching up with friends and posting your family vacation photos – this is your networking hub. This is where you keep up with people you've met at networking events, keep abreast of what's going on in the industry and potentially gain new clients.

LinkedIn Best Practices

Rather than filing away those business cards you collected at your last networking event, go through the stack and connect with those people on LinkedIn. Once you're connected, it's easier to stay in touch because you can now see their activity in your feed.

LinkedIn has a great feature that allows you to write notes for each one of your contacts so that you can remember things like where you met, and what your last conversation entailed. Building relationships with people is one of the core concepts of networking. They may not become a client, but they may refer others to you, or there may be someone in their network you have been trying to meet. Connecting to people on LinkedIn gives you the advantage of seeing everyone that person is connected to. It also helps keep you – and that new contact – from being another business card lost in a pile somewhere.

Button Up Your Profile

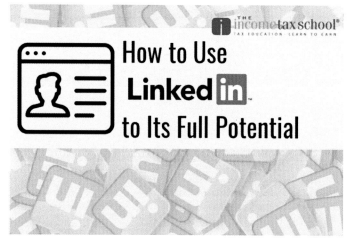

How you present yourself is important. Your LinkedIn profile is essentially your CV (Curriculum Vitae) or resume. You want people to be interested in you, not turned off by a lackluster profile. Make sure you have a professional picture, your profile is filled out completely, and you've added any certificates or credentials you have earned.

Take some time crafting a compelling headline that catches people's attention. Something like… "Saving taxpayers hassle and money for 30+ years".

Another feature that helps you stand out is adding a header image. Use this space to create an image that shows off and promotes your business. www.canva.com is an excellent and easy program to create images.

Chapter 13 – Social Media Marketing

Finally, get endorsed for your skills and ask clients and connections for recommendations. This will provide a little social proof and help make you look legit and professional.

- **See Who's Viewed Your Profile**
  Send these people a message through LinkedIn to thank them for visiting your profile, tell them you are looking to grow your network, and ask them if you can connect with them on LinkedIn. This will help to grow your connections on LinkedIn.

- **Join LinkedIn Groups**
  Groups are another great way to network online. Join industry related groups to chat and stay in the loop about things happening in the tax and/or accounting industry. Join community groups like your local Chamber of Commerce and other networking organizations you are involved in to stay connected to people in your community. Join eclectic groups where your industry expertise would be insightful to conversations or where you can draw insight from others outside of your industry. Interacting within different groups on LinkedIn not only helps you network online, but it also keeps your mind sharp by keeping your ear to what's going on within your professional network. Start by joining LinkedIn Group, Tax Business Owners of America: https://www.linkedin.com/groups/1868452

- **Post Regularly**
  Do you write a blog? Post it as an update in your LinkedIn feed. Share what you have to say with your connections to bring people back to your website and remind people to stay connected to you. Your posts shouldn't always have to be self-serving – share interesting articles you find, start a discussion, or share an event you hope to attend.

- **Share Content**
  The purpose of LinkedIn is to share knowledge and connect with other professionals. Share updates about your business and tax tips your network will find professional – just like you would on a company Facebook Page.

  LinkedIn Pulse is a great place to publish long-form content that will reach your network. Even if it's a re-post of a blog from your website, getting your information out there on multiple channels helps to establish yourself as a subject matter expert and increases your potential reach.

- **Connect with Others**
  Throw those business cards you've been collecting out! Instead, connect with those people on LinkedIn. Not only will you add them to your growing network, but they'll also get updates from you. This is a great way to stay top of mind with both old and new connections. If you really want to get organized, you can tag the profiles of your connections with things like industry or networking group, so your contacts are sortable. Here's where LinkedIn gets really cool. Are you looking to add clients in a specific industry? You can search for people who work in specific

fields in your area and then see if you have any mutual connections. It's a great way to get a warm lead.

- **Follow influencers**
  LinkedIn has a great list of "influencers" that you can follow. These people are very well known in their industry and produce articles exclusively for LinkedIn. Browse the influencer section and follow a few that interest you. If you really want to get the creative juices flowing, follow some people outside of the industry (like marketing or social media people). These people can give you ideas and tips in areas of business that you may not be as well-versed in. Here are a few suggestions:

  - Brian Solis – Principle Analyst of the Altimeter Group
  - Richard Branson – Serial Entrepreneur
  - Walt Bettinger – President and CEO of Charles Schwab
  - Naomi Simson – Founder of Red Balloon

Twitter

Twitter is a fast-paced social media platform that communicates in 140 characters at a time. Twitter is used by bloggers, business owners, and journalists as a networking tool, and is very popular with journalists who use it to find story leads.

Twitter Best Practices

- Set aside time to read your feed and interact with people daily or weekly.
- Follow local news media (and the journalists who write about the industry).
- Follow businesses and individuals in your community.
- Use a tool like Hootsuite to listen for conversations and mentions of your company and to schedule tweets.
- Write 5-10 tweets to promote each blog post you write. Schedule these to post every other day after each blog is written.
- Respond when others tag you.
- Sharing is caring. RT (retweet) others and tag people when you tweet their articles.
- Plan and write tweets ahead of time and then schedule them weekly.
- Use hashtags.

Chapter 13 – Social Media Marketing

o Definition per http://www.wix.com: A hashtag is a keyword or phrase preceded by the hash symbol (#), that people include in their social media posts. Essentially, it makes the content of your post accessible to all people with similar interests, even if they're not your followers or fans. For instance, let's say you're an Apple fan and that you're playing with the idea of buying an iPhone 5. A simple "#iPhone5" search on any social network will open a dedicated news feed with all iPhone 5 latest updates, deals, rumors, and hacks. The results you see on this feed are the aggregated posts of any users who used "#iPhone5" in their posts. But usually, users don't actively search for hashtags, but simply spot them. Hashtags appear as clickable links on posts they see, and a mouse click will display a real-time live feed of every other post tagged with the same hashtag.

Blog

A company blog is a great way to show off your knowledge, provide value to your clients and potential clients, and give people a reason to keep coming back to your website. Your blog posts can also provide you with great content for your social media channels.

Blogging Best Practices

- Maintain an editorial calendar to plan topics ahead of time.
- Speak in plain language – no legalese or complicated tax terms.
- Keep your posts between 500 and 700 words.
- Use headers to break up your posts into easily digestible or scan-able chunks.
- Blog about topics that your clients are interested in or ask questions about.

Management Tools

So how do you manage all of this and run a tax business? There are some great tools out there that will help by allowing you to monitor everything in one dashboard and schedule posts. If it's just too overwhelming, you can hire a professional.

Chapter 13 – Social Media Marketing

Hootsuite and Buffer are two great tools that help you monitor your social media channels and schedule posts. Tools like Canva can help you create stunning visuals. Pocket can help you save and discover shareable content, and https://www.BuzzSumo.com can help you research blog topics and keywords. Of course, there are other tools out there in addition to the ones mentioned above, and more pop up all the time!

TIP: If you can afford someone to help you with social media, it can be very helpful to your business. Ashley Ray is the Social Media Marketer for The Income Tax School. Find out more on her website http://www.BeEmergent.com or follow her on Twitter: @BeEmergent

A Social Media Checklist is on the next page for you to help you get started managing your business on social media!

Chapter 13 – Social Media Marketing

Prepare for Tax Season

- ☐ Check all social media profiles for proper logos, descriptions, and images.
- ☐ Check that LinkedIn personal profiles are complete with updated headshot, compelling headlines and linked to the company LinkedIn page.
- ☐ Add social media info to marketing materials (flyers, business cards, brochures, email signatures, in your newsletter, etc.)
- ☐ Create an editorial calendar for newsletters, blogs, social media ads, graphics, and social media posts.
- ☐ Define your audience to ensure all content is written to that specific audience.
- ☐ Research social media tools to help you get more done.

Daily Checklist

- ☐ Check for and respond to comments and messages.
- ☐ Monitor Twitter and Google Alerts for mentions of your company name.
- ☐ Spend 10-15 minutes reading your feeds and engaging with others.
- ☐ Follow people back.

Weekly Checklist

- ☐ Collect and curate shareable content.
- ☐ Write and schedule content for the upcoming week (posts, blog posts, newsletters) .
- ☐ Find and follow new people.
- ☐ Engage with influencers, partners and clients.
- ☐ Check and record weekly stats.

Monthly Checklist

- ☐ Plan out editorial calendar
- ☐ Analyze metrics and plan for the upcoming month.
- ☐ Plan and set-up social media ads.

Chapter 13 – Social Media Marketing

Advertising through Social Media

Facebook Ads

Facebook ads are a great way to help boost special announcements and promotions, or to just give you some increased reach. The great thing about Facebook ads is you can target very specific demographics. Here are some interesting ways you can target people on Facebook:

- Location – you can choose a specific radius around your business
- Income level – you can target taxpayers within a specific income range
- Newlyweds, new home buyers, new parents, and other life-changing events that change a tax situation
- Business Owners
- People on your email list
- Specific households, job titles, and interests

Facebook Insights is a great place to go for metrics. Metrics you should be looking for:

- Likes
- Engagement
- Reach
- Referral traffic to website (you can find that metric in Google Analytics)

LinkedIn Ads

Just like Facebook, LinkedIn has a very robust ads platform that can help you get in front of the right people. Because of the business nature of the platform, there are different targeting capabilities on LinkedIn. You can target by location, occupation, industry, seniority, company, and much more.

LinkedIn has insights as well for both pages and for people. Here are some metrics to pay attention to:

- Who's viewed your profile (personal)
- Views of your post (personal)
- Article views (personal)
- Followers (company page)
- Engagement (company page)
- Reach (company page)

Twitter Ads

Get your messages in front of people not yet following you by paying to promote certain Tweets. You can reach the right audience by targeting based on interests, geography, gender, device, or users similar to your followers. In addition, you can maximize the relevancy of your message by targeting through keywords in other users' Tweets.

You can quickly grow your community of high value followers and drive word of mouth by promoting your Twitter account. This will enable you to get your Tweets and your account in front of more people who are interested in you.

It's easy to track the growth of your follower base and see how people engage with every single Tweet. You only pay when users follow your account or retweet, like, reply, or click on your Promoted Tweet. You're in complete control. There's no minimum spend, and you can start and stop at any time.

Twitter analytics is a great place to go to see how you're doing on the platform. Here are some analytics you should pay attention to:

- Followers
- Impressions
- Mentions
- Top Tweets

Items that spark the most interest often make great topics for future blog posts!

Other Social Media Channels

The key to social media is not to be on every channel imaginable. It's all about finding the channels that your target audience uses the most, suit your business, and mesh well with the type of content you are able to produce. Know your strengths and only focus on the channels you are capable of managing. That said, here are some best practices for other social media channels that might suit you.

Instagram

Instagram is a social media application that allows you to share photos and videos right from your smartphone. The content is much more visual-based than Facebook. Instagram can work for your business if you are good at taking pictures and videos for your business. You can also use it to share industry relevant quotes or images, special offers, your company culture, and more. Here are some tips to help you get started:

- Upload high quality images.
- Stick to a particular look for all of your Instagram photos so your feed is consistent and compelling.

Chapter 13 – Social Media Marketing

- Research relevant hashtags in your community and use no more than 10 per post. These will help people find your posts.

- Post regularly throughout the week.

- Comment and like other Instagram photos.

- Follow influencers and people in the community.

- Tag others in photos when it makes sense.

Pinterest

Pinterest is a web and mobile application that allows you to discover and share ideas with other people on just about anything. You can create pin boards to save things like recipes, clothing, quotes, vacations, arts and crafts, decorating ideas, and even tax tips! Here are some tips to help you get started with Pinterest:

- Make sure your photos are high quality.

- Use target keywords in file names and pin descriptions.

- Pin blog posts as well as images.

- Create compelling infographics that break down processes or explain complicated tax topics. An infographic is a way to show information in a more visual way. It breaks down text and uses image to help explain data.

- Re-pin other pins and follow people who follow you.

- Use taller images that take up more space in the Pinterest feed will show up more!

- Credit your sources by linking to their site.

YouTube

YouTube is a free video-sharing website that allows you to upload and share your videos with anyone and everyone! You can create a channel for your business and load all of your videos there at no charge. This can be used to create "How To" videos for simple tax returns, to tell your company's story, and more. Here are some tips if you decide to use YouTube for your business.

- Make content, not ads.

- Tell stories.

- Make sure your videos are high quality and shorter in length (under two minutes).

- Include descriptions with keywords for each video.

- Link back to your website in the about section.

Chapter 13 – Social Media Marketing

- Create videos that teach and engage.

- Read and respond to comments

Tip: Expand Your Social Media Arsenal in the Summer Months

Beyond the most popular options, there are some channels growing in popularity that could be effective marketing tools for tax preparers. What better time to learn and test these tools than during the summer months when business is slower? We're talking about Alignable and Nextdoor. Here's what you need to know about them.

Alignable

Alignable is a networking platform for small businesses that focuses on building relationships locally. The platform goes beyond asking people for recommendations and connecting to other businesses. On Alignable, you can:

- Ask questions

- Show off your expertise by answering questions

- Get and give recommendations

- Tell your story and explain your services

- Connect your Facebook page

- Rate the services you use

- Research other services like Mailchimp and Yelp by looking at their ratings

- Highlight upcoming events and promotions

The platform uses geolocation features to recommend other businesses in your neighborhood to connect with. Use these to find and recommend people you already do business with, and find new people to meet and network with online. It's a great way to get to know the businesses around you and a great tool to help share your expertise or ask others for theirs.

Chapter 13 – Social Media Marketing

Nextdoor

Nextdoor is a social network designed to connect you with your neighbors and community in order to build stronger, safer neighborhoods. It's hyperlocal, and a great resource for communicating what's happening (i.e. alerting people to a lost dog, a garage sale, a plant exchange, etc.).

Local businesses are just as important to the neighborhood as residents are so, in addition to having a personal account, you can *"claim your business"*. Once claimed, businesses can get recommendations, include information about their location and hours, and reply to comments and messages. Nextdoor doesn't require as much attention as other platforms, but is a passive way of getting referrals and recommendations from locals who love you.

Unlike other social media platforms, these two don't require a constant need for writing posts. Claim your business on these channels and give them a whirl! If you're already using them, we'd love to hear what you think.

Conclusion

Social media marketing is a great way to promote your business. Try to focus on sharing valuable information. This will be appreciated and help you gain traction as an expert in your field. Follow the one-in-seven rule, where you only truly promote your business one out of every seven posts. The other six posts are used to give tips, provide information, and ask questions to engage current followers and create new ones! Creating followers will take time, but if your content is helpful and valuable, it *will* help to increase your business in the long run.

Chapter 14

Neighborhood Marketing

"Our job is to connect to people, to interact with them in a way that leaves them better than we found them, more able to get where they'd like to go."

- Seth Godin

Chapter 14 – Neighborhood Marketing

What is Neighborhood Marketing?

Neighborhood Marketing is specifically targeting a community of people around your physical office or storefront. Your promotional messages are geared toward that local group of people rather than the mass market.

You can be the best tax preparer in the world, but no one will know about your presence in the community unless you market your services to the people in that community. This doesn't mean spending thousands on conventional mass media advertising. It means doing the research to know your neighborhood and then using certain tactics to spread the word within networking groups, word of mouth, or through local promotions.

Marketing with Limited Resources

Independent tax businesses cannot compete with the vast marketing budgets and sophisticated mass-media advertising campaigns of the national tax firms. Therefore, independents must find ways to market effectively with limited resources. The key is to spend the tax firm's limited marketing dollars effectively and measure the results. Mass media advertising is not feasible for most independent tax firms; targeted advertising is the alternative. To ensure the effectiveness of advertising, each ad campaign should be tested before it is fully rolled out. A direct response ad is usually desirable so that results can be measured. Many advertising options are available, but relatively few are effective. An effective advertising vehicle will only work with a well-designed and compelling ad. Many times, business development can generate more business for independent tax firms than advertising. Direct selling and networking can bring in new clients, and these activities are not done well by many local national tax firm managers or franchisees. Here are a few low-budget local marketing tactics.

Seminars

Conducting seminars can be an effective method to recruit new clients for a tax service that caters to middle-income and upper-end taxpayers. You could partner with a financial services professional to conduct joint tax and financial planning seminars. Often the entire seminar cost, including lunch or dinner, will be paid for by the financial services professional's broker-dealer. Your small business banker is a key person to approach about providing seminars for the bank's small business customers. Partnering your local Chamber of Commerce or Retail Merchants Association to educate their members is also a good option. You can conduct seminars on tax tips and new tax laws for individuals and/or small businesses to create awareness of your expertise and build credibility. Often seminar participants will immediately convert to clients. Conducting joint seminars with a complimentary professional such as a financial planner can increase attendance, especially if their clients are invited. Having the seminar hosted and/or sponsored by a large employer, bank or association can also increase attendance and reduce cost.

Bartering

Trade Associations are cropping up in many communities. The association serves as a broker for small businesses to legally exchange goods and services. The value of services or goods provided by a member to another member is credited to the members account and used to buy products and services from other members. Essentially, this is a non-monetary exchange. The trade association receives a percentage (5-15%) of all exchange purchases and, possibly, a monthly membership fee. The association helps to match purchasers with providers. The service benefits members in two ways:

1. By marketing its products and services to those who might not otherwise buy them.

2. By conserving cash.

Client Refer-A-Friend Program

More new clients come from referrals than from any other source, including advertising. The client referral process can be facilitated by providing an incentive for clients to make referrals, or simply by just asking clients to make referrals. The idea is simple:

- Give each client a client referral form (or 2 or 3) and ask the client to refer a friend or relative.

- The referral form includes spaces for the client to enter his or her name and address.

- When the referred client brings in the card, which provides a special new client discount, the form is turned into management or your accountant and the client who made the referral receives a "fee rebate" check for $10-$25.

Chapter 14 – Neighborhood Marketing

Traditional advertising can also be used, but it should be targeted to prospective clients. The key is to determine the methods that work best in the tax practitioner's community and to devote more resources to these effective marketing strategies and tactics. Growth will be greatly impacted by a tax firm's client retention rate. If only 65% of last year's clients return, 35% of those clients must be replaced before any growth can be shown. For example, if you had 1,000 clients, you would need 350 new clients just to break even! The most effective way to grow is to provide true value to your clients so they will return.

Public Speaking

A great way to get new clients is to offer to be a guest speaker at a group event, a church, an assisted living facility, etc. You should consider speaking on tax topics to targeted business and consumer groups that can drive business to your tax firm. You can contact local business groups and offer to be a guest speaker. Groups such as Jaycees, Business Networks International (BNI), Toastmasters and Rotary, as well as small home business professionals who work for organizations like Mary Kay, Pampered Chef, and Stella & Dot, are always seeking speakers for their meetings. You should never turn down the opportunity to be a guest speaker, especially during tax season. You should strive to be known as the first person such groups will call when they are seeking a tax expert. Be sure to have an outline of what you wish to address and why their members will benefit and, if appropriate, a PowerPoint presentation.

People always have questions about their own personal tax situation, which you can answer afterward. Be sure you know who your audience will be. Come prepared to talk about something tax-related that most people in the group will have an interest in. Some examples include recent tax-law changes, year-end tax tips, senior tax tips, business tax tips, and the top 10 things most taxpayers don't know they can do to help save on taxes, etc. Once they see you as the expert in your field, you will be top of mind when a need arises. Be sure to bring business cards and handouts of the information that you covered.

Public Relations (PR) and Publicity

PR can be your most cost-effective marketing strategy. A feature article in the major local newspaper on your tax firm could produce more business than an expensive ad campaign. However, getting such an article published rarely just happens. Obtaining good publicity takes planning and preparation. A tax business owner who is not skilled in PR, or who does not have the time, might consider hiring a PR professional.

You can learn to become your own PR person. PR, in addition to being the most effective strategy to market your business, costs nothing except your time. You could also become a guest on your local TV and radio news and consumer affairs programs. Contact the reporters and program directors and make them aware of your expertise and willingness to serve as a resource on income tax topics. Invite them to meet you for coffee or buy them lunch, or introduce yourself at networking events. Taking time to develop relationships with local media representatives can pay big dividends. Become the "Go To" person for commentary on income tax in your community.

Although your business may be home-based, your public image can make a huge difference in bringing in new business. As a professional, the image you portray in the community you serve is critical to your success. Your public image is shaped by a number of factors including the following:

- Personal appearance

- Appearance and atmosphere of your office

- Quality and professionalism of the service you provide

- Appearance and professionalism of any advertisements and literature

- Public activities and community service

- Academic and professional credentials

- Professional affiliations

- Personal references and friends

- Reputation for reliability, honesty and integrity

- Media reports about you

Because you are providing a personal service, you must be especially sensitive to all these factors - remember that perception is reality...without a good image, you are out of business.

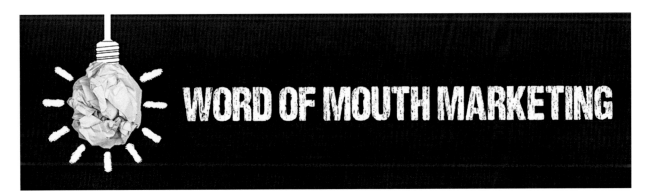

Create New Business Through Word of Mouth

Generating word-of-mouth business is important, but it's certainly not easy. Your tax firm may have the best tax professionals, the best client service, and the best deals in town, but that does not automatically mean you will generate word-of-mouth about your firm. As a tax business, it's obvious that the best source of referrals is satisfied clients, especially "raving fans." However, there are a few things that need to be in place before you can get the referrals rolling.

The Raving Experience

A tax preparer's goal should always be to provide excellent service to every client and make the experience very positive to develop raving fans. While you may already expect your staff to give every client a raving experience have you trained them to know what that involves?

Giving a client a raving experience starts at the front door. How are they greeted when they come in? Are they immediately acknowledged, given a wait time and offered a beverage? Is the reception area remarkable? Remarkable could mean toys to keep children entertained, a television, coffee station or any number of things. Was the client prepped before they came in the door? Do they know what they need to have when they come in for their appointment?

How about the process with the preparer? Do your tax preparers have strong interpersonal skills? Do they work to build relationships with their clients? Finally, are your preparers trained to ask if the client needs anything before they leave? Not only should your preparers ensure the client's needs have been met, they should also review what has been done to minimize the client's taxes and remind the client to refer them to others. If you have a referral program, this is an excellent time to tell the client about it.

Give Them Something to Rave About

If the raving experience doesn't get them, maybe they need something else to rave about. Ask yourself, what do you offer that no one else does? These are the things you should be talking about on social media and other channels of communication.

A few great things you might be able stress in your communications:

- A "Refer a Friend" program. Clients love participating because it saves both parties (the client and the person they referred) money on tax preparation.
- Year-round service. Offering assistance to your clients year-round, whether they are being audited by the IRS, have been contacted by the IRS, or just have questions after tax time, you should always be available to help.
- A Q&A Group for taxpayers. You could form a LinkedIn Group open for anyone to join and ask tax questions that are answered by their tax preparers.
- A top-notch guarantee that removes all doubt or uncertainty someone might have. Your guarantee should cover accuracy, satisfaction, and year-round service.

Chapter 14 – Neighborhood Marketing

You should provide taxpayers (clients or not) with helpful information that they'll want to share with friends and family. This comes in the form of blog posts, email newsletters and whitepapers. This will help people see you as a tax expert.

Give Them a Way to Talk About You

Even if a client has had an amazing experience, they need to know how they can spread the word. If you're on social media, make sure that the information is readily available whether in your newsletter, email signature or at the reception desk. You can also send an email after the appointment with a survey and call to action to refer a friend – making the referral process easy.

Highlight Your Raving Fans

One great way to show some love (and increase your chances of being raved about) is to highlight your raving fans. You can do this in customer testimonials on YouTube, in blog posts or on your social media channels in general. Do you have clients who own businesses? Why not rave about them – or at least share information about them? As they say, "Sharing is Caring".

Be a Resource

Positive publicity is another effective way to create awareness and get people talking about your tax service. A feature newspaper article about you or your tax firm will help to keep you top-of-mind, especially if it is published during tax season. Doing local radio and TV interviews or writing a column on tax tips are also possibilities.

Opportunities to Engage

Don't miss opportunities to interact with your clients. Tax season or not, you are their "tax person". Being as helpful and informative as possible is key. Here are a few ways to keep in touch and offer a higher level of service:

- Newsletters that offer tax reminders throughout the year.
- Tax Appointment checklists with appointment reminders.
- Reminders to schedule their appointment in the New Year.

Giving Back to the Community Helps Grow Your Business

Outside of preparing taxes for your clients, how involved are you in your community? Maybe you get out and network at your local Chamber; maybe you're in a BNI group. While those two things are great for networking and relationship building, they don't count as giving back to the community.

Chapter 14 – Neighborhood Marketing

Getting involved in community events is a great way to meet people and build relationships outside of the general "What do you do? Let me give you a business card" networking events. It's also a great way to meet people outside of your normal business sphere. Have you ever noticed that the same people attend the same networking events? This is a great way to break the mold and meet some people you wouldn't normally see at a Chamber event.

You should give back to the community. Being a good company citizen is very good for business. Volunteering to serve on non-profit boards and committees and providing the encouragement and time for your employees to do so can really pay off. Your reputation and the image of your company are very important to your success. You should always strive to be a good corporate citizen and utilize your resources, especially when you can meet both company goals and social goals at the same time.

One of the advantages you have over a national franchise as a local business owner is that you can market to your community as a local business owner. So why not embrace your local roots by digging in and giving back to the community that you live and work in? Giving back is not just a good thing to do, it can help your business a great deal.

What Does Giving Back Look Like?

- Offering your services free of charge to an underserved population in your community.
- Donating to a local charity that your company/team is connected to.
- Volunteering your time or expertise.
- Mentoring small business owners/startups.

Here are some great reasons to give back to your community as a business owner.

You Build Respect Within the Community

Business owners who are involved in their local community earn the respect and backing of the very community they give back to. Not only do you build strong relationships with the people you are giving back to, you begin meeting and building relationships with other leaders in the community who share the same passion for that cause or organization as you do. When you give to the community, you get back respect and loyalty. People within the community tend to back and support businesses who support the community.

You Enrich the Community

When community members take ownership of their community, it only helps to improve the community and the lives of people living within the community. Whether it's helping raise funds for a park or helping people within the community, you are making the community you live in a better place to live. That's a win-win.

It Improves Moral

Making community stewardship a part of your culture helps improve your work environment. Volunteerism gives employees a purpose and takes them away from the daily grind to remind them of issues that are important.

A study by the University of Exeter found that "volunteers had a 22% lower mortality rate than non-volunteers, and they also had higher levels of self-esteem and happiness."

- http://www.fastcoexist.com/3016549/volunteering-makes-you-happier

Getting your employees involved is a great way to keep them engaged and motivated to continue working for you. It improves moral and helps develop more respect for the company and its leaders and creates cohesion between everyone in the company as they work together to enrich the community around them.

Press Opportunities

Giving back to the community is always a great way to get local press around your business. There are usually exposure opportunities available for businesses who sponsor, donate or volunteer at local events. If you plan to host an event to raise money for or build awareness around a cause or a charity, make sure your local media outlets know about it. Local businesses giving back always makes for a great story!

Here is another reason: **giving back your community is just the right thing to do!**

> **TIP:** Have Some Heart with Cause-related Marketing

Consider adopting a local charity by offering free tax preparation to give back to your community. You and your employees will feel great about giving back and it will bring in new clients to your tax office.

Chapter 14 – Neighborhood Marketing

Letters

Sending letters to targeted prospects is a great way to increase your client base. The more personal you can make the letter the better your chances are of gaining a new client. Some mailing lists can be obtained in electronic form, which makes it easy to import and produce personalized letters with your letterhead. Envelopes look more personal by laser printing them, or by using clear laser printed labels that give a typed appearance. You might also use postage stamps instead of a meter (available for first class or bulk rate). Finally, signing each letter individually in blue ink makes it obvious that you took the time to personally sign the letter. Customized form letters can be used to appeal to taxpayers with special needs. You can write them yourself or purchase sample letters from tax professional suppliers. Try to be selective and have a special offer as many of these people are getting offers from many different services and some of them are your competitors. Your letter will need to stand out. Letters such as the following types are available from such suppliers:

- Prospective client introduction: Use this letter to introduce yourself to potential tax prep clients.

- New business: When new businesses move into your neighborhood [or start-up], let them know your services are available.

- Referral: Referrals are a great source of new clients. Thank your clients and reward them for every referral they send to you.

- New home: New homeowners are often listed in your local paper. Take the initiative to let them know that you can help with the special tax needs related to a new home purchase.

- Retirement: Remind recently retired clients (and prospective clients) to come in and discuss their changing needs.

- New baby: Look in your local baby or birth announcements. Parents often don't know how their tax situations will change with the birth of a child.

- Recently Married: Look in your local paper for newly engaged or married couples. Their tax situation is about to change.

- Recently divorced or separated individual: Send this letter along with the brochure on the same topic and offer your help with changing tax needs.

Chapter 14 – Neighborhood Marketing

You could add to the above list a variety of additional categories of taxpayers with special needs. Such as ministers, military personnel, police officers, outside sales reps, doctors, etc. Almost any list can be purchased for a moderate cost from list brokers or trade and professional associations.

Press Releases

Some activities, events, and accomplishments pertaining to you are newsworthy, and you should be sure all appropriate media in your community are made aware of them. The most efficient way to accomplish this is to compile and maintain a personalized media mailing list and send each media contact a press release every time you have news. Instead of mailing your press releases, fax them or send them by E-mail whenever possible. Here are two websites that enable you to send out your press and news releases to specific media of your choosing.

- http://www.prweb.com
- http://www.prnewswire.com

Become a valuable source of tax information for your media contacts. Be the "Go To" person for commentary on tax news stories.

Discounts, Incentives, and Special Promotional Offers

Changing tax professionals is not something that a person wants to do every year. People get comfortable with their tax preparer and know what to expect from them. Many will stay with the same preparer for as long as that person is willing and able to serve them, until the client moves away, or one of them dies. Even when a client moves away, communication is so easy now with fax machines and email, there really is no need to find a new preparer. The taxpayer should continue as a client unless the person is not satisfied with the service they are receiving, their situation becomes too complex for the preparer, or the preparer is charging too much.

With that information in mind, people are motivated by many different things. A flyer with a special coupon may work well for one potential client while another would rather have a personal referral to a high-level professional and would be willing to pay full price. The more you know about the types of clients you want to serve, the easier it will be to determine what will work with them.

The most effective way to measure the results of an advertising program is through a direct response device such as a discount coupon. The discount, of course, also serves as an incentive for a taxpayer to use your services. For these reasons, discount coupons should be incorporated into most print ads and flyers – along with a call to action. A discount on tax preparation services may look better if stated as a dollar amount instead of a percentage. Someone considering using your service will not know what your fee would be. Therefore, one cannot translate a percentage discount into a dollar amount. In addition, because of this uncertainty about price, your ad should probably invite prospects to call for a free price estimate. To reduce uncertainty, you could include a statement such as "fees competitive with those of the national tax firms."

Group Tax Program

Providing group tax services is a great way to recruit and retain clients. You could contact major employers and membership organizations in your community and offer to provide a *special* "Group Tax Discount" program for their employees or members. Explain that tax preparation is a service that all employees and most association members need and offering this valuable "fringe benefit" costs the organization nothing. Ideally, the employer will provide the tax preparer with an office to meet with employees or members on-site by appointment. Donating some portion of the fees to the organization's favorite charity could enhance the tax firm's image and increase participation. For associations, this arrangement is usually referred to as an "Affinity Program" and the association (or church) might be expecting a small "revenue-share" for the association in addition to a smaller discount being extended to their members. The idea is to make a compelling value-proposition about your services to the organization and let the organization "sell" your services to their employees or members.

Become an Author

Offer to write articles, columns and/or blog posts for local publications. You could write a weekly or monthly column on tax tips and timely income tax topics. You would not need to create all of the content yourself. You could subscribe to tax news articles provided by a tax professional association and/or a tax industry vendor to get ideas. Public domain articles may be published verbatim without permission, but proper attribution should be given to the author. Again, you will be perceived as the tax expert and the "go to person" for tax information and advice. As a tax expert author, you will be top of mind when members of your audience have a need for tax preparation services.

Friends, Family, Neighbors

Your friends and family are great prospects for your new tax service. Perhaps you already prepare their tax returns and that is what motivated you to start your own tax business. The trust factor is already there and they believe that you will do a good job. So, how do you move on from there? How about your neighbors? Like your family and friends, neighbors probably trust you if you have been in the neighborhood for a while and they know you. Many neighborhoods have an association that holds social networking events, publishes a monthly e-newsletter, have a Facebook page, and/or has a community networking website, such as Nextdoor: http://www.nextdoor.com. If your neighborhood does not subscribe to such a group, you could start a subscription. There are no fees. Neighbors are a great place to start offering your services. If you have a

Chapter 14 – Neighborhood Marketing

home-based business with little to no overhead, you are able to charge a much more affordable rate than a tax business with a storefront office. Another advantage you have is convenience. You can schedule your client interviews in the evenings or on weekends when it is convenient for your neighbors. You can also offer to meet them at their house or yours. Then down the road you can offer a pick-up and delivery service and call them to see if there have been any big changes that you should discuss in person.

Churches

Another great place to find clients is at your local church. People from your church tend to fall in line with friends, family and neighbors. If you attend regularly and have been there for a while, the trust factor will be there or will be easier to create. Asking for the business outright might be a little awkward at church. Consider offering a free seminar at the church's facilities, and make a donation, to kick things off. From there you may get questions and people who want to try your services.

Networking and Relationship Building

People do business with people, not brands. Often, someone may choose your tax business because they've met and liked the owner or an employee. You can't hide behind that monitor all day. Networking events give your business more exposure by making other professionals aware of your expertise and capabilities so they will think of you whenever the topic of income tax comes up with their clients and professional contacts.

Although it may be difficult as a tax professional to attend networking events during tax season, it is essential for you to do so. As the tax business owner, you are the "face" of your firm and people must get to know you and your firm's capabilities before they will use your service or make referrals. Becoming a member of key business organizations in your community such as the Chamber of Commerce and local business leader groups can pay dividends. However, to realize value, you must be actively engaged in attending networking events and participating in committees. Being actively involved in one or two key groups may be more effective than simply attending events of multiple groups.

Meeting other business and professional people in a social setting is one of the best ways to recruit new upscale clients. You would be wise to take advantage of every appropriate networking opportunity that you can make time for in your schedule. Many tax professionals neglect this important method of attracting new clients - especially during tax season, when people are thinking about taxes.

Chapter 14 – Neighborhood Marketing

Finding a last-minute excuse not to attend a networking function is all too common. Those tax professionals who attend important functions and follow through will be the benefactors.

Types of networking functions include events sponsored by your local Chamber of Commerce, Retail Merchants Association, civic clubs, business clubs, tips clubs, etc. Your major newspaper or website may publish a weekly list of upcoming events, and you can get your name on the mailing or email lists of appropriate organizations. You can get a head start by meeting with someone who is well connected in the community and active in networking and asking that person to help you "plug in" to the network and introduce you to key people.

When attending a networking event, follow these few simple rules:

- Bring plenty of business cards

- Wear your name tag on your right side so people shaking your hand can read it easily (also put your company name on the tag)

- Don't spend all your time with one or two people, after a brief discussion, move on to make a new contact

- Collect business cards and make notes on the backs of special interests or follow-up action needed

- Talk to your competitors too (you may learn something); but be careful not to divulge trade secrets

- Seek opportunities for professional referral relationships, group tax arrangements, joint marketing agreements, etc.

- Add key names to your networking email list

- Try to ask questions about the other person – people love to talk about themselves

- Really listen to what people are telling you to help them solve the right problem. Also, listen to people when they tell you what they do. Ask them who their target audience is and what kinds of problems they solve for, in case you know someone who would be a good match for them.

- Take notes in a notebook, on your phone, or on the backs of business cards, however you decide to do it, make notes about whom you speak with – notes about physical characteristics (to help you remember them) as well as what you talk

Chapter 14 – Neighborhood Marketing

about and what problems they want to solve. Also take good notes about what you can do for them and what they can do for others in case you run into someone who can use their services.

- Follow up on all important contacts with a phone call, letter or email…or better yet, connect with them on LinkedIn!

> **TIP**: Develop your 60-second elevator pitch… (the amount of time you typically have on an elevator) you have 60 seconds when you meet someone to really get their attention and tell them what you do. Make sure you know what you want to say when someone asks, "What do you do?" What will you say to spark their interest and make them want to continue the conversation? Be sure you are ready, so your next networking function is a success. Be creative! You don't want to be put in the tax professional box with all the other tax pros they know. How will you be different?

Develop a networking database of your key contacts and customers. Periodically (about twice a year) send a company development update email to all network contacts. The email should be personalized. Always ask your network contacts for referrals in your letters or emails. Late January is a good time to send an email with a referral coupon enclosed.

> **TIP**: If you do lots of networking and collect cards by the dozens, consider investing in a card scanner. It can save you a lot of time and ensures that the content is entered into your contact database accurately.

Influencer Marketing

Today, you'd be hard-pressed to find someone who hasn't used or heard of social media. Facebook is a driving force in the way brands do business. Instagram and Twitter are changing the way consumers discover new products. If you're not actively devoting time to getting your message out on these channels, you're missing out on a huge potential client base. After all, 81% of all Americans have at least one social media profile, with 68% of American adults on Facebook alone. But with such vast platforms, how can your message break through the noise?

Enter influencer marketing. Whether you're looking to dip your toes in the social media pool for the first time or improve your long-term marketing efforts, influencer marketing is an essential tool. Influencer mentions go a lot farther than a tweet or post from a company account. Why is this?

Influencers are powerful because they meet consumers where they are. They provide a trusted voice to brands and products in a way that many businesses simply can't. It's important to recognize the distinction - the sooner you do, the sooner you can understand just how much of an impact influencer marketing can have on your tax business.

It's also important to note that influencers aren't just famous celebrities or people with massive online followings. Influencers are personalities who are **actively engaged with their audience.** Engagement is the mark of a true influencer, not follower counts or video views. For example, a product review YouTube channel with 1000 subscribers, or a mommy blogger with 100 followers could both help you gain new clients with the right message. Working closely with influencers can afford you 3 great marketing opportunities:

1. **Earning credibility with a new audience** who might not have given you any attention or trust otherwise.

2. **Gaining exposure to new potential clients** who might not have heard about your business otherwise.

3. **Generating quality content to help promote your business,** which can be used again and again.

Reaching out to influencers directly to start building a relationship is one method, but the reality is that you'll need to spend either time or money to establish a fruitful relationship for both parties. Because every business is unique - with a unique set of problems to solve - there's no magic formula for influencer marketing. **Patience Is key.**

It's also important to reach out to influencers that can actually be of help to you, whether in your niche or community. In other words, sending a DM to Dwayne 'The Rock' Johnson on Instagram probably won't magically transform your tax business overnight.

To get started, try researching who's active in your area. **Reaching out to local/regional influencers** is a great way to make an impact in the community while spreading the word about your tax business. For example, reaching out to an engaged freelancer or startup on Instagram could be a great way to spread the word that you specialize in taxes for freelancers and startups!

Chapter 14 – Neighborhood Marketing

Here are some helpful ways to start building relationships with influencers:

1. **Ask for their perspective.** What would they like to see in a tax business? Starting and maintaining a two-way dialogue is an excellent way to conduct market research (and get your business on their radar).

2. **Create an experience or product of value.** This could be a quick informative video, infographic, tax prep resource, or an e-book like the one you are reading.

3. **Pay for a product review or placement.** This tried and true method is the most direct means of influencer marketing. Many influencers are willing to negotiate prices, especially about products they believe in.

4. **Offer additional exposure to their content channels.** Influencer marketing is a two-way street. Find unique ways to leverage your channels to drive traffic to an influencer's, and you'll lay the foundation for a fruitful relationship.

Become a Connector

Have you heard of the philosophy "Givers Gain"? It's a BNI principle based on the law of reciprocity. Networking should be an important part of your business. It's a tried and true way to build your network, spread the word about your company, and essentially gain new clients.

The Benefits of Being a Connector

You've likely encountered a number of different approaches to networking. Some people work the room in an attempt to get business cards in everyone's hands, some people focus on meeting and talking to certain people, and some people just go with the flow. While there are different approaches to networking, there's one approach we've found to be extremely effective – being a connector.

A connector is someone who always has a recommendation and is always willing to offer up an introduction to someone who might help your business grow. They have a huge network of people and are always willing to help.

Not only is helping people awesome. Helping other people helps you, because generally, those people will reciprocate your generosity.

Chapter 14 – Neighborhood Marketing

Benefits of Being a Connector

1. You Have a Big Network

Connectors are always developing relationships. They have a huge network of people which means LOTS of people know who they are and what they do. Alec Baldwin was close but not quite when he said, "ABC, always be closing." But instead of "always be closing," at networking events you should "always be connecting." Look for connections between people you know and people you've just met. Find opportunities to introduce people to each other and connect them to information and resources they need. Not only will it boost your reputation as a person people can trust and go to as a resource; it's how you build bonds in your community.

2. You are THE Person

When someone needs a referral, they come to you. That makes you a trusted advisor and someone who is always at the forefront of people's minds. If you're talking to a small business owner who needs to meet a contractor, and you happen to know a really good one who is there at the same event, introduce them to each other then and there. If the two parties aren't in the same place, make an email introduction later. Make it a habit to connect as many people as possible. It will help your friends and build those community ties.

3. "Givers Gain"

When you adopt a giving philosophy and focus on giving business to your fellow networkers, people naturally become eager to repay your kindness by sending business your way in return. Giving doesn't have to mean that you're giving up money or services necessarily. It's more of a mindset that if you give of yourself by sharing energy, knowledge, and connections that can help the people you're networking with, good things will come to you in return. It works on two levels. On the first level, you'll build up a reputation as being a helpful, generous person. People will remember how you helped them and return the favor if an opportunity comes up. On another level, whether you believe in things like karma or not, generally the energy you give to the world is the energy you get back. So, even if the people you helped don't directly "pay you back," somehow it all works out in the end and good things come to you.

4. **It Makes Networking Easier**

   If striking up conversation makes you feel uneasy, take the connector approach. It's easier to introduce two people who may not know each other but would be good connections for each other.

5. **It's Good for You**

   Studies show that giving is good for the giver. It boosts your mental and physical health, it makes you more mindful and appreciative, and it's fulfilling. Try being a connect and you'll reap the benefits!

Host a Holiday Open House and Gain Exposure

You may already plan a company Christmas party for your staff – but have you considered making it an open house? Holiday open houses are a great way to celebrate with staff, thank your clients for their business and invite new contacts and potential clients to see what you're all about. Hosting a holiday party can be very beneficial for future business in the very near tax season. Here are some ideas to help you plan.

Who to Invite to an Open House

It's an open house so the more the merrier! Here are some ideas:

- Staff and their families
- Current Clients
- Prospects
- New contacts
- Social media fans and followers
- People you've been meaning to reach out to – this is a great way to reach out with a personal invitation
- Any business partners you may have in the community

- Contractors who do work for you

- Referral partners or members of networking groups you are involved with

Include a Charity Drive

A great way to show community involvement and to give back for the holiday season is to give your party a charity tie in. You could do this by hosting a Toy Drive, a canned food drive, or doing a silent auction with proceeds going to a local charity.

Have a Holiday Office Tour

Host a tacky light tour in your office for the holiday party. Have employees decorate their cubicles/offices and guests can vote for the best ones. You can even award prizes. It can be lots of fun and it gives people an opportunity to check out the office and meet all our employees.

Give Party Favors

You got them in the door, don't let them leave without something to remember you by or a reason to contact you. That could be refer-a-friend cards, a discount card for first time appointments or a brochure with helpful tips and your contact information. Bundle it with treats and marketing swag so that guests will want to take it home to see what's inside.

How to Promote It

There are several different ways to promote your holiday open house – it all depends on your time and resources. Here are some suggestions:

- Send out personal emails to clients

- Create an evite for free online and send invites to your contacts that way

- Include a blurb about it in your newsletter or e-newsletter

- Post about it on your social media channels

- If you have a Facebook page, be sure to create a Facebook Event so that people can RSVP that way.

- If you are a member of any networking groups, see if your event can get a mention in their newsletters or on their social media sites.

- Do you have a list of leads you've been meaning to catch up with? Sending a personal email to invite them to your open house is a great way to reach out.

However you decide to do it, make it fun, do it in the spirit of saying thanks to your employees and clients, and open it up to potential clients or partners to ensure more business in the upcoming season.

Conclusion

There are various Neighborhood Marketing efforts that can be effective and beneficial for small businesses, and many are inexpensive or free. The key is to target your audience. Additionally, it helps to make connections in your community through networking and PR opportunities. Giving back shows that you are community-minded, which creates positive PR, higher employee morale and improved connections. A win-win for everyone! These Neighborhood Marketing tactics will help you become known as the "go to person" for tax preparation in your area.

Chapter 15

Client Retention Strategies

Being on par in terms of price and quality only gets you into the game. Service wins the game.

- Tony Allesandra

Chapter 15 – Client Service and Retention Strategies

This chapter focuses on serving and keeping your clients commonly referred to as Customer Retention.

Distinction between Customer and Client

As a tax preparer, CPA, or accountant, do you have customers or clients? Most would say clients without hesitation. But the distinction is an important one. Strictly defined, a customer is someone who buys goods or services from a store or business. They may buy from you once, infrequently, or on a regular basis but the relationship is not a deep one. Typically, the relationship never gets further than the transaction. The word "client" can also mean "customer," according to the American Heritage Dictionary, but it has a separate definition as someone who receives professional services. In business, the two terms are often applied differently based on the types of relationships built and the type of transactions that occur.

Clients, however, purchase services that are personalized to them. The relationship is deeper. The client depends on the skill and expertise of the business they are getting service from. This distinction is very important for professionals in our field because it speaks to the expectation and level of service we need to provide.

Just something to think about during the tax season as you see client after client. Each one relies on your skills and expertise. Each one demands relationship building so that you know more about them, their families, and their specific financial situations. Each one requires personalization when preparing their returns. These are not customers, they are clients. They are taxpayers who come to you in need of a professional who they can rely on year after year and trust that their returns are prepared accurately.

Make it a point to be personable and build better relationships with your clients this tax season and they will surely come back to you, year after year!

Client Retention

Every year, millions of people pay someone to prepare and file their tax return and if they are not satisfied, for whatever reason, they can and <u>will</u> find someone else. Retaining clients is vital for business growth.

Did you know?

- The average company loses half of their clients/customers every five years.

- A 5% reduction in client/customer defections can increase profits up to 25%.

- It is 5-7 times more expensive to gain a new client/customer than it is to retain an existing one.

Chapter 15 – Client Service and Retention Strategies

Many tax businesses take their existing clients for granted or forget that they may have other needs that could create new revenue streams for them. Most are too busy pursuing new clients. The business world is extremely competitive today and your direct and indirect competitors are not just sitting idly waiting for new clients. They are out there every day, pushing very persuasive offers to clients to make a switch. If you're not doing your best to satisfy your clients' current and potential needs, you may lose them.

13 Tips to Retain Your Clients and Grow Your Tax Business:

1. **Pay Attention to Your Existing Clients**

   It is five to 10 times more expensive to attract new clients than it is to retain your existing clients. Plus, word of mouth is the best form of advertising, and happy clients will tell their friends and family about you!

2. **Stay in Touch with Your Clients on a Regular Basis**

   They need to be reminded that you are there year-round and that you care enough to send them important and timely tax information.

3. **Get to Know Your Clients Well**

   The more connected you are, the less likely they are to leave and the better you'll be at serving them.

4. **Always Follow Through on Commitments Made to Your Clients**

   You must deliver what you promise if you want your clients to trust you and be loyal to you.

5. **Be Consistent and Professional**

   This goes for the office image, your image and all contact you have with your clients. Inconsistencies and unprofessionalism can cause you to lose valuable clients.

Chapter 15 – Client Service and Retention Strategies

6. **Learn from Other Leaders in the Tax Industry**

   They are leaders because they have figured out what works. There's no need to always reinvent the wheel.

7. **Request Feedback and Suggestions from Your Clients**

   You'll learn so much from your clients – both good and bad. Try to duplicate the positive things and eliminate the things your clients find most frustrating. Consider conducting a client survey.

8. **If You Have Employees, Hire People that Enjoy Serving Other People**

   You can teach people taxes, but you may not be able to teach people to enjoy serving others. Look for outgoing, client-oriented people.

9. **Focus on a Target Group and Become an Expert for Them**

   When you become an expert in a specific field, you become the go-to person and word of mouth will bring your new business.

10. **Share Ideas, Resources and Contacts with Your Clients**

    This is considered adding value to your clients and it can be priceless.

11. **Reward Your Clients for Being Loyal**

    It doesn't always have to cost a lot of money. Your clients will appreciate being recognized for their loyalty.

12. **Continue Your Education in Taxation and Other Areas That Will Enhance Your Knowledge and Skills**

    Increasing your knowledge will benefit you and your clients.

13. **Track What Is and Isn't Working**

    You'll never know what you should continue doing and what you should end without tracking your results.

Chapter 15 – Client Service and Retention Strategies

Client retention efforts are essential to realize the growth you need to succeed. You should know your Client Retention Rate, which is the percentage of last year's clients that have returned this year. Here is how it works:

- If you prepared 1,000 returns last year and 850 returned this year, your retention rate is 85%, which means you lost 150 clients and need 150 *new* clients before you can show any growth over last year.

- If you increase your retention rate to 95%, and you add the same 150 new clients, you will realize 10% growth in clients.

- Check your own Client Retention Rate and see if you are happy with the results!

It is much easier and less costly to retain a prior client then to get a new client. Clients are retained by delivering real value when preparing their tax returns accurately, and by communicating with them year-round. Retaining good tax preparers is also a key factor in retaining clients.

> **TIP:** Reach out to past clients who have not returned. Getting a new client is a very expensive proposition, but the lifetime value of each client makes the cost of reaching out a worthwhile investment. When a client leaves, it is a very big loss. You should do everything you can to get non-returning prior clients back. One tactic is to mail a personalized letter to all non-returning clients each year with a 50% "Special Re-Introductory Offer."

Think about the reasons why you hesitate when you are faced with an offer to buy something. Many times, the reason is because you perceive risks associated with that purchase and those risks are greater than the possible benefits you *might* receive. For a tax client, it could be that they are afraid they will choose the wrong preparer, be charged too much, may not see the value in the service, or might not be satisfied with the service and will be unable to get their money back.

Service Guarantee

Offering a guarantee can be a wonderful way to minimize the perceived risk that prevents people from choosing to do business with you. It's amazing how many businesses shy away from a guarantee because they fear that a large percentage of their clients will take advantage of it. In fact, just the opposite is true. A very small number of your clients will actually take you up on your guarantee.

Chapter 15 – Client Service and Retention Strategies

Before creating a guarantee, check out your competitors for patterns in the industry. When you get ready to create your own guarantee, focus on your strengths and the results that your clients want. Don't be afraid to offer a hassle-free, money back guarantee for unsatisfied clients.

Below, is an example of an excellent guarantee that covers the main concerns of tax clients.

- **Assistance**

  We are available all year-round to answer any tax questions you may have. Should your income tax return be audited, we will help you prepare for the audit and serve as your advisor (not your legal representative) throughout the audit process. (If you should require or request that we represent you, we will be glad to do so for an additional charge.)

- **Accuracy**

  Thorough employee training and double-checking of every return safeguards the accuracy of your tax return. However, if we make an error we will correct our error and reimburse you for any penalties and actual interest damages you incur. You will still be responsible for any additional taxes that would have been due had the error not been made.

- **Satisfaction**

  If you are not pleased with the service you receive in the preparation of your tax return(s) and you choose to neither file them nor allow us to redo them, we will refund your fee in full

Chapter 15 – Client Service and Retention Strategies

Positive Experience

When was the last time you had a **great** experience as a client or customer? A time when you were amazed at how friendly and helpful the people were? Or how easy and painless they made everything seem? People want to have positive experiences and many will go out of their way to have them. When a person is looking for a good tax professional, they are likely to ask around for referrals to someone that comes highly recommended with a proven track record. They are seeking a positive experience.

People value their time and money and don't want to waste them on someone mediocre or worse. When they are looking for a tax professional, they are looking for someone with whom they can have a longstanding relationship; someone who will provide a consistent, positive experience.

When someone has a positive or negative experience, it can be based on many things – not just the actual face-to-face meetings you have with them. Every encounter or interaction your client has with someone helps to shape your client's experience. That includes phone calls, emails, visits to your website, your brochure, any mailings you send them, your business card, other clients they may meet, etc.

Your clients are looking for real value, which includes much more than just an accurate tax return. If you can provide them with a positive experience and deliver consistent, valuable service, it will lead to repeat business and positive word of mouth, which means referrals! Creating positive experiences and delivering consistent value will grow your business.

Encourage Clients to File Their Tax Returns Early

As their trusted advisor, it's up to you to inform them of the benefits of filing early. It's also advantageous of you to get them in your office as early as possible. First of all, you want to reduce the number of late season appointments. Secondly, you may need some early revenue to pay off-season bills. Lastly, you want to keep them coming back to you and not be swayed by an offer from another tax business.

Chapter 15 – Client Service and Retention Strategies

So, how will you convince them? Give them these four reasons to file early.

1. **Filing Early Prevents Tax ID Fraud**

   ID thieves are out in full force during tax season. If they file a client's return first, you've got a big mess to clean up! First off, they'll use all the unlawful tricks in the book to get the most money back, putting a red flag on your client. Second, it often takes years before your client will see that refund money. Filing as early as possible can prevent all of this from happening.

2. **They May End Up Owing**

   That surprise is better to get in January or February than in April when there's less time to come up with the money. As you know, they don't actually have to pay any tax they may owe until the true tax deadline, April 15.

3. **Your Schedule is MUCH More Open Early in Tax Season**

   It's important to communicate to clients that making an appointment now will be much easier than in late March or April. Waiting until the last minute to get an appointment is never a good strategy – because that's what too many others do! And your fees might be higher in April.

4. **It's Off Their Plate**

   It feels good to not have to worry about things, doesn't it? Remind your clients of that. Filing early means all their worries about tax returns are over.

January is the time to get messaging out to your clients and potential clients about filing early. Write a blog post, put it out on social media channels, put it in an email, give them a call, mail them a tax planner, or a reminder card. Whatever it takes to get them through the door!

Year-round Service

Most people never want to think about taxes. However, during tax season they must, and it's your job to make it as painless as possible. Although you may only want to be available during tax season, it's important that your clients are able to reach you during the off-season should issues arise. Some clients may need your assistance in dealing with the

Chapter 15 – Client Service and Retention Strategies

IRS or for tax planning. If you are not accessible to these clients when issues arise, they will find another tax professional that is available and you will likely lose their business. You may not even need to meet with the client in person, but you should definitely find a way for your clients to connect with you when the need presents itself.

Year-end Tax Planning

Tax clients who have more complex tax returns could be invited to come in for a year-end tax planning session. This meeting provides another "touch point" opportunity to ensure client retention. Tax planning can also be a source of additional revenue if fees are charged for the session or if fees or commissions are earned for financial planning. A tax and financial planning checklist could be used to conduct these sessions, with consideration for such strategies as:

1. Deferring income.
2. Prepaying deductible medical, business, education, and employee expenses, unless the impact of Alternative Minimum Tax (AMT) would be negative.
3. Selling securities to book paper losses and offset any capital gains and realize a capital loss of up to $3,000 to offset ordinary income. Consider the different tax treatments of the sale of long and short term stocks, and the taxability of December mutual fund payouts.
4. If applicable, consider a "bond swap" to increase a bond rating and book a loss to offset other gains.
5. Making charitable contributions of stock or other property (be aware of AMT
6. Maximizing contributions to retirement accounts.
7. Ensuring compliance with IRS withdrawal rules for taxpayers who reached age 70-1/2 by June 30th of the current year; consider making the required distribution a Qualified Charitable Distribution (QCD) from an IRA account to avoid reporting the additional income.
8. Consider the tax advantage of gifting stock to children before selling to reduce tax to the Kiddie Tax rate.

Chapter 15 – Client Service and Retention Strategies

9. Capitalize on income tax and Social Security tax savings through employer Flexible Spending Accounts, if applicable.

Convenience (Appointments, Walk-ins, Drop-offs, Off-site)

In today's complex society, there is rarely enough time to accomplish our daily tasks. Businesses that provide greater convenience, all else being equal, will attract more clients. Most taxpayers prefer to have their taxes prepared near their homes rather than near their jobs. This rule follows consumer-shopping patterns. Locations in or near community retail shopping centers are very convenient because taxpayers visit these centers frequently to shop. Tax offices in regional malls can attract taxpayers of all kinds from surrounding communities who shop at these malls frequently. However, those taxpayers who come to the mall occasionally from a distance do most of their shopping in their own community retail centers and are less likely to bring their W-2s to the mall. Therefore, not all of the mall traffic represents prospective clients.

Appointments should be offered, not only for client convenience, but also because they enable you to schedule your client flow and staff the tax office properly. However, walk-ins should also be welcomed and worked in between appointments, to avoid losing clients. Procedures should be established to handle bottlenecks in a professional manner. These include a system to:

1. Take drop-off returns.
2. Schedule later appointments.
3. Have tax associates available on call. An off-site service can also be arranged for convenience during scheduled days and hours at major employers and other facilities such as adult homes.

WALK-INS WELCOME

DROP OFF SERVICE AVAILABLE

Letters and Postcards

You should write to every client at least once a year. Clients with complex tax situations and small business owners should be contacted two or three times per year. The annual letter or postcard should be a reminder that you are available and interested in serving your client and should include a summary of the benefits they will realize by using your service. This reminder should also advise your clients of any important tax changes and any changes in your firm that will affect them. For example, they should be advised if you have moved, or if you are assigning a specific new tax associate to serve them.

Chapter 15 – Client Service and Retention Strategies

For upwardly mobile, executive and small business clients, a personalized letter is recommended. This letter can come from the company president or the office manager. For budget-service and bank product clients, a postcard can be more effective and will cost less. The annual letter or postcard should be mailed in early January to arrive prior to the time clients are receiving their W-2s.

TIP: Consider including refer-a-friend discount information. You could use this letter to thank them for their business and to ask them to refer business to you. Including Refer-a-Friend Certificates is a great way to ensure success!

Essentials of Developing a Client Newsletter

Email newsletters are a great way to keep in touch with clients year-round. They add a personal touch, keep clients in the loop, and are sharable. The following are some suggestions to create newsletters that will have real value for your clients.

Planning

As with any marketing effort, the first step is planning. You should have an editorial calendar that maps out important dates, holidays, promotions, etc. This is the skeleton for what will become your newsletter. Start with a spreadsheet that has important dates (like start to the tax season, filing deadlines, etc.), seasonal topics (like Back to School or Tax Season), and holidays (Labor Day, Christmas, etc.). These will be the bare bones of your calendar and will help you plan out what to put in each email. There are a lot of editorial calendar templates online that can be downloaded and used – it all depends on how detailed you want to get and how much content you are planning.

Topics

Once you have a general idea of seasonality, it's time to start planning specific topics to talk about. You don't want a newsletter full of self-promotion and you also don't want to be boring. Think about what your clients will find interesting or useful. What do they need to know? How can you offer up advice seasonally? What's top of mind for them right now?

Take a look at your editorial calendar and start planning out specific topics. For example, September is Back to School season, what tax tips can you offer up for parents or students? Write down your content ideas either on a separate tab in your spreadsheet or within the spreadsheet itself. Make sure you cover topics that will appeal to all of your clients. For example, you can also include a section specifically for small business clients.

Chapter 15 – Client Service and Retention Strategies

Frequency

During the off season, a monthly newsletter is probably the best frequency. Once tax season starts, consider sending out weekly or bi-weekly newsletters to make sure you are top of mind during your peak season.

Important Items to Include

Make sure you include the following essential items in your newsletters:

- Links to your social media channels
- Links to any blogs you've written
- Links to important articles of interest to your clients
- Information about tax law changes
- News about you or your employees
- Offer to speak or provide a speaker on tax tips
- Reminder to contact you if they hear from the IRS
- Your Guarantee
- Refer-A-Friend requests
- Contact information
- Important dates

Email newsletters are fun to put together and a great planning tool. Once you've gathered all of the content together, you may find you have plenty of material to use for posts on your social media channels. Keep your clients informed, stay top of mind, and help yourself plan for the months ahead by creating regular email newsletters.

Loyal Client Discount

The most effective annual client-mailing piece you can develop is a loyalty program. A loyal client discount serves several important purposes:

1. It is your annual prior client reminder.

2. It communicates the benefits of your service to your clients.

3. It provides special benefits for client loyalty.

4. It makes your clients feel they are special and are part of an exclusive club.

Chapter 15 – Client Service and Retention Strategies

Consider a special discount similar to the following:

- 3% per year returning
- 15% maximum in 6th year (valid with one other discount; maximum total discount not to exceed 25%)

- Clients receive their loyalty discount in the mail in January of their second year with you. New clients benefit from this program in subsequent years!

TIP: New Client Gift Cards - One easy way to promote your tax service is to carry gift cards with you. When you meet new people looking for a tax service, you can give them a gift card to be used toward their first visit with you.

Client Brochures

Many tax firms provide brochures on tax tips and tax information to help their clients become better informed about their tax situations. Some firms provide tax organizers or checklists (often on a 9" x 12" envelope) and tax record books (rental property, business, etc.) to help them compile tax information needed in preparing their returns. If your name is on an IRS list as a tax professional or electronic filer you will undoubtedly receive catalogs and brochures in the mail offering such products. Unless you need a very large quantity, buying client brochures is probably more economical than producing them yourself. Such brochures and record-keeping aids are a nice touch for your clients.

TIP: Client Presentation Folders - Providing the client's tax return copy in a professional folder enhances the image of your service. The folder can also be used to provide year-round service information and to present the details of your guarantee.

Giving Away Free Services and Information

Your time, talent, and knowledge are valuable. This is why many professionals hesitate to give anything that involves those things away for free. But free does not equal loss. In some cases, it can benefit or help grow your tax practice. There are ways to be smart about it. If you're asking yourself "Why should I give *anything* away?" Here are some things to consider:

- **Free Tax Information**

  Tax information comes in many forms. While you shouldn't sit down with someone line by line and show them how to prepare their tax return for free, there are many

Chapter 15 – Client Service and Retention Strategies

forms of free information that could benefit your practice or firm by showing off your knowledge and raising your credibility.

- **Free Tax Tips Seminar**

  Presenting a free tax seminar is one great way to network and instill confidence that you know what you're talking about. Seminars are a great way to get your foot in the door at a new networking organization and get in front of new audiences. Hosting a seminar at your office is also a great way to get new people into your office. The few pointers you give won't solve all of their tax problems but it will show your tax knowledge.

  Giving away tax information on a blog or in a forum is also a way to give yourself credibility. Offering up valuable info on your blog builds trust, adds value for current clients and gives people a reason to keep coming back to your website. Offering up information or tips on a forum builds relationships and is a great way to network with people online. If you're offering information in this way, make sure you follow up with a way for people to contact you.

- **Communicating with the IRS for Your Clients**

  You should encourage your clients to contact you as soon as they receive any correspondence from the IRS. Clients are usually unnerved by a notice from the IRS and are very anxious to resolve any issues. Stress the importance of contacting you before responding to the IRS. These situations may often be resolved with a telephone call to the IRS, an amended return, or a letter of response from the client. Sometimes the notice will require preparations for an audit. All of these situations present an opportunity for you to assist your client, add value to your services and, possibly, increase your revenue.

NOTE: There are rules around who may engage with the IRS on certain matters on behalf of a taxpayer. Please review the IRS website and Treasury Department Circular 230 for current information on this topic. For additional information about this topic, from the IRS website, please follow this link: http://www.irs.gov/pub/irs-utl/pcir230.pdf

Chapter 15 – Client Service and Retention Strategies

Handling Paperwork Professionally

You'll need a professional environment and a filing system for handing your clients' paperwork. You don't have to start out with a home office but you will need a place to meet with your clients and a secure place to store records. The last thing clients will want to see are piles of paperwork or another client's information lying out in plain view. Not only does it give them a bad impression of you, but it is also a violation of the IRS rules to share or disclose in anyway another client's

information, knowingly or otherwise. It's imperative that you handle each client's paperwork in a systematic manner. File it away before meeting with another client. If you are not finished with a client's tax return, you can put it into a pending file to work on later. If you have finished a tax return but are waiting for the client to come by and sign, you could put it in a different file labeled "waiting for client's signature." All client files must be kept in a *locked* file cabinet, file drawer or file room when not in use, as required by IRS privacy rules. Your clients will appreciate that you are handling things professionally and protecting each client's privacy.

Managing Client Expectations

Be sure to communicate with your client as to how long you expect it will take to prepare their tax return. If you come to a bump in the road, keep them in the loop. Communication is so important. You will also want to tell your client right away if there will be any delays or if you need to file an extension. It's also important to tell them as soon as possible if they are going to owe money to the IRS, and that any tax balance due must be paid by the filing deadline to avoid stiff penalties. The biggest thing is to communicate with your client. No one wants to feel like they are in the dark.

Associates' Sales Efforts

Increasing tax office revenue benefits the company and, especially, tax preparers who are compensated based on revenue they generate. Your tax preparers are in an excellent position to help bring in new clients. First and foremost, providing excellent client service is the real key to building your clientele. Everyone will benefit in the long run if you provide true value to each and every one of your clients. However, many times you will only get referrals or repeat business if you ask for it and actively overcome objections and dispel myths and misconceptions some people have about the services offered. Here are a few basic actions you can take to build your business:

- Call all prior clients who came in within two weeks of the current date last year.

Chapter 15 – Client Service and Retention Strategies

- Try to convert each phone inquiry into a client by making an appointment. Explaining your guarantee can help reduce the prospective client's perceived risk. Explain any added benefits a client would receive by coming to your company.

- Tell each one of your clients what you've done to save them money on their taxes, and explain your guarantee and other services.

- Ask for referrals, ideally through a Refer-A-Friend program.

Phone Etiquette

- Remember the phone is **not** an interruption. It is our link to your clients.

- Concentrate on the call. Get the person's name the first time.

- Answer properly. Use "comfort words" or warm phrases, such as "Thank you for calling (Company name)." Be sure to tell the caller your name.

- Answer promptly. You should have a policy to answer by the third ring or less.

- **Never** put callers on hold before finding out who they are and **never** leave them

- on hold for more than 30 seconds without checking back with them.

- Control tone of voice. **Smile**--it really does work!

- **Always** get the caller's name. **ALWAYS!**

- Avoid slang.

- Let the caller hang up first.

- The client signs the paycheck, not the boss. The telephone can be a profitable

- piece of equipment if used professionally and properly.

Chapter 15 – Client Service and Retention Strategies

Build Better Client Relationships During Tax Season and Beyond

The beginning of tax season is a great time to reflect on the importance of knowing your clients since you're about to see all of them within the next few months!

For tax preparers, *really* knowing your clients is important. On the one hand, you need to build strong relationships with each one in order to build trust and loyalty. On the other hand, the better you know your clients, the better tax preparer you can be when it comes to making sure their tax liability is minimized and they will be provided with tax planning strategies to ensure that their result will be as good as possible when they file their tax returns next year.

Here are seven ways to build better client relationships, starting with actions you can take during the tax season.

1. **Conduct Thorough Tax Prep Interviews**

   For new clients, the tax prep interview is crucial to building a relationship. Your interview shouldn't feel like an interrogation, it should be a conversation that makes them feel comfortable and confident in your tax preparation skills.

2. **Ask Extra Questions**

   Asking questions seems so obvious but for some tax preparers it's not. Ask questions beyond the standard things you need to know to file their taxes this year. How was their Christmas? What are their plans for the coming year? How are their kids, husband, wife, family?

3. **Listen more**

   Your clients likely haven't seen you since last tax season. A lot has probably happened in their lives since then! Listening more means paying attention to everything that is said. Their stories, questions and answers to your questions will tell you a lot about them and give you more insight that will help you be of better service.

4. **Survey clients**

   Knowing your clients better also means knowing their preferences and their impression of your services. A great way to learn this is by sending out a company

187

Chapter 15 – Client Service and Retention Strategies

survey to clients. Making it anonymous helps clients feel more comfortable sharing their thoughts and gives you a good look at how your clients feel overall.

5. Have an open house for clients

It can be hard to get to know clients in a tax situation when both parties have limited time. Hosting an open house is a great way to mingle and chat with clients in a social setting. Open houses are great to hold at the beginning of tax season or even right before the holidays.

6. Keep notes

It can be hard to keep track of everything a client tells you, especially when you have multiple clients. Keeping notes on things you talked about with each client is a great way to remember. It's a nice to touch to be able to recall that last year your client was planning a big family vacation so that you can ask them about it when you see them this year. Take notes after your client leaves and then review your notes from last time before they arrive each year. Consider buying and implementing a Customer Relationship Management (CRM) system to keep electronic records that you can review when you are meeting with your clients and update with new information.

7. Build demographic profiles of your clients

Getting to know your clients is also important from a marketing standpoint. It's important to know who your clients are so your marketing can be targeted to a certain demographic of people. Trying to market to *everyone* is not a smart way to spend your marketing budget. Take what you know about your current clients and build demographic profiles so that you can zero in on a few specific groups of people.

Getting to know your clients is important. Make it a point to build stronger relationships this upcoming tax season!

Chapter 15 – Client Service and Retention Strategies

The list above includes things the client should expect and receive automatically. They are all part of just being professional and running a good business.

TIP: It's OK to Say No: How and When to Fire Problem Clients (Nicely)

Sometimes someone special walks through your door – someone so special that they make you want to scream in frustration. Some clients are problem clients and they can be toxic. This is the person who does nothing but cause you problems and agony. The one who makes you question why you went into business for yourself. Well, these moments are precisely why you went into business for yourself. When you work for someone else at a company you don't own, you might have to put up with an awful lot of ridiculous behavior and situations from coworkers and clients. You don't get to decide who gets the boot. But when you own your own tax business, you can decide when a client has crossed a line – and then take action to correct the situation. It's both a drawback and a perk of being the big boss. (But ultimately, it's more of a perk, because at least you get to be in charge of making the call!) That's why it's important to **learn how and when to fire problem clients.**

First, determine if they are actually a problem

Part of working for yourself – or really just part of life – is getting along with different kinds of people. Some of your clients will become your friends. Some of your clients will be just that – clients – and you will have a pure business relationship with them. That leaves a handful of others who may not always be as easy to work. However, "not as easy to work with" doesn't actually take them to the level of toxic clients who are so bad you need to fire them.

Ask yourself these questions:

- **What is the client actually doing wrong?** Is it something you can coach them to be better at? Maybe you can help teach them the best ways to work with you (for example, teaching them the right timelines for submitting documents). **If the client expects you to prepare a fraudulent tax return, then you must refuse.**

- **Is your ego getting in the way?** Do you feel that they are somehow questioning your work? Don't let pride get in the way of a client relationship. Listen to what your client needs and see if they have a valid point – and if you can fix or improve upon whatever they're asking for.

- **Is it still possible to resolve the issue?** Are you both still communicating well enough that you can sit down and listen to each other? Is it possible to reach an understanding and move forward?

Chapter 15 – Client Service and Retention Strategies

Depending on the answers to these questions, you might be able to work things out. Have you tried absolutely everything you can to salvage the relationship? If the answer is "yes" and it still isn't working, keep reading …

Problem client red flags to look for

Sometimes you will not be able to resolve things. Four of the biggest, most glaring red flags are:

- **Poor Communication**

  Is your client really listening to you? Can you understand each other? Does your client let lots of time pass between responses or give no response to your queries (time sensitive or not)? Do they refuse to use efficient ways to communicate (for example, they insist on talking on the phone or visiting in person when an email would do)?

- **Poor Understanding of What the Problem Is**

  This point is related to poor communication, but it's worth talking about separately. Do you understand what the problem is – and is your client able to articulate it to you in a constructive way? Can you understand well enough to fix the problem? If you can't even work together well enough to understand the issue and you reach a communication impasse, that's a bad sign.

- **Know-It-All Attitude**

  Does your client tell you how to do your job, whether they know anything about taxes or not? You need their input about their financial situation, yes. However, once you get that info, you're the expert and they are there to get advice from you. After all, if they already knew the best way to file their taxes, they would not have come to you, right?

- **Overly Harsh Criticism**

  Does the client give unnecessarily harsh – and often unhelpful – criticism? Is their attitude hostile or are they making accusations against you?

Chapter 15 – Client Service and Retention Strategies

When you see too many of these red flags in your client relationship, it's time to cut your toxic client loose. Otherwise, you risk digging yourself in deeper, losing more money, increasing your stress levels, and making the situation worse overall.

When It's Time to Have the Conversation

Once you've decided to let a client go, how do you tell them?

- **Be direct, but not cruel.** It's alright to say something, such as, "This doesn't seem to be the best fit for you or for me." It's not alright to call someone out and say, "I hate working with you. You're a …"

- Give as much or as little detail as you feel comfortable with but remember sometimes less is more. You don't have to outline every disagreement you have had with each other. You don't really owe them an explanation beyond, "This doesn't seem to be working for us." However, if you would like to give any additional detail, feel free. Just don't cross the line into giving away too much personal information.

- Offer helpful recommendations for another tax advisor. Feel free to make suggestions of other offices or individuals they may want to contact.

- Wish them all the best, and always try to leave things on a positive note whenever possible.

Also, please note that if your client has actually done something really bad or even illegal, such as sexually harassed you or your staff, provided false documentation, or somehow put you and your staff in danger or in any legal risk, all bets are off.

Assuming this is simply a toxic client you need to let go, we recommend talking on the phone or in person; but if you have to do a letter or email, a script might look like this letter to the right.

Dear [Client],

After much thought, I regret that My Tax Company, LLC, will no longer be able to help you with your tax preparation.

As much as I'd like to be able to help you, I think another tax preparer may be a better fit for what you need. You may want to reach out to [Competitor A] at [contact info] or perhaps [Competitor B] at [contact info] to see if they can help you.

Thank you again for your business. I wish you all the best!

Sincerely,

Your Tax Preparer

Why Client Surveys are Important

When tax season is over, you'll want to take some time to reflect. How did you do? What were your revenue? Did you increase or decrease over last year? You can determine your success or lack thereof by looking at revenue, number of new clients, number of referrals, or marketing metrics but how do you judge how well you did with service? How did your clients feel after leaving your office? The only way to know is through client surveys.

Client survey scores may not seem as important as the other metrics listed above, but they are. In fact, they are one of the most important pieces of information to study after tax season. Here are some reasons why.

1. Gauge your firm's level of service after tax season. Generating referrals means creating raving fans through exceptional client service!

Chapter 15 – Client Service and Retention Strategies

2. Get demographic information from your clients. You can gather a lot of information from a client survey if you ask the right questions. Some questions you should ask are key demographics like location, age, gender, and occupation. Knowing the actual demographics of your client base is key to more effective marketing next tax season.

3. Gauge the effectiveness of marketing campaigns. An important question to ask in your survey is how they heard about you. This information will give you an idea of what worked and what didn't.

4. Pinpoint strengths and weaknesses. You can't improve if you don't know your strengths and weaknesses. You should ask questions like: What did you like most about us? What can we do to improve?

5. Determine your net promoter score (the percentage of clients that would recommend you). This score is important to track simply because you want people to recommend you. It can be tracked by asking the simple question: Would you recommend us to others?

6. Inform clients of other services and/or get testimonials. The end of your client survey can include information about other services you may offer and can also include a call to action for a written testimonial, or even reminder to follow you on social media.

7. It shows you care. Asking clients for input shows you care about their experience and the level of service you provide.

8. Operating a tax business isn't all about numbers, it's about relationships and client service! Client surveys can help you to provide great client service!

Conclusion

It is your responsibility as a business owner to ensure that your clients are receiving the service and respect they deserve. If you do not take care of your clients' needs and manage their expectations, they will take their business elsewhere!

In order for you to be able to effectively compete with others in your market, you need to:

Chapter 15 – Client Service and Retention Strategies

- Truly work toward understanding each client's business and personal situation so that you can anticipate problems and seek new ways that your services can help the client.

- Touch base with your clients several times a year and give them helpful tips throughout the year.

- Establish and reinforce a sense of mutual understanding and trust. Let them know they can call you for tax advice and planning any time of year.

- Understand that if your clients don't perceive quality in terms of their needs, then your service can be the best there is, but they won't see it, and they will leave.

- Always have your clients' best interests in mind.

- Be flexible and ready to change to meet your clients' needs.

- Listen to your client.

Remember, it is much less expensive to retain a current client than it is to find a new one. Client retention rate is an important measure of the success of your business. You, your tax preparers and your tax firm are rated by that measure.

Chapter 16

Recruiting & Training Tax Preparers

Great vision without great people is irrelevant.

- Jim Collins

Chapter 16 – Recruiting & Training Tax Preparers

When I began my career in the tax business over 40 years ago, obtaining good tax preparers was not very difficult. My employer, H&R Block, Inc., had developed their income tax school a few years earlier as an ingenious method of recruiting and training tax preparers to support their rapid expansion. As a district manager and later a regional director, I was able to find plenty of good people who were willing to pay to take our Basic Income Tax Course with no guarantee of employment. We could observe the students in class for several months and determine which graduates we would hire based on grades, participation, attitude, attendance, punctuality, and other qualities demonstrated in the classroom. We rarely had trouble staffing our seasonal offices with intelligent, competent, friendly people whom we had taught how to prepare income tax returns. Today, virtually all national tax firms and many regional and local tax firms offer income tax classes to recruit and train tax preparers. Obviously, operating an income tax school has become recognized as a "best practice" for tax preparation firms wishing to grow. Although an income tax school may still be the best way to recruit and train seasonal tax preparers, the environment is very different today.

Today's Personnel Challenge

In recent years, unemployment rates have been low, and finding and keeping good employees has been a challenge for many businesses. Tax preparation firms have been no exception. Extended unemployment benefits results in some unemployed people opting to continue collecting benefits rather than take a seasonal or entry-level job. Basic demographic and economic trends reduce the available pool of prospective employees, especially for tax firms. Stay-at-home parents and early retirees had always been prime candidates for employment during tax season. But increases in two-wage-earner households and full-time post-retirement careers have caused these pools to shrink. Employees are working longer hours and being paid more. With less spare time and more money, part-time jobs are not as appealing to many workers. At the same time, more tax firms have been operating income tax schools and competing for fewer prospective students. Yet, without an adequate staff of qualified trained tax preparers, a tax firm cannot grow.

Good tax preparers tend to be loyal to their clients and, due to employment contract non-compete provisions, they usually can't legally bring their clients with them. Hiring an experienced local tax preparer who has left his or her clients behind often results in acquiring someone else's problem. At the very least, the employee may have to unlearn

Chapter 16 – Recruiting & Training Tax Preparers

some bad habits. Occasionally, we've been lucky and picked up a good experienced tax preparer, usually someone who has just moved into town. Overall, finding individuals with good people skills who meet all other employment criteria and teaching them tax preparation is still the best way we've found to staff our growing tax business.

Operating Your Own Tax School

Operating your own tax school may be your best option to obtain qualified tax preparers. Students can be recruited and required to pay a modest fee to cover the cost of books and materials. It's helpful to run the school with no obligation for students to work for your tax firm and no commitment for your firm to hire graduates. Your opportunity to observe students during the tax course can help to avoid costly hiring mistakes. Qualified graduates who have demonstrated competency in tax preparation and who also meet your tax firm's employment criteria can be hired. Teaching your own tax class can provide you with a pool of qualified entry-level seasonal tax preparers who have been pre-screened and are likely to fit in with your company culture.

Identifying the Best Tax Preparer Prospects

The best prospective tax preparers are not necessarily accountants. Accountants and other financially oriented professionals sometimes tend to be more numbers-oriented than people-oriented. Taxation is not accounting; it is law. Preparing tax returns is a very personal process that requires someone with strong people-skills to satisfy their clients. For your client, the interview *experience* can be just as important as your preparer's tax knowledge. This fact is why I named my tax business *Peoples* Income Tax. Amazingly, the trademark search firm I hired when I founded the Company in 1987 could not find another income tax firm named Peoples anywhere in the United States!

Why People Skills are Paramount

While serving as regional director for the Block New York City Region, I visited tax offices in many neighborhoods. When entering a storefront office, if I was not immediately greeted, I would take a seat in the "waiting area" (which I now prefer to call the reception area) and observe the tax preparers. Typically, they had their heads down focused on "cranking out" tax returns and were totally oblivious of me entering the office. Often, the preparers I observed were aloof and arrogant. They may have been very capable of preparing accurate tax returns, but they lacked people skills. I refer to these tax preparers as "tax technicians." I could see that the tax interview experience was not positive for their clients. If your clients do not feel good about the experience, they may not be likely to return. You can teach someone tax preparation if they have the aptitude to understand the tax laws, basic arithmetic skill, and the interest in learning; however, it's much less likely that you can teach people skills to a "tax technician." Because people skills cannot usually be taught to someone who lacks them, we seek individuals with the aptitude to learn and strong people skills, and we teach those people how to prepare tax returns.

Chapter 16 – Recruiting & Training Tax Preparers

Buy-in to Your Company Philosophy

You should only hire people who wholeheartedly agree with your company philosophy or they will not be long-term employees and will cost your business time and money. Hiring and training a new employee is very expensive. Be sure to hire the right people!

Finding the Right People

Clients don't like to see new faces every year. Most clients want to establish a relationship with a tax preparer who will be available year-after-year. Ideally, the tax preparer will also be available to handle any tax problems and questions during the off-season. Continuity of tax preparers may be less important to low-income clients who seek refund advances and are primarily concerned with convenience, cost and speed. However, relationships are important to everyone. Also, keep in mind the high cost of training and developing a new tax preparer. High employee retention can be difficult to attain when you can offer only seasonal employment, but there are methods that work.

Sources of Experienced Tax Preparers

1. **Help wanted advertising** usually comes to mind first. Classified help wanted ads are inexpensive and can be effective. Your major local newspaper, as well as local printed employment guides and Internet job listing sites should be considered. If your city has a daily newspaper, advertise only on Sunday (or Saturday if the newspaper is published only six days a week). Placing your ad with internet job boards would probably be more effective. We have found placing our help wanted ads with Indeed to be the most cost-effective way to recruit employees.

2. **Temporary Employment Agencies** may seem like a viable source of temporary help, but the reality is they usually can't meet the needs of tax preparation firms. Most accounting and finance professionals registered with temporary employment agencies are not experienced in preparing individual tax returns for the general public and would need to complete a tax course to become qualified. Occasionally temp agencies have former employees of tax or accounting firms. However, unless the tax preparer has recently moved into town, you may be picking up someone else's problem, for a higher hourly rate!

3. **Employees of Other Tax or Accounting Firms** might be your best source of

qualified experienced tax preparers. Hiring a tax professional who is currently employed may result in a better hire. Your challenge is to identify employed tax preparers who might not be completely satisfied with their current employer. If you attend local or regional tax continuing education (CE) conferences, you could meet some prospects. Also, seasonal tax preparers may be seeking employment after tax season. If any of them post their resumes on Indeed, you can find them by doing a search of "Tax Preparers" *by the date* they were posted.

4. **LinkedIn or Facebook Groups for tax preparers** can also be a good source to find tax preparers who may not be satisfied with their current employer.

Long-term Seasonal Career Candidates

Your goal should be to hire people who will become long-term career employees. The best long-term tax preparer prospects are people whose personal needs can be met through seasonal careers, such as the following prospects:

- Homemakers with young children in school
- Early retirees who travel or spend time with their grandchildren during summers
- Financial services professionals who can make their own hours and may benefit by meeting prospective clients
- People with complementary seasonal occupations
- Moonlighting professionals who want to earn extra money every tax season
- College seniors and graduate students who need business experience
- Blue-collar workers who want to break into a new white-collar profession

You should look for people who view tax preparation as a rewarding career because they like to help others and avoid hiring someone whose primary motivation is money. Seek people who are likely to stay with you for years. Hiring someone who is "between jobs" may provide a quick fix to a personnel shortage. However, unless you can reasonably expect the person to return next tax season as a part-time tax preparer (after finding a year-round job) this will usually prove to be a poor hiring decision. Such dilemmas can be prevented through proper planning and preparation during the off-season. The best strategy is to find good people with the desired qualities and interest and then teach them to become tax preparers. If you cannot operate your own income tax school, you could arrange for your candidates to complete an income tax course offered elsewhere. The

Chapter 16 – Recruiting & Training Tax Preparers

Comprehensive Income Tax Course offered by The Income Tax School may be a good option and can be completed anytime from anywhere with Internet access.

Low-cost Ways to Recruit Tax School Students

In this economy, given the recent high unemployment, a great source of prospective tax school students is unemployed workers. Unemployed people might be interested in learning to become tax preparers if they were made aware of this opportunity. Other good candidates are stay-at-home parents with school-age children who need to be home in the summer when the kids are in school, but still want to maintain job skills. Early retirees are also good prospects since they may like to travel or spend time with grandchildren during the off-season. College students may view tax preparation as an opportunity to gain experience and enhance their resumes. Below are some tactics you can use to make such prospects aware of your opportunity.

1. **Newspaper Help Wanted Ads**

   You can place classified ads in the help wanted section of your local major newspaper. Here are some tips:

   - Advertise for Tax Preparers and indicate that training is available.
   - Consider "Tuition-Free (fee for books)."
   - Place the ads under the heading of "Accounting", if possible
   - Run the ad when most help wanted ads run (usually Sunday or Saturday).
   - Keep the ad very short and run it sparingly to minimize the cost.

Keep in mind that a candidate will probably have no idea that his or her career objectives could be met by learning to become tax preparer. Remember that you are offering a rewarding seasonal career, with flexible hours and pleasant working conditions, using computers and interacting with people. You are not seeking accountants, although some accountants may be interested and qualified if they have good people skills. Consider that many people who read help wanted ads

Chapter 16 – Recruiting & Training Tax Preparers

are looking for a job now, and may not have the patience to take a tax course in the fall to qualify for a job starting in January

2. Online Job Postings

Usually, you can also place your help wanted ad in the online help wanted listings of your major newspaper, as well as other internet job boards, including those of non-profit support groups that help unemployed people find work. Craigslist.com can be very effective and is free in many cities (although nominal fees are now charged in some cities). You could place a detailed ad for tax preparers to start in January and indicate that training is available. You will also need to specify the pay rate. You should have applicants reply by email to you with their resumes.

Paid online job postings are also an option. Job sites such as Monster.com and Careerbuilder.com are costly, and Snagajob.com is primarily for non-professional hourly workers. However, good results can be obtained at a nominal cost from job sites such as Indeed.com, which charges a fee "per click", i.e., you pay a small fee for each prospect who clicks on your ad. Your ad can be as detailed as you'd like since you are paying for viewers, not for the length of your ad. You can also suspend the ad at any time.

> **TIP:** A sample job description is located at the end of this chapter.

3. Temporary Employment Agencies

In a competitive market, you might find a temp agency that is willing to recruit and screen prospects to attend your tax school without compensation as a requisite for them being placed with you after graduation. However, you should be able to find tax school candidates without their help. Also, remember that employing a temp is like hiring someone who is "between jobs" and your clients don't like to see different faces each year. While the higher hourly rate of a temp includes payroll taxes and benefits, and the agency handles the screening and hiring, you are still paying the extra cost of the agency's profit. Using an agency should probably be your last resort.

4. **Employee Outplacement Services**

   These services aid employees who have lost their jobs due to restructuring and downsizing. Some services are private businesses to which employers refer their displaced employees, and often pay the fee to ease the transition. Some larger employers provide in-house outplacement services. In addition, many communities offer outplacement services provided by nonprofit organizations. Often, displaced employees are nearing retirement, may have retirement packages, and could become good long-term seasonal tax preparers. All such services should be contacted and made aware of your seasonal employment opportunities.

5. **Social Media**

   You could post your opportunity on local groups to which you belong or can join, including local LinkedIn job search and professional groups. While on LinkedIn, you might consider joining the group that I founded, "Tax Business Owners of America." Facebook, Twitter, and YouTube can also be effective to make local people aware of your job opportunities.

6. **Signage**

   If you operate your tax office(s) in a storefront, you can capitalize on the visibility by putting a sign in the window advertising your tax school. You can also mount posters on the wall in your client reception area. You might also consider magnet signs for your vehicle to advertise your tax school

7. **Job Fairs**

   You can set up a table at your local job fairs. Some job fairs are free for

Chapter 16 – Recruiting & Training Tax Preparers

employers and some require employers to pay a nominal fee. Be sure to have brochures or flyers describing the opportunity.

8. Employment Offices or Services

You can display flyers or brochures at your local state employment office and any other employment services (e.g. 50+ job counselors). You can provide a job description. Most communities have nonprofit support groups for people who are unemployed that help their members find jobs and introduce them to prospective employers.

9. Networking

At local networking events, you can tell people about your job opportunities and available training. Every community has many opportunities for networking such as the Chamber of Commerce, BBB, Retail Merchants Association, and various business and professional organizations.

10. Seniors & Women Groups

To reach early retirees and women with school-age children who are prime candidates, you could ask senior & women's groups to make their members aware of your opportunity, possibly in a newsletter. An article on the advantages of a tax professional career is available free from The Income Tax School. You can find the article here:

- https://www.theincometaxschool.com/resources/free-whitepapers/

You should be able to find such organizations through an online search using terms such as "Senior Services" and "Women's Support Groups."

Chapter 16 – Recruiting & Training Tax Preparers

11. Military Personnel

If there is a military base nearby, you can make the director of the Army Career and Alumni Program (ACAP) aware of your opportunity for retiring military personnel and military spouses. ACAP helps retiring military personnel transition from  military to civilian careers. Our article on the advantages of a career as a tax pro and our tax preparer job description can be provided to the ACAP manager. Military personnel are a source of prime candidates for second careers in tax preparation. If there is a military base in or near your community, you should contact the career transition center. Some of our best long-term office managers have been retired military officers. Tax preparation can also be an attractive option for military spouses.

12. Colleges and Career Schools

You could advise the campus career placement office at local colleges and career schools of your opportunities for mature students (ideally seniors or graduate students). You can post flyers on approved campus bulletin boards. Establish relationships with business school faculty members who are in a position to refer their best students to you to obtain practical career experience. Most private career schools need to demonstrate a high level of career placement to maintain their state license requirements and provide statistics for their literature.

Chapter 16 – Recruiting & Training Tax Preparers

13. Employee Referrals

In-house referrals are always an excellent source of good new employees. Your employees should be encouraged to refer prospective employees to you. Many companies offer substantial financial rewards for referrals that  result in new hires. One suggestion is to offer a finder's fee equal to $5-$10 times the average hours worked per week during tax season by a referred employee who successfully completes the tax season. Our employees are also authorized to award full-tuition scholarships to people who they know would be qualified and willing to become employees upon successful completion of our Comprehensive Income Tax Course. Again, the scholarship student is required to pay the cost of the books and materials. If there is room in the class for another student, this costs the company nothing.

14. Recruit Your Own Tax Preparation Clients

We all have some clients who come in with their tax returns already prepared and just want you to prepare them on your tax software and e-file. If you publish a client newsletter, you could include an article about your income tax course and offer a tuition scholarship for any client who wishes to take the course. They would pay only for the cost of their books and materials. Who would be a better ambassador for your tax service than a person who chose you over all their other options? You would lose a tax preparation client but gain a more valuable asset!

How to Set Up a Tax School

To operate your own tax school, you will need to consider the following:

1. **The instructor** should be you or a veteran tax preparer of your tax firm who has good communication skills. Adults are much easier to teach than children or

Chapter 16 – Recruiting & Training Tax Preparers

adolescents. If you have solid tax knowledge and communication skill, you should be a good tax course teacher. If you charge tuition, your firm may need to be licensed as a private career school (check the laws in your state). Many tax school operators offer their courses tuition-free if doing so would avoid the requirement for licensing. They can usually charge a fee for books and materials to cover their costs. If you are operating a licensed tax school, your instructors may have to meet education and/or experience requirements of the licensing agency. Be sure to research the laws governing private career schools in your state.

2. **Course Curriculum** is a critical element. The Income Tax School (ITS) Comprehensive Income Tax Course is comparable to the basic income tax preparation courses offered by national tax firms. In fact, both Jackson Hewitt and Liberty Tax Service outsourced their tax schools to The Income Tax School during their first two years of existence. The ITS Comprehensive Tax Course consists of sixteen 3-hour lessons, ideally taught over eight weeks (two morning or evening classes per week). ITS licensees have the option of teaching the courses face-to-face or online and are provided with an online Instructor Resource Center (IRC), a student manual to follow along with the students, and answer keys. The ITS Comprehensive Income Tax Course covers Form 1040 and all related schedules and statements, including more complex forms such as sale of property and self-employment. The course also covers e-filing, IRS Due Diligence and client interview techniques. Corresponding local state and locality income tax preparation should be taught along with the Federal. The Income Tax School also offers advanced courses for in house instruction.

If you create your own course curriculum, topics should be presented in a logical sequence, beginning with the basics, and gradually progressing to more complex tax situations. The course curriculum should also include exercises and quizzes, homework problems and reading assignments, plus mid-term and final exams. Students should not be permitted to use computer tax preparation software to do their tax course problems as then the software is making the decisions for them.

Chapter 16 – Recruiting & Training Tax Preparers

Course graduates can be taught how to use your tax preparation software before they are scheduled to prepare tax returns. Tax preparers should be encouraged or required to complete advanced Continuing Education (CE) annually after completing the basic course and working as tax preparers.

3. **Instructional materials** can be developed in-house or purchased. Students should have access to reference books. For a basic tax course, IRS Publication 17, *Your Federal Income Tax* is the best reference book. For advanced courses, a comprehensive fiscal interpretation reference such as the Commerce Clearing House (CCH) *U.S. Master Tax Guide* can be used as a text. The student course text should include a syllabus (course outline), a lesson-by-lesson summary of the subjects emphasizing key points, special advice and interview tips for tax preparers, examples, illustrations, tables and charts, in-class quizzes, homework problems, reading assignments, a glossary of tax terms, and also a student survey and evaluation forms. Students will also need tax return forms, schedules, and statements to work out all the problems in the course. These forms are available for downloading and printing, or as online fill-in forms, from the IRS website.

Another critical element is Instructor Resources, which could include lesson plans with examples to use in class, key points to emphasize, role playing exercises (to teach interview techniques), and student attendance and achievement forms. Instructors should have answers to all student text quizzes, problems, homework assignments and mid-term & final exams, plus grading criteria. It is highly recommended that before each lesson the instructor read the reading assignments and do the problems assigned to the students to properly prepare to teach the lesson. The instructor should also be provided with an LCD projector to display completed tax returns and forms prepared by computer. Fillable PDF forms are available on the IRS website and can be displayed and completed line-by-line for this purpose. A projector screen will also be needed, unless a white surface is available as a projection surface. A white board used for teaching could double as a screen.

Chapter 16 – Recruiting & Training Tax Preparers

The Income Tax School materials include a Tax School Licensee Handbook with a One Year License to use the training materials, an Instructor Resource Center (IRC) including Answer Keys and PowerPoint presentations to display using an LCD projector, and Student Texts.

4. **The Classroom** should be functional, comfortable, and clean. A large open room is ideal. A conference room can also be used. If adequate space is available, folding tables can be provided for students to open their books in front of them. Three students  can fit at a 30" x 72" table and two can fit at a 24" x 48" table. If you have a large group, the 24" x 48" tables take up less space and are easier to arrange. Tables can be configured in rows, a U-shape, or as a conference table. Folding tables are inexpensive and can be purchased from suppliers such as Office Depot, Staples, Home Depot, Costco, and Sam's Club. Most tax offices have enough chairs, but additional inexpensive stacking chairs can be purchased if needed. Furniture can also be rented or borrowed. If your office is not large enough, you will need to find an outside classroom. A hotel meeting room is an option, but, unless you can work out a special deal for multiple 3-hour sessions, a hotel may be cost-prohibitive. A better alternative may be to reserve a room, for minimum or no cost, in your local community center, Chamber of Commerce, YMCA, Knights of Columbus, library, school or church. If this fails, you might be able to use the conference room of another business, or a vacant office or store. Having your students take the course online is also an option, with instructor support provided by e-mail and phone. You can also have your students complete their lessons and have their homework assignments graded online and provide supplemental classroom reviews of the lessons to reduce the number of classroom hours for the instructor and the students.

Chapter 16 – Recruiting & Training Tax Preparers

5. **Your plan to recruit students** would include the suggestions made earlier in this chapter. The Income Tax School package includes optional marketing materials (prospective student brochures, window banners, posters, sample ads, and inquiry & follow-up forms). A successful student recruitment campaign involves a multitude of activities. The key strategy is to think about organizations and places where you will find the ideal type of people you desire as long-term employees. You could then determine how to reach them with information about your opportunity, and how to entice them to consider enrolling in your tax course.

Alternatives to Operating Your Own Income Tax School

If you lack the resources or time to operate your own income tax school, or if you need only one or two employees, there are other options. Many tax firms have sent their employees to tax courses operated by national tax firms. H & R Block no longer allows anyone to take their tax courses unless they sign an agreement to work for Block if offered a job after graduation. Many Jackson Hewitt and Liberty Tax Service franchisees have adopted comparable policies. Some colleges offer practical courses in income tax preparation, but most college tax courses focus more on theory than practical application, and they rarely cover state income tax preparation. However, the foundation provided by a college tax course can reduce the amount of additional training needed. It's also possible for two or more local tax firms to pool their resources together to offer a tax course. One firm might provide the teacher, while the other provides the classroom. Both firms share in the cost of advertising, promotion, and instructional materials. This strategy will work best if the firms are not competing directly for clients in the same local market.

Distance learning is another option. Employees can complete home-study tax courses, although independent learning requires greater self-discipline and many home-study students do not finish. However, with encouragement and support from you as the employer, the success rate should be much greater. Each year, The Income Tax School enrolls numerous online students nationwide in Comprehensive and other tax courses that are available via the Internet. ITS offers special group pricing when two or more students are enrolled at the same time in the online Comprehensive Income Tax Course with ITS as the instructor. More information is available from the ITS website:

- https://www.theincometaxschool.com/train-employees/

Chapter 16 – Recruiting & Training Tax Preparers

Internships are another option. You and/or a veteran tax preparer employed by you could work with a college student or receptionist to teach the understudy taxes on the job. This would be a slow process, and it requires patience; but the result could be a highly qualified, loyal tax preparer who has learned tax preparation the right way!

Guerilla Tactics

Suppose tax season is just around the corner and you realize that you will not have enough tax preparers to staff your office. Maybe a key tax preparer decided not to return; or worse, you've learned that he/she plans to compete with you and solicit your clients that he/she served in prior years. If you had properly planned and prepared, you would not be in this situation. You should have had your tax preparers sign employment agreements including a legally enforceable confidentiality provision and non-solicitation for a period of time and a certain area. You should not let it happen again. However, if you are in such a predicament, what can you do?

It's time to use guerilla tactics. Fortunately, some qualified tax preparers seem to "come out of the woodwork" during December and January. You could run help wanted ads for *experienced* tax preparers. If ads are grouped by job title, run separate ads under both "Accountants" and "Tax Preparers." Advertise continuously through mid-January. Obtain a mailing list from a list broker or tax industry supplier of tax practitioners within commuting distance of your office(s) and send out a job opening notice on your letterhead, assuring complete confidentiality for respondents. Contact reputable temp agencies that place accounting and financial professionals for experienced tax preparers. Be very specific as to the practical and extensive tax preparation experience you require. Screen prospects by phone and schedule qualified candidates to take a tax test. Most applicants who apply from help wanted ads fail a tax test and realize that they need to take an income tax course to become qualified. If you need several preparers, consider conducting a free "accelerated" income tax course for new applicants, including daily lessons over several weeks. Schedule the successful graduates for additional training in your computer software and company policies and procedures.

You should also take measures to maximize the productivity of your existing tax preparers by providing them with adequate tools to do the job, including (if tax office volume justifies it) tax office assistants to greet clients, schedule appointments, answer telephones, pull files, conduct pre-interviews and process and transmit tax returns. Ask experienced tax preparers to work extra hours, even overtime if necessary. If you have part-timers who are employed full-time elsewhere, they may be willing to take vacation time from their regular jobs during peak periods. If you serve "walk-ins," call your prior clients to schedule appointments and spread out your workload. Ask your priors to come in during slower days and times. Take drop-off returns and complete them after hours. Extend your office hours. In short, do whatever it takes to serve your clients and keep from losing business. After you get through the tax season, begin planning early so you will not be in this situation again next year!

Chapter 16 – Recruiting & Training Tax Preparers

Conclusion

Finding and keeping good tax preparers is essential to building and growing a quality tax service. Qualified seasonal  tax preparers are scarce and competition for experienced tax preparers is stiff. Experienced tax professionals command a high price and may not become your best long-term employees. Excellent people skills are the most important attribute of a good tax preparer. Adequate planning conducted well in advance of the tax season is essential to ensure proper tax preparer staffing during the tax season. Retention of tax preparers is essential to maintain client relationships and retention, and to minimize recruiting and training costs. A proven "best practice" is to operate an income tax school to recruit and train entry-level tax preparers and provide continuing professional education for experienced tax preparers. There are alternatives to operating your own income tax school, but "growing your own" tax preparers is the "best practice" to ensure an adequate staff of competent, people-oriented tax preparers who will continue year-after-year to serve your valued clients. The Income Tax School makes it easy for you to recruit and train tax preparers without having to create your own curriculum year-after-year.

Chapter 16 – Recruiting & Training Tax Preparers

Tax Preparer
SAMPLE JOB DESCRIPTION

POSITION: Tax Preparer (entry-level)   **REPORTS TO:** Office Manager

LOCATIONS & HOURS:

- Offices throughout the city
- Flexible hours, days, evenings, and weekends

RESPONSIBILITIES:

- Attend pre-work training
- Prepare federal and state income tax returns
- Check, process, and e-file tax returns
- Advise taxpayers of tax planning strategies
- Prepare daily reports
- Complete recommended annual continuing professional education
- Learn and adhere to Company Policies and Procedures (see P&P Manual)
- Help with all other tasks necessary to maintain Company image and organization

EXPECTATIONS:

- Work efficiently; be productive and self-directed
- Represent the Company professionally to the public and to other Associates
- Place quality client service above all other considerations
- Function as a loyal member of the tax office team
- Maintain confidentiality of client information and Company proprietary information
- Availability for agreed upon hours, dependability

EXPERIENCE, SKILLS & QUALITIES REQUIRED:
- Knowledge of tax preparation (relevant experience or completion of tax course) *
- Maturity, sensitivity, and integrity
- Detail orientation, strong organizational skills
- Strong interpersonal skills, concern for people, a team player
- Computer proficiency or aptitude (training in tax preparation software provided)
- Initiative, self-reliance & perseverance
- *Tuition-free tax course available for qualified candidates

COMPENSATION:

Associates receive a base hourly pay rate, plus bonuses for personal production, achieving office growth (Office Bonus Pool).

Chapter 17

Employee Pre-Work Training

We learn to do something by doing it. There is no other way.

- John Holt

Chapter 17 – Employee Pre-work Training

Tax Preparer Training

Your tax preparers will be much more productive and less frustrated when the pressure is on if they receive proper pre-work training. Your clients will also be impressed by the efficiency of your operation.

Tax preparer training should include the following four elements:

1. Income tax preparation training, where they learn how to correctly interview clients and prepare federal and local state income tax returns. The Income Tax School incorporates interview training and tax laws updates in their courses.

2. Tax preparation software training using provided computers.

3. Pre-work training in your firm's policies and procedures, including customer service.

4. On-the-job training.

Tax Preparation and Client Interview Training

One of the most important things you will need to do is make sure that your tax preparers truly have the tax knowledge that they say they do. This topic was covered in detail in Chapter 16 on Recruiting and Training Tax Preparers. However, another key point is to make sure your employees know how to conduct an accurate and thorough client interview. Your preparers may have great tax knowledge, but without a good client interview, they could be missing key details that make a huge difference on the outcome of a client's tax return. Set aside some time for role-playing with your tax preparers and go through a few typical scenarios that are likely to occur at your tax office. This will quickly show you who is ready and who needs more training. It's often eye-opening, everyone learns a lot, and it can even be fun to do.

Chapter 17 – Employee Pre-work Training

New Tax Laws

Every year some of our tax laws change. Some years the changes may be extensive. Your tax preparers must be educated in the changes. You should hold a session with your tax preparers before the start of the season on federal and local and adjacent state income tax laws that have changed. Seminars on new tax laws are available each year from various providers of continuing education (CE), including the annual Tax Law Update online CE seminar provided by The Income Tax School.

Tax Software Training

Your new tax preparers who have just completed their first basic income tax course will need comprehensive training in the tax software they will be using. They will need to be provided with computers, either individually, or if you must train a number of new tax preparers, they can work in groups of 3 to 4 sharing one computer. You or your most experienced tax preparer should conduct the training. They can practice by entering tax return problems from their tax course into the tax software you are using.

When you update your tax software, you will also need to train your experienced tax preparers in the changes. Both your prior and new tax preparers should also be taught shortcuts and special features of your tax software that will enable them to prepare tax returns more efficiently.

Scheduling of Pre-work Training

Years ago, all tax office employee training had to be completed by December 31st, because tax season started the first business day after New Year's Day. However, now that the IRS does not begin accepting e-filed tax returns until late January, pre-work training can be conducted during the first two weeks of January, which is much better.

Prior Employee Reorientation

Prior employees will not need as much pre-work training as new employees. However, you should go over any new policies or procedures your office might have developed, and any changes such as an increase in pricing and new marketing campaigns. You should also stress your key policies and procedures and any issues you've experienced in employees adhering to them. Hopefully, at the end of last tax season you took some time to reflect on shortcomings or opportunities to work on for the current season. You also may have sent out a customer survey. Reviewing any issues is a great way to help prior employees grow and get better. During your review, you may want to set some goals for this tax season.

New Tax Preparer Training

You should devote adequate time to train your new tax preparers in all of your tax office policies, procedures and practices, including company philosophy and client service based on your tax office operations manual. If you don't have a Policy and Procedure Manual (Operations Manual), there is no need to "reinvent the wheel." Consider obtaining a Tax Office Operations Manual from another source, such as The Income Tax School (ITS). The ITS Operations Manual is provided in hard copy, as well as in digital form to enable it to be customized by any tax firm. Pre-work training is one of the most important ways to ensure that your tax preparers will understand and adhere to your policies and procedures.

- https://www.theincometaxschool.com/product/tax-office-operations-manual/

Pre-work Training Topics

Before tax season gets underway, after having completed training in tax preparation, proper client interviewing techniques, new tax laws, and tax preparation software, your tax preparers should also be trained in all of your policies, procedures and practices, including the following topics:

- Company Mission, Vision, and Philosophy
- Guiding Principles
- Image
- Personnel Policies & Procedures

Chapter 17 – Employee Pre-work Training

- Marketing Campaigns
- Tax Office Policies and Procedures/Operations
- Administrative Procedures
- Electronic Filing
- Pricing of Tax Returns
- Confidential Information
- IRS Circular 230
- IRS Due Diligence
- Client Service

Tax office receptionists and other clerical employees should be included in the portions of your pre-work training that are relevant to the duties they perform.

Company Vision and Philosophy

As the "CEO" of your tax firm, you have a vision for the mission, growth and success of your business. Your vision and philosophy should be communicated to all employees as often as possible. This should be the first topic of your annual pre-work training. Relaying your company vision and philosophy sets the tone for your company culture. If you spend time reviewing your expectations and the history of your company, you will find that your employees will be more passionate about your business and the work that they do.

Company culture is also extremely important. It sets the tone for how employees interact with management, with each other, and with your clients. Company culture is also linked to employee morale and happiness. Happy employees are more productive, better at providing excellent customer service, healthier, more loyal and less likely to leave.

Guiding Principles

Guiding Principles provide a structure by which to operate your business. Your Guiding Principles should be designed to create the following four conditions:

1. Deliver needed services and true value to all clients.
2. Integrate the goals of the Company.
3. Produce a fair return for the company owner(s).
4. Contribute to the community.

Chapter 17 – Employee Pre-work Training

Image

Your tax office should be designed to provide a neat, efficient, professional and inviting atmosphere. All of your tax office employees should portray an appropriate image in their personal appearance and behavior at all times while representing your company. Your employees should be responsible to keep their personal workspaces and the entire office clean, uncluttered, and organized. Papers should not be taped or pinned to walls, equipment or office furniture. Smoking or chewing gum while in the office should not be permitted at any time. Soft music can enhance your professional office atmosphere.

Personnel Policies & Procedures

You should have a personnel manual that spells out in plain language all your policies and procedures that pertaining to your employees. Your personnel manual should cover topics such as attendance, time cards, payroll, dress code, phones, substance abuse, harassment, breaks, absences, benefits, etc. Each employee should be issued a copy of your personnel manual and asked to sign an acknowledgement that they have received and read it. Any questions they may have should be addressed to their supervisor. You can obtain a customizable personnel manual from several sources, including The Income Tax School and decide which policies and procedures you will adopt, change, or delete.

- https://www.theincometaxschool.com/product/tax-business-personnel-manual/

Marketing Campaigns

Everyone in your office should be aware of the marketing campaigns you plan to implement during tax season. These initiatives should be explained during training and provided in writing for future reference. Make sure each employee understands all promotions and that you answer any questions they may have. If a client comes in with a discount coupon, they should already know about the promotion and not cause the client to feel uncomfortable while they look into how to handle it. Asking them for ideas can also make them more engaged and they may come up with some great suggestions.

Tax Office Policies and Procedures

Tax office policies and procedures include topics such as your hours of operation, how to answer the phone, how appointments can be scheduled, how to determine the pricing of tax returns, payment options, IRS privacy and Due Diligence requirements, etc. These are simply the day-to-day rules and practices that keep your business running and in compliance with the law and with IRS regulations. Making sure that your employees understand your tax office policies and procedures is one of the most important objectives of your pre-work training. The proper preparation and handling of tax returns and serving

Chapter 17 – Employee Pre-work Training

your clients professionally is the lifeblood of your business. You must spend ample time training your tax office employees on the following topics.

Administrative Procedures

There are many administrative aspects involved in running a tax office. Below are some topics that should be covered in your employee training and included in your tax office P&P or Operations Manual.

- Payroll & Timecard
- Daily Report
- Client Information
- Payment Options
- Bank Deposits
- Answering Phones
- Appointments

- Drop-off Returns
- Price Inquiries
- Work Schedules
- Work Station Set-up
- Ordering Office Supplies and Equipment

Electronic Filing

The IRS has very specific procedures for electronic filing that should be reviewed. Your tax preparers should know how electronic filing and direct deposit of tax refunds are done. They should also be trained in the precautions that need to be taken, how to tell their clients what to expect, and how to detect fraud.

Pricing of Tax Returns

Your tax preparers need to know how to properly charge clients for the work they do. Go over your pricing philosophy, procedures, and your schedule of charges. Explain how to provide price estimates, when to allow price reductions, etc.

Confidential Information

The Company's Policies and Procedures, including the complete Schedule of Charges, Company newsletters and intra-Company correspondence are confidential and should not be divulged to anyone not associated with the Company. Competitors may try to obtain confidential information. Be cautious about providing in-depth information about your company to callers until you are comfortable with whom are you speaking. Some unusual inquiries may represent opportunities, so be courteous. **Client names, addresses and tax return information are strictly confidential and disclosures of this information are prohibited by law.**

Chapter 17 – Employee Pre-work Training

IRS Circular 230

All client tax return information, including names, addresses and tax return information are strictly confidential and must never be visible to anyone other than the tax preparer while preparing a tax return. Client files must always be kept in locked file cabinets or desk drawers, or a in a locked file room. Disclosures of this information are strictly prohibited by IRS Circular 230. The IRS can impose severe fines for violations.

IRS Due Diligence

The IRS requires that all tax preparers adhere to specific Due Diligence requirements while preparing tax returns. The IRS Due Diligence rules and regulations are designed to uncover and prevent prevent fraud

Client Service/Courtesy

Each client or prospect that enters or calls the office should be **recognized immediately** and treated with **courtesy**, **respect** and **friendliness**. You should treat each client's tax needs as if they were the most important concerns in the world to you. Simply treat each and every client's tax return as if it were **your** tax return.

Remember the client is the boss. The client signs your paycheck. Clients notice everything about the office, you, appearances, cleanliness, attitudes, courtesy, organization, confidence, handling of the phones and phone calls, etc. All of these things and more can make or break a client relationship.

Providing World-Class Service

The following employee practices are from the Ritz Carlton Hotels, which are renowned worldwide for the extraordinary experience they consistently deliver to their guests.

The 3 Steps of Service

1. A warm, sincere greeting; use the client's name.

2. *Anticipation* of and compliance with the client's needs.

3. A fond farewell; give them a warm goodbye and use their names.

"I have a customer on the line,
but I'm not trained on what to say to them!"

Chapter 17 – Employee Pre-work Training

Our Credo

Our firm is a place where *genuine* care and concern for our clients is our highest mission. We pledge to provide the finest personal service, professionalism and atmosphere for our clients. The experience we provide enlivens the senses, instills peace-of-mind and fulfills even the *unexpressed wishes and needs* of our clients.

The 20 Basics of Service

1. Our Credo will be known, owned and energized by all Associates.

2. We are ladies and gentlemen serving ladies and gentlemen.

3. All Associates will practice the 3 Steps of Service.

4. *Smile*, we are all on stage; always maintain *positive* eye contact.

5. Use the proper vocabulary with guests; avoid crude language and slang expressions.

6. *Uncompromising* levels of cleanliness are the responsibility of every Associate.

7. Create a positive workplace environment; practice teamwork.

8. Be an ambassador, both inside and outside of the office; always talk positively about our firm.

9. Any Associate who receives a client complaint *owns* the complaint and must see that it is promptly and properly resolved.

10. Instant pacification of irate clients will be insured by all Associates (within 10 minutes).

11. Use the Problem Resolution form to communicate details to associates and document errors.

12. Introduce clients to other associates or professionals who can meet their needs instead of telling them to call someone else.

13. Be knowledgeable of our services and other information in order to answer client inquiries.

14. Use proper phone etiquette; answer within 3 rings and *with a smile*; ask permission to put the caller on hold; do not screen calls; eliminate call transfers whenever possible.

15. Recommend our service at every opportunity.

16. Always be well-groomed and professionally dressed when representing the firm (see guidelines).

17. Insure that all Associates know their roles in emergency situations.

18. Notify your supervisor of hazards, injuries, equipment or assistance needs you have.

19. Practice energy conservation and proper maintenance and repair of property and equipment.

20. Protecting property of the Company is the responsibility of every Associate.

The above principles and practices complement the Company Philosophy and Guiding Principles which appear on the preceding page. Employees should be advised that their success and advancement would be determined by their belief in and willingness to internalize and practice these values and principles of integrity and interaction with their peers and clients.

Goals to Strive For

- This is your business; treat it as such.
- Provide a warm welcome.
- Listen intently.
- Be knowledgeable about your services.
- Balance efficiency with courtesy.
- Thank clients sincerely.
- Demonstrate a passion for client service.
- Build long-term relationships with clients.
- Seek opportunities to enhance our success.
- Always treat your clients as you would like to be treated.
- Be sincere.
- Strive to make the Company better tomorrow than it is today.
- Proceed boldly; give it everything you've got!
- Show respect to others.
- Take responsibility for the day to day results; don't fix blame; fix the problem.
- Always do more than your fair share.
- Demand continuous improvement for yourself.
- Look for opportunities to add value to everything you do.

Chapter 17 – Employee Pre-work Training

- Listen to suggestions from others; everything can always be improved upon.

- Always strive to provide excellent client service.

- Smile.

- Keep your word; deliver more than you promise.

- Be personally responsible for the satisfaction of every client.

- Learn from others.

- Be dedicated to doing the best you can for you and your clients.

- Respect others; show appreciation of the efforts others make for you.

- Recognize and celebrate success.

- Thank people.

- Communicate honestly and completely with accurate information.

On the Job Training

Training should be ongoing so that tax preparers are continuing to learn throughout the tax season. New tax preparers should be trained under the supervision of you, your office manager or a veteran tax preparer. Schedule on-the-job training early in the season before the office gets busy. Have new tax preparers prepare practice tax returns, by computer, using tax school problems, your tax software firm's tutorial and/or actual prior year file copies of tax returns.

Conclusion

Conducting timely and comprehensive employee pre-work training will ensure that your tax office operates smoothly and professionally. Taking the time to adequately train your employees will save you a great deal of time and frustration during tax season. Adequate employee training will also result in much greater client satisfaction and set your tax firm apart from your competitors. Employee morale will also be greatly enhanced due to the training. Pre-work employee training is one of the best uses of the time of a tax business owner. This investment in time will pay big dividends during tax season.

Chapter 18

Motivating & Retaining Employees

"Always treat your employees exactly as you want them to treat your best customers."

- Stephen R. Covey

Chapter 18 – Motivating & Retaining Employees

Employee retention is essential to maintain customer relationships and minimize recruiting and training costs. The keys to employee satisfaction and retention are founded on strong leadership and sound management practices. By mastering these arts, you should have happy, loyal employees and customers, resulting in growth, profits and personal gratification.

Operating Systems

As explained in Chapter 6—Tax Office Operating Systems, the foundation of an efficient and effective workplace is the structure, discipline and consistency provided by well-conceived systematic operating methods. A policies and procedures manual (or operations manual) is critical to ensure that employees understand what is expected of them and know how they should handle the myriad of duties and responsibilities in the day-to-day operations of the business.

Employment Agreements and Job Descriptions

Legal agreements are often a "necessary evil" to ensure there is a "meeting of the minds" as to exactly what the parties agree to when they enter into an employer-employee relationship. The agreement should specify the term, termination, restrictive covenants, duties, responsibilities and compensation.

Tax Preparer Employment Agreements

Employment agreements should be prepared or updated prior to interviewing and hiring or rehiring tax preparers. If you do not bind tax preparers to the restrictive contract provisions described below, you are risking the preparers taking clients with them, should they leave; and having these provisions in place could discourage them from leaving.

1. **Non-Competition**

    A non-compete provision that is construed as being unreasonable will not be upheld by most courts. Non-compete agreements that extend beyond the employment term may not be legal in some localities and some states, such as California. Tax preparers should never be permitted to compete while employed, and non-competition while employed is legal anywhere. A non-competition provision beyond the term of employment must be reasonable in terms of:

Chapter 18 – Motivating & Retaining Employees

    a. **Duration**, usually not more than 2 years,

    b. **Distance**, usually not beyond a 25-mile radius, and

    c. **Livelihood**, not restricted.

Developing an independent tax practice while employed as a tax preparer is a conflict of interest and should not be allowed. If an experienced tax preparer applies for employment and has a handful of long-term personal clients, buying the clients might be an option. Another alternative might be to exclude existing clients specifically by contract addendum from your non-compete provision.

2. **Non-Solicitation**

   Even more important than a non-compete provision is a "Non-Solicitation" clause that survives beyond the term of employment, as well as beyond the non-compete restriction. This provision is perpetual.

3. **Confidentiality**

   Equally important to a non-solicitation clause is a confidentiality provision that is also perpetual. Confidentiality typically pertains to trade secrets and client information.

Such restrictive covenants can effectively prevent tax preparers who leave from ever taking your clients. Removing client information from your office to solicit clients they served while employed by your company is a confidentiality breach. A breach of the confidentiality provision is also a violation of IRS Circular 230 Privacy Regulations and could jeopardize a preparer's IRS credentials.

You might be able to obtain a copy of an employment agreement of one of the national tax firms. You could also obtain a sample tax preparer employment agreement from a provider of tax practice management products, such as The Income Tax School. In any event, you should hire a qualified labor law attorney who is familiar with your state and local laws to ensure the employment contract is likely to be upheld by the courts in the localities in which your tax firm operates.

Tax Preparer Compensation

Tax preparers can be paid a straight hourly rate, a fixed salary, a percentage of revenue, a wage as a draw against a percentage of revenue, or a wage plus a percentage of revenue. There are other options, but these are the most common. Regardless of which method you choose, tax preparer compensation should be based on the revenue the preparer generates. Having tax preparers paid either a wage as a draw against a percentage of the revenue they generate, or a wage plus a smaller percentage of revenue generated usually works very well.

Training and Tools to do the Job

As discussed in previous chapters, adequate employee training and providing all the necessary tools to do the job are essential. Ensuring these things will reduce employee frustration and increase job satisfaction. Following these principles will result in increased employee retention and greater business success.

Company Culture

Business profit is a byproduct of meeting the needs of customers and employees. A business also has a responsibility to give back to the community, and most employees want to make meaningful contributions through their work. They also like to take pride in their work and deliver quality products and services. Employees also need to continue to learn and grow professionally. A world-class company culture enables employees to combine their strengths to meet these mutual needs as part of a dynamic team.

Benefits

Even if your profit margins are thin, you can provide benefits that are not cost-prohibitive, or even free. Giving benefits puts you in a better competitive position to attract and retain employees. A profit sharing plan based on *growth in profits* is a win-win. You could offer a 401k plan or a pre-tax benefits savings plan. Group insurance, group discounts and other benefits can be provided through your local Chamber of Commerce. Your company can also become a member of a credit union to enable employees to qualify for benefits. Little perks, like buying pizza for the staff on a hectic day, help to make your employees appreciate their jobs. Be creative!

Chapter 18 – Motivating & Retaining Employees

Recognition

Numerous studies have documented the fact that money is not the primary motivator for most workers. In fact, people who are motivated primarily by money may not be good employees. Recognize your people frequently for their good work and they will repeat the performance often. Praise must be sincere and should be distributed equitably, if warranted. When possible, praise people publicly in meetings or employee newsletters. Be sure to give credit and rewards for good ideas that benefit the company. Reinforce the right behaviors. Avoid saying "Great, but." Look for key measures to recognize employees, such as production or customer retention. Come up with contests to recognize your people. Give recognition certificates, plaques and prizes other than money, such as tickets for the movies or a sports event, or gift certificates for merchandise or dinner. A tangible reward makes a more lasting impression. Praising your best performers (the top 10-20%) will raise the bar for your weaker people. The goal is to encourage behaviors that build your business and recognize your people as often as possible for practicing those behaviors.

Communication

Lack of effective communication from superiors is often the greatest cause for employee dissatisfaction and premature departure. The best managers listen to and communicate frequently with all employees; and they make it easy for employees to tell them about problems and concerns. Communication should include training, group and individual meetings and, most important, daily dialogue with employees. As the manager, you should make the time to talk regularly with everyone. E-mail is a good communication vehicle, but the phone is more personal; and neither can replace face-to-face meetings. Even virtual meetings can work if you can't meet in person.

Employee newsletters can enhance communication. Keep communication simple, provide adequate information and give examples for clarity. Show your trust in your people and make them feel included by sharing financial and other inside information. Management can make much better decisions by getting input from front-line employees. If your people know their voices are heard and feel like they are part of the decision-making process, they will be much happier, loyal and more likely to support new programs.

Having Fun to Boost Morale

People like to work in an environment that is enjoyable. They can get burned out if the work environment is totally serious and strictly business. Great companies like Southwest Airlines have come up with creative ways for employees to have fun. If you're not naturally good at getting people to have fun, designate a key employee to assume this role and be your official or unofficial cheerleader.

Chapter 18 – Motivating & Retaining Employees

Laughter and humor are an important part of the workplace. Laughter has been proven to reduce stress, draw people together, boost your mood, increase productivity, relax your entire body, and most importantly is contagious.

At The Income Tax School, there is a designated "Fun Committee" to help ensure that the morale in the office is high.

Here are some fun and inexpensive things you can do to boost the mood/moral during tax season.

- Order pizza for the office on busy days.
- Purchase adjustable standing/sitting desks for those who need/want to move more.
- Have a donut taste test day from competing donut shops.
- Take a walk during breaks.
- Play positive/uplifting music in the office and take turns choosing the music.
- Celebrate holidays.
- Have theme days like sports day or funny t-shirt day.
- Have a potluck luncheon.
- Host an office Olympics.
- Tell corny jokes.

Keep Your Employees Motivated Through the Busy Tax Season

If one of the reasons you decided to open (or are thinking about opening) your own tax preparation business is because you've had miserable experiences working for others, ask yourself this very important question: What are you doing not to repeat those same mistakes with your employees? Especially during tax season. What are the best ways to keep your employees motivated through the busy tax season?

If your office atmosphere is dull, dreary, or even abusive, throwing a pizza party or some gift cards at your employees is throwing a bandage on the problem. It won't actually heal anything. On the other hand, if you provide the right balance of leadership, a focused work environment, and fun, you'll have a positive, productive atmosphere that people enjoy working in. What's more – if your employees feel happy and fulfilled, they are more

Chapter 18 – Motivating & Retaining Employees

likely to provide superior service to your clients. Finding the right way to motivate and retain your employees really is a win for you, a win for them, and a win for your clients. To have satisfied clients, you must first have satisfied employees. So, how can you have a top-notch staff, show them you care, and keep them motivated.

Recognize Their Needs

Remember that your employees are not there just because they love you (although hopefully that's part of it). Your employees need jobs. They also have lives outside of work that need attention. If you're able to support them in accomplishing what they need to get done outside work, they'll be better able to focus on work at the office.

Today, flexibility at work is key for many people, whether it's because they want to fit in more exercise, they have hobbies they're passionate about, or they have families to take care of. Whatever you can do to help recognize the needs of your employees will make it more likely to retain them. Finding a positive work environment that gives someone the freedom and flexibility to both be productive at work and have a life outside work is hard to do. Can you offer flexible hours? Could some people be allowed to work from home by setting up a cloud-based, virtual office? What's the secret sauce for helping them be more productive at work and at home?

Now, that doesn't mean you should let employees come and go as they please. You have work to get done and clients to answer to. If an employee misses too much time from work or frequently comes in unfit to work, they're not holding up their end of the bargain. You'll have to figure out what's going on and find a solution – keeping in mind that the solution may be as easy as letting someone come in 30 minutes earlier so they can leave 30 minutes earlier. Or, perhaps someone can make up time from home after hours.

The main point is, if you recognize your employees' needs, more often than not, they'll be more productive and focused.

Provide Pre-work and On-the-job Training

Make sure your employees are prepared for each tax season and are growing as tax preparation professionals. Provide access to resources and opportunities to grow their skill sets. Be sure to include training in customer service and technical skills. Doing any kind of training as a group can be a great team-building exercise, too! You'll win on both a professional and an interpersonal level!

Reward Hard Work with Bonuses and Fun

There are so many ways to make your work environment fun, show employees you really appreciate their hard work, and reward them with a little something extra.

- Give bonuses based on individual, team, or overall office performance so they know that the better the company does, the better they'll do.

- Hold fun contests with prizes for top performers and top learners. The contests can be work-related or not.

- Bring in food. Whether you have snacks around or you provide lunch or dinner during a busy day, keeping everyone fueled can go a long way. Provide healthy options and make sure to consider people's food allergies and preferences. No one likes to be left out, and there are many options that can make everyone happy.

When you're thinking about what kinds of bonuses and incentives your people will like, consider the whole picture. Money is great – but money is soon spent and forgotten. However, gift cards to the movies, dinner, or other experiences will create memories that last longer than cash. Doing something together as an office to celebrate the end of tax season or realizing revenue goals lets you all make memories together and sends a signal to your employees that they really are an integral part of the business.

Communicate

Everyone likes to be "in the know." Make sure you keep your employees updated about big changes, help you need, and how the business is doing overall. Likewise, encourage your employees to communicate with you when they are struggling, have questions, or can take on more work. When the going gets tough (and it always does at some point), keep a sense of humor, remember your priorities, be there for each other, and order a pizza. You all will get through this tax preparation season together.

Consider Adopting a Servant Leadership Model for Your Tax Business

Servant leadership is at the heart of how business is done at The Income Tax School. It's so important as a business owner that you set strong values for your organization to follow.

As a business owner, the way you lead your people could make or break you. But leadership is more than just managing people, it's about making a difference and leading change. Business owners who embrace servant leadership have the opportunity to make an impact in their business, the lives of their employees and their own community. In turn, the impact that you make will help strengthen and grown your own business.

What is Servant Leadership?

Servant leadership is a philosophy and set of practices that enriches the lives of individuals, builds better organizations, and ultimately creates a more just and caring world. Servant leaders put the needs of customers, employees, and communities first.

It's about…

- Serving others.

Chapter 18 – Motivating & Retaining Employees

- Leveraging your company or resources to produce worthwhile change.

- Transforming your business into a successful enterprise by inspiring people to excel and helping them grow. personally, and professionally.

Servant Leadership in Practice

A servant leader focuses primarily on the growth and well-being of people: employees, community members, clients, etc. Practicing Servant Leadership includes implementing the following practices in every action, decision, or interaction.

- Always put integrity and ethics first.
- Show empathy and genuine concern for others.
- Communicate openly.
- Demonstrate mutual trust & respect for each other, for clients, and for the community.
- Lead a purposeful life.

When you focus on caring and having compassion for others, your employees and clients will be happier, and your business will grow.

Conclusion

You cannot motivate your employees; to be productive, your employees must be self-motivated. Your objective should be to create an atmosphere where your employees will act in the best interest of your clients and the company without being directly supervised. They should want to do the right things even when you are not looking. This requires creating a company culture for your tax office to be a rewarding and fun place to work, with the opportunity for career and professional advancement. You should also provide the benefits you can afford to be competitive with other employers to retain your employees. You must also protect your client base and help to ensure retention through restrictive employment agreement provisions. In addition, your employees must be provided with adequate training, retraining and continuous communication, as well as systematic operating methods and all of the tools they need to do their jobs.

Chapter 19

Continuing Education

There are no great limits to growth because there are no limits of human intelligence, imagination, and wonder.

- Ronald Reagan
  Actor and 40th President of the United States

Chapter 19 – Continuing Education

This is an exciting time to be a tax preparer and it is important to your business to stay current with the ever-changing tax laws. But in addition to keeping up with the changes, you should also consider expanding your tax knowledge. Learning advanced individual and small business tax information will enable you to grow your business and take on more complicated tax returns. You will gain confidence as a knowledgeable preparer, continue to grow in the field, and expand your tax practice.

Preparing More Complicated Tax Returns

Many tax preparers decide to limit their practice to the preparation of simple tax returns. They see this market as their "bread and butter" and have been able to develop a successful business. However, one important consideration in today's marketplace is the fact that the simple returns can be prepared by more people, including the clients with inexpensive software such as TurboTax. Therefore, it's easier for a competitor to take the clients away from you.

As you become more educated, you will be able to prepare more complicated tax returns. Clients with complicated tax issues know that they need professional help and want a reliable, professional that will take care of everything for them. These types of clients are going to be more loyal to you and harder for your competition to persuade to leave. In addition, you can charge a higher fee when you are preparing more complicated tax returns. You may charge $150 for a fairly basic tax return. While, depending on the amount of work involved, you could earn $500 or more preparing a more complicated tax return. More clients + more complicated tax returns = more revenue for you!

Consider taking advanced individual and small business income tax courses and Continuing Education (CE) seminars for the following reasons.

10 Reasons to Earn CE and Tax Pro Credentials

As a tax professional, you have a responsibility to your clients and, equally important, to yourself to develop a strong base of tax knowledge and to always be current on all new tax laws. Having a tax professional credential is also important. Below are 10 reasons why you should complete annual Continuing Education (CE) and earn at least one tax professional credential.

1. Gain Pride and Self Confidence

Even if you are not required to be well versed and current in tax laws pertaining

to the types of tax returns you prepare, you must have this knowledge in order to

consider yourself a true tax professional and to take pride in your work. Tax

Chapter 19 – Continuing Education

preparation software has enabled many tax preparers to complete tax returns without really knowing the tax laws. This is a key reason why tax preparer regulations have been repeatedly proposed by the IRS, Congress and consumer protection groups. Having this knowledge will provide you with self-confidence.

2. Gain a Competitive Advantage

Taxpayers have many options when choosing a tax preparer. A smart taxpayer will always choose a tax professional who is knowledgeable and current in tax laws. Professional credentials and current educational certificates should be displayed in your office, advertising materials, website, and business cards to demonstrate your competency to potential clients. If you have credentials that your competitor does not have, the taxpayer will probably choose you, even if your fees are higher.

3. Earn More Money

The more tax knowledge you have, the more types of tax returns you can prepare. The Income Tax School (ITS), the National Standard in Tax Professional Training, offers a series of five hands-on courses in income tax preparation, plus dozens of Continuing Education (CE) seminars. Completing the ITS Comprehensive Tax Course will provide you with the knowledge you need to prepare Form 1040 tax returns for the vast majority of individual U.S. taxpayers. You could then take advanced tax courses (levels I and II) or seminars to learn to prepare more complex individual returns resulting in higher fees. If you want to go beyond only preparing Form 1040 individual returns, you could complete the Small Business I Tax Course and then the Small Business II Tax Course to learn to prepare Form 1120 and 1120S corporation and Form 1065 partnership returns to add another source of revenue.

4. Avoid Making Mistakes and Losing Clients

The easiest way to lose valued clients is to make mistakes on their tax returns. You do not want to put yourself in that position. The cost of acquiring a new

Chapter 19 – Continuing Education

client is substantial and the lifetime value of each client is significant. Client retention is critical to your success. Continuing education will allow you to gain more tax knowledge, keep abreast of the constantly changing tax laws and possibly remind you of some tax regulations you may have forgotten. Investing in education will help you and your employees reduce the possibility of making errors in your tax practice.

5. Avoid Refunding Fees and Incurring Interest & Penalties

When you make a mistake on a tax return that costs your client money, you will be responsible for any penalties and interest incurred due to your error. To retain a client whose return you prepared incorrectly, it is often necessary to give the client a full or partial refund and/or a credit toward next year's tax preparation. This adds up to a significant loss of revenue.

6. Avoid IRS Tax Preparer Penalties

Tax preparers can be assessed stiff penalties by the IRS for making errors on tax returns. The penalties for preparing an inaccurate tax return can be very costly. For example, the IRS penalty for failure to be diligent in determining eligibility for earned income credit" is $500. IRS Due Diligence is covered thoroughly in the ITS Comprehensive Tax Course.

7. Earn Professional Credentials

Many taxpayers specifically look for a tax preparer with credentials because it adds a level of trust and shows the preparer cares enough to go the extra mile. By obtaining a tax professional credential such as The Income Tax School's prestigious Chartered Tax Professional (CTP®) designation,  you will enjoy the status of being a true tax professional and including the CTP® designation after your name. After earning the CTP® certification and gaining more tax preparation experience you should have the knowledge necessary to prepare for the IRS Enrolled Agent (EA) Exam, sit for the EA Exam and also become an EA. The IRS EA designation is the most significant professional credential in the tax preparation industry. ITS offers two lesser Charted Tax certificate programs (the CTA® and CTC®) as steppingstones toward the CTP®.

8. Earn Certificates of Completion

Certificates of Completion are great to display in your tax office and are wonderful tools that show clients you are taking the time to complete relevant courses to stay abreast of the everchanging tax laws. After completing every tax course and seminar at The Income Tax School, you receive a Certificate of Completion

for your tax office. Our most impressive certificate is awarded for completion of the prestigious Chartered Tax Professional (CTP®) certificate program. You should be proud of your efforts and these Certificates of Completion should be displayed in your tax office to instill the confidence of your clients in you.

9. Meet Current or Future IRS or State Preparer Requirements

If you plan to prepare tax returns in California or Oregon, you must complete the required Qualifying Course and annual CE, in addition to other requirements imposed on tax preparers by these states. While the IRS Preparer Requirements are currently suspended by a Federal Court Injunction, the IRS is appealing, and Preparer Requirements could resume in the future. Meanwhile, the IRS has implemented their voluntary Annual Filing Season Program (AFSP). Attaining the AFSP Record of Completion provides important benefits described below.

The AFSP aims to recognize the efforts of non-credentialed return preparers who aspire to a higher level of professionalism. Benefits include:

- **Represent Your Clients:** AFSP participants have limited representation rights, able to represent clients during an examination of a return they prepared.

- **FREE Marketing:** AFSP participants are listed on the IRS Federal Tax Return Preparers Directory with professional credentials or other select qualifications.

- **Promote Your Credentials:** Participants can market themselves as a credentialed preparer by adding, "as seen on IRS.gov" or "AFSP – Record of Completion" to their tax designation.

- **Certificate from the IRS:** Participants receive an IRS record of completion.

- **Set Yourself Apart:** Participants are set apart and have the means to show that they are qualified to prepare taxes by completing the program.

10. **Peace of Mind**

Having a solid base of tax knowledge and keeping current on the tax laws will give you the peace of mind in knowing that you are able to competently prepare accurate tax returns and meet the needs of your valued clients as a highly-qualified tax professional.

TIP: Learn More about the AFSP Available at The Income Tax School:
- https://www.theincometaxschool.com/irs-annual-filing-season-program-afsp/

Tax Business Owners

If you are thinking about going out on your own, or you already have a tax business established, now is the time to learn some business strategies and tactics. There are tax practice management tools and resources available to help you build and grow a successful tax business. You can also take business courses and seminars to help you in all aspects of your business. The Income Tax School offers a set of four Tax Practice Management Manuals (TPMs) specifically for this purpose. The TPMs discuss the top strategies and tactics national tax firms use to fuel growth, as well as other topics such as marketing and day-to-day business operations, plus so much more. These manuals are the "how-to" guides for running and growing a tax business. The key is to learn from others already in the tax industry and avoid reinventing the wheel when possible.

Chapter 19 – Continuing Education

TIP: Learn More about the Tax Practice Management Manuals Available at The Income Tax School:

- https://www.theincometaxschool.com/build-your-tax-business/tax-practice-manuals/

Conclusion

It's always a good idea to continue your education. It's paramount to stay on top of the tax law changes that occur each year. But you can always learn new things in other areas that will help give you new ideas and help you to grow as a person. Learning new things can help you gain confidence and keep you motivated and excited about what you do. It can also help you become more qualified in your field and make more money. Education is always a good idea!

Chapter 20

Diversification for Year-Round Revenue

"The only thing we know about the future is that it will be different."

- Peter Drucker

Chapter 20 – Diversification for Year-Round Revenue

How Will You Earn Money After Tax Season?

Diversification is important to consider before starting your own tax business. Operating a tax business can be a very rewarding career, or a great additional service for someone in a complimentary business. Tax season is less than *one-fourth* of the year, which means unless you are in the position to take that much time off without income, you've got to have a plan. As the saying goes, "Don't put all your eggs in one basket."

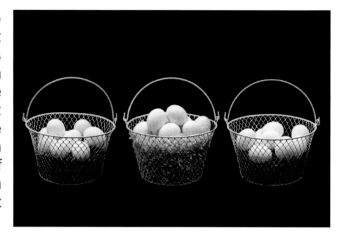

One way to ensure year-round revenue is to acquire business clients who need bookkeeping and payroll services and must file tax reports quarterly. You could also offer IRS taxpayer representation services, which are described in Chapter 22, but remember that to represent a taxpayer before the IRS who is not your client, you must have status as an Enrolled Agent, a CPA or an attorney. Below are some other ideas for you to earn income during the off-season, or year-round.

While you can still bank on the fact that some people who missed the deadline or applied for an extension because they did not have everything necessary to complete their tax returns will need your help after tax season; this most likely won't carry you through to next year. How do other tax professionals generate revenue? They diversify.

Diversification means that, unless you have other business skills, you'll need to learn how to do more than just taxes. There are a good number of options out there for tax preparers. Here are some of the most common.

Bookkeeping Services

Bookkeeping is a great complimentary business to tax preparation because it is a year-round necessity for small business taxpayers. If you are already preparing taxes for the business, bookkeeping could be an easy add-on. Conversely, you may acquire clients for your bookkeeping services that could become tax preparation clients as well.

Becoming a bookkeeper does not require any special certification, but it does require accounting knowledge. There are many options to learn to become a bookkeeper. The Income Tax School partners with Penn Foster to offer their bookkeeping course.

You could also consider a course in bookkeeping offered by a local community college or workforce development program. The course must be hands-on and designed for a bookkeeper and not just a small business owner seeking to learn how to do their own bookkeeping.

Chapter 20 – Diversification for Year-Round Revenue

If you currently offer bookkeeping services, you should make sure you market those services throughout the year to current and potential clients. Continuing to market your services throughout the year and being strategic about marketing and communications, will help keep business coming in after tax season ends.

Bookkeeping software will also be needed such as Intuit's QuickBooks, which is the standard used by most bookkeepers and small businesses. Although you will need to learn QuickBooks to help business clients who use QuickBooks, many bookkeepers use a different "write-up" software product for clients who do not use QuickBooks.

TIP: For more information on the Penn Foster Bookkeeping Course, visit: www.theincometaxschool.com/build-your-own-successful-tax-business/become-a-bookkeeper-in-as-little-as-5-months/

Payroll Services

Another great service to add for business clients is payroll. Intuit offers great payroll solutions to consider. You would need a relationship with a bank to set up an account to process ACH payroll deposits. A local community bank may be easier to work with because a small bank would be less bureaucratic. Learn more about Intuit payroll products at: http://accountants.intuit.com/payroll-payments/

Bill Paying Services

Offering a bill paying service to clients can be an easy addition to your business. Staying organized and keeping up with monthly payments is a huge source of frustration and stress for many people. The bills aren't going away and if they're not paid on time, late fees will pile on and could even cause the threat of bankruptcy if it gets really bad.

Financial Services

Chances are that your clients are already asking you questions pertaining to financial planning that go beyond taxes. Adding financial planning to your list of services will help deepen the relationship with your clients and generate more revenue. Unless you provide only fee-based financial services, you will need to obtain securities licenses and you must have a relationship with a broker-dealer such as H.D. Vest that specializes in working with tax preparers.

Chapter 20 – Diversification for Year-Round Revenue

- www.hdvestdev.com/business-models/partners-program

Drake Software, which provides professional tax software, has partnered with broker-dealer HD Vest Financial Services to help its users offer financial planning services. Drake and HD Vest's combined offering aims to encourage Drake's 50,000-plus client firms to explore tax-focused financial services, including planning, securities, insurance, money management services and banking solutions, to expand their practice. HD Vest supports a network of tax and non-tax professionals who provide financial planning and wealth management services.

- https://sites.hdvest.com/campfinancial/products/

Tax Planning Services

After tax season, taxpayers should begin planning for next year to ensure they pay their minimum legitimate tax. A great opportunity would be for you to contact your clients and educate them on the benefits of tax planning. Providing tax planning is another great way to recruit new clients for next tax season. Bringing new people in for free tax-planning sessions will ensure that they file with you when the time comes. Offering an initial tax planning session for free is a great way to recruit tax preparation or bookkeeping clients.

Taxpayer Representation

If you are a CPA, attorney, or an Enrolled Agent (EA), you have unlimited representation rights before the IRS and the ability to represent your clients on any matter. Without the CPA, attorney, or EA certification, only tax preparers who participate in the voluntary IRS Annual Filing Season Program (AFSP) have representation rights – and those are limited. This means that tax preparers who are not CPAs, attorneys or EAs (known as "unenrolled preparers") but participate in the AFSP may only represent clients whose returns they prepared and signed. All other tax preparers have no representation rights. The Income Tax School offers education on the tax topics on the EA Exam through the ITS CTP® Certificate Program, plus ITS partners with Surgent to offer **EA Exam Review Courses** that will help prepare you to pass the EA Exam. Learn more by visiting:

- https://www.theincometaxschool.com/continuing-education/ea-review/

You can learn more about taxpayer representation at https://www.irs.gov. You should also become educated in the Taxpayer Representation process by taking courses such as the seminar titled "Responding to the IRS" offered by The Income Tax School.

Chapter 20 – Diversification for Year-Round Revenue

Keep Business Coming After the Deadline

By offering some of the services described above, business doesn't have to end after the tax filing deadline. There are also other opportunities to gain business after tax season. Here are some ideas to help keep business coming in after the tax season.

Some Less Common Areas of Diversification Include:

Outsourcing Tax Preparation

There are many accounting firms out there looking to outsource tax preparation for their clients. This could be a great way to add additional revenue and keep idle employees busy. Some accounting firms outsource all their tax preparation, while others only want to outsource the less complicated tax returns. However, this option is also seasonal.

QuickBooks Training Services

QuickBooks is very popular with small businesses and they need help learning how to use the QuickBooks software. If you become QuickBooks certified, you can earn revenue by providing QuickBooks training and assistance for small businesses in your community. Businesses using QuickBooks for their daily bookkeeping may still need help with their bank reconciliations, financial statements, quarterly reports, payroll, budgeting, tax return preparation, and managerial finance.

Real Estate

Becoming a real estate agent is another way to diversify and add a revenue stream. The licensing requirements vary from state-to-state. You could be an independent broker or work for a broker. Real estate licensing requirements differ from state to state.

Insurance

To become an independent insurance agent, you must obtain a license in the state in which you want to sell insurance and become associated with insurance companies and satisfy their requirements. Working for an insurance agency can provide a fast track.

Tax Education

The Income Tax School evolved out of a need to recruit and train tax preparers for a tax business and to diversify and generate off-season revenue. The Income Tax School has continued to grow and evolve and now teaches students directly through eLearning. You too can offer tax education. ITS offers turnkey solutions to recruiting and training tax preparers. Find out more about ITS tax education options on the ITS website.

- https://www.theincometaxschool.com/train-employees/

Chapter 20 – Diversification for Year-Round Revenue

Amended Returns

There are plenty of taxpayers who make errors on their returns or need to make a filing status change each year. It could be for the current year or for previous years. Send out a dedicated email to clients with information about amended returns and who may need to do so. You should also include information about amended returns on your website.

People Who Filed an Extension

There are plenty of people who have filed an extension but still need to come in to have their taxes prepared.

Business Owners

Businesses still have quarterly taxes and other deadlines. Consider targeting business owners as clients. Now that the season is over, you could do some dedicated marketing to this segment. Business returns are more complicated and will result in a higher fee.

Conclusion

Unless you don't need year-round income, you should start planning right away to generate off-season revenue. Many opportunities are available to generate revenue year-round. The easiest businesses for a tax preparer to start are those related to tax preparation or financial services. Cross-selling to your existing clients will eliminate the need for you to find new clients. In addition, the more services that your clients depend upon you for, the less likely they are to leave.

Chapter 21

Circular 230, Due Diligence & Fraud Protection

"The expectations of life depend upon diligence; the mechanic that would perfect his work must first sharpen his tools."

- Confucius

Chapter 21 – Circular 230, Due Diligence & Fraud Protection

The IRS takes Circular 230 and due-diligence requirements very seriously. In fact, to ensure compliance during the tax season, they send letters to paid tax preparers whom they suspected have been noncompliant in meeting their Earned Income Tax Credit (EITC) or other Due-Diligence requirements.

According to The Journal of Accountancy, the IRS estimates that between 22% and 26% of all EITC claims contain some sort of mistake, costing the federal government between billions in tax revenue each year. No doubt the cost has increased considerably since then.

Due Diligence requirements have become stricter and tax preparers must strictly adhere to these IRS regulations. "Due Diligence is more than a check mark on a form or clicking through tax preparation software." – IRS Publication 4687

Have a Set of Written Policies

The best way to ensure you and everyone in your office is following IRS due-diligence requirements is to have a set of written procedures that everyone is required to follow. It should also be a big part of your pre-work training for new and prior tax preparers.

Most Common Errors

The three most common errors made in EITC claims are:

1. Claiming a child who doesn't meet EITC age, relationship, or residency requirements.
2. Filing as Single or Head of Household even though the taxpayer is married.
3. Reporting income or expenses incorrectly.

Errors happen when tax preparers do not do a thorough job conducting interviews, fail to ask the right questions, have not been trained properly, and/or don't have standard procedures written down.

The Penalties

To err is human but know that the penalties are severe. Failing to meet Due-Diligence requirements in 2020 is $530 per credit, per return. That means that if you fail to meet Due Diligence for all four tax credits your penalty would be $2,120 per return!

Chapter 21 – Circular 230, Due Diligence & Fraud Protection

Confidentiality

Income tax preparers have access to confidential information pertaining to their clients. Tax preparers may not disclose such confidential information to anyone. Tax preparation firms are required by the Gramm-Leach-Bliley Act to post a notice to clients like the example below to confirm compliance with the Act.

A Notice to All Clients of (Your Tax Firm)

Regarding Our Privacy Policy

Re: Compliance with the Gramm-Leach-Bliley Act,

Public Law 106-102 (FTC 16 CFR Part 313)

To meet the requirements of the Gramm-Leach-Bliley Act of 1999, (Your Tax Firm) is sending this notice to ensure you are aware of the privacy policy of (Your Tax Firm). We collect nonpublic information about you from the following sources:

- Information we receive from you on employment applications, tax preparation organizers, worksheets, and other documents we use in tax preparation or providing financial service, or other forms. Information about your transactions with us, our affiliates, or others; and

- Information we receive from a consumer reporting agency.

We do not disclose any nonpublic personal information about our clients or former clients to anyone, except as permitted by law. We restrict access to nonpublic personal information about you to members of our firm who need to know that information to provide services to you. We maintain physical, electronic, and procedural safeguards that comply with federal regulations to guard your nonpublic personal information.

Tax Preparer Circular 230 Regulations

All tax professionals are required to comply with Circular 230 and Section 7216 of the Internal Revenue Code of 1986. Preparers who fail to comply or who violate Circular 230 and Section 7216 will be subject to penalties by the IRS. As part of the Circular 230 rules all tax professionals are required to register with the IRS and obtain a Preparer Tax Identification Number (PTIN).

It is critical that all necessary paperwork for Earned Income Tax Credit (EITC) filers be completed and kept in the client's file. Most tax software programs have all the Due Diligence forms necessary to complete extensive Due Diligence for all clients.

Chapter 21 – Circular 230, Due Diligence & Fraud Protection

State forms are available through the tax preparation software and the instructions are available on the appropriate state website. Your tax preparation software should also provide online IRS website access, which includes the most current information regarding tax laws.

Checking Tax Returns

It is critical that all tax returns be checked for accuracy. Ideally, the tax return should be checked by a tax preparer other than the one who prepared the return. If another tax preparer is not available, the return should be carefully double-checked by the preparer.

Sample Checking Policy

After the return has been input, prepare the return for checking. Make sure copies of all W-2s and 1099s are in the case file. Fill in all information on the client envelope and client folder if the client has requested a printed copy of their return. Enclose the client documents, envelopes, receipt, the client folder, and the client envelope (for printed copies of the return) in the client's file. Place the entire file in the designated office-checking file, positioning your return behind those already in the "to be checked" file.

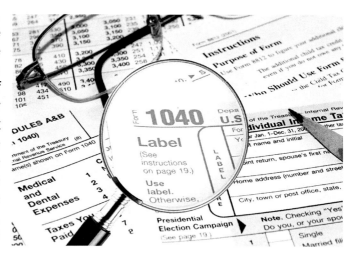

Another tax preparer in the office then checks the return thoroughly, verifying all W-2 information, Social Security numbers, etc. (see procedures below). If the return is free of transposition, and math and theory errors, put your preparer number in box 2 on the Preparer Use screen, sign the "Client Action Form" and give the return back to the tax associate who prepared it (or put it in his or her box) to be processed. If you discover any error(s), make a notation on a "Client Action Form" (see example which follows) and give the return to the preparer for correction. Your checking procedures must include reviewing either a printed copy of the return or a PDF file of the return. It is possible to miss an error if you check only from the computer software.

Checkers must verify that necessary copies of IDs, EIC eligibility and other worksheets are correctly and completely filled out.

After the return has been corrected and the client notified by phone of any changes affecting the refund or balance due, prepare a "Client Action Form" listing any corrections made and put the return back in the file for rechecking.

Chapter 21 – Circular 230, Due Diligence & Fraud Protection

If the return is correct, it should be given back to the preparer for processing, which may include printing copies of the return, burning a copy to a CD or creating a PDF file. After processing, the client should be notified that the return is ready to be picked up. It is then placed in the pick-up drawer in alphabetic order.

Chapter 21 – Circular 230, Due Diligence & Fraud Protection

CLIENT ACTION FORM

Client Name: _____ Date: _____

Preparer Name: _____ Preparer #: _____

Checker Name: _____ Checker #: _____

Please Check and Send to E-File   Please Check and Return to Preparer

Notes: _____
_____
_____
_____

Need to Call Client for Pick-up: Yes ☐   No ☐   Date Called: _____

Need Signatures on Documents:
    Fed 8879   Yes ☐   No ☐   Date Signed: _____

    State 8453   Yes ☐   No ☐   Date Signed: _____

    1040/760   Yes ☐   No ☐   Date Signed: _____

    ERC/ERD Form   Yes ☐   No ☐   Date Signed: _____

Need to Collect Payment: Yes ☐ No ☐   Amount: $_____   Date: _____

Collected By: _____

Payment by: Cash _____   Check _____   Credit Card _____   ERC _____

After Collection:
    Paper Return _____   E-File _____   ERC _____

Copies Given to Client Yes   No ☐   Documents Scanned: Yes ☐   No ☐

Additional Comments:
_____
_____
_____
_____
_____

Federal Return Filed On: _____   Date Accepted: _____

State Return Filed On: _____   Date Accepted: _____

Chapter 21 – Circular 230, Due Diligence & Fraud Protection

Computer Program Errors

At the beginning of the season, check each return the computer has calculated; there is always the chance of a bug in the program since the software is updated each year. If a bug is found, notify your Office Manager and the Tax Division Manager or Corporate Office immediately.

Computer Input Errors

You must double-check each data entry you make. This is especially important when the original source data is not available to the person checking the return. All W-2 information should be directly entered into the computer to reduce transposition errors. Do not skip some of the boxes. Enter all information whether you think you need it to prepare the return or not.

Checking Computer Returns

The following elements of each computer return must be checked:

- Data entries from any source documents

- Data entries from all Forms W-2, etc.

- Theory of all data entries

- Errors of omission (e.g. overlooked income, deductions, etc.)

- Preparer's signature and Preparer Tax Identification Number (PTIN)

- Correct pricing of return including applicable discounts and coupons

Checker's Responsibility

The checker must enter his or her Associate Number on the flap of the envelope containing the tax return (for printed copies), and the "Client Action Form." Doing so indicates that the return has been checked and found to be correct. Additionally, the preparer must enter his number in the section for Preparer's ID on the Preparer Use Screen of the tax program. **(The Preparer's number should go on line 1 and the checker's number on line 2.)** The Preparer's share of the Office Bonus Pool will be calculated on the volume of returns checked as well as the volume of returns prepared. These amounts will be determined from the data entered by preparers in the appropriate tax program screens. If a preparer has not placed his number on the right line, he **will not receive** credit for checking the return and will lose credit for the Office Bonus Pool.

Chapter 21 – Circular 230, Due Diligence & Fraud Protection

Marking returns checked when they have not been will result in disciplinary action.

Fraud

Fraud is a deliberately practiced deception to secure unfair or unlawful gain. Tax preparers have an obligation to prepare tax returns as honestly and accurately as possible. If a preparer has reason to believe the information given to them to prepare a taxpayer's return is fraudulent, they should either research the situation through questioning the taxpayer or refuse to complete the return. The tax preparer should have the suspected taxpayer sign the tax return or Form 8879, so there is no question of the intentions of the taxpayer. However, the tax preparer should not file the return electronically. The preparer also has an obligation to alert the IRS concerning fraudulent returns or potentially abusive returns. If the preparer feels a fraudulent return has been filed by a taxpayer or another tax preparer, they should contact the Criminal Investigation Division (CID) of the IRS. Form 3949-A, *Information Referral,* may be used to report fraud in the IRS e-file Program to the IRS via the internet.

Warning Signs of Fraud

1. Forms W-2 that are handwritten, photocopied, typed, duplicates; substitute Form W-2s, absence of Form W-2s, attempts to use a note from an employer as a Form W-2 or an attempt to use a final pay stub instead of a Form W-2.

2. Unusually high withholdings for which there is no explanation.

3. High dollar amount for refund.

4. Self-prepared return.

5. Computer generated Form W-2 that differs from others from the same firm.

6. Social Security number that is different from the taxpayer's or which has been altered or a Social Security card that has been altered.

7. Forms W-2 for out-of-state firms or firms with which the preparer has no familiarity.

8. Forms W-2 with copies "A" for Social Security and "D" for the employer still attached.

9. Suspicious persons accompanying the taxpayer at check pick up and observed on prior occasions.

10. Similar returns – the same amount of refund, same number of dependents, etc. or returns generated by the same firm, in the same area of by the same preparer, which have similarities or expenses that appear unrealistic. Example: Mortgage interest deduction in the amount of $12,000 for a single taxpayer who earns only $15,000.

11. Multiple refunds with the same address or P.O. number.

12. Unrealistic income for the number of dependents ($4,000 total income with 3 dependents).

13. Last name of child is different from taxpayer (although this is not uncommon, it may be a warning sign of fraud, especially when accompanied by suspicious behavior or questionable information).

14. Different taxpayers claiming the same dependent or using the same Social Security number.

15. Taxpayer cannot spell or has difficulty spelling the children's names, does not know the child's age or date of birth.

16. Man and woman are present with children calling them "Mommy" and "Daddy"; however, both filing Head of Household with each claiming some of the children (again not uncommon; however, the tax preparer should ask the taxpayers if they are married. You never know, the child might actually answer the question for his parents!)

17. Person is present or calling to pick up bank product check for his spouse who filed Head of Household

18. A couple claims they just live together and have children--especially in a common-law state.

19. Person wants to file Head of Household with EIC but has no child-care expenses.

20. The same taxpayer changes dependents from year to year (an aunt who claims her niece this year, stating she has custody of the child who then uses a different child as her dependent the next year).

Verifying Taxpayer Identification Numbers (TINS)

An Electronic Return Originator (ERO) should verify identities and taxpayer identification numbers of everyone listed on each tax return (taxpayer, spouse, and dependents) prepared by their firm to protect IRS *e-file* from fraud and abuse. Types of TINs include SSNs, EINs, Individual Taxpayer Identification Numbers (ITINs), and Adoption Taxpayer Identification Numbers (ATINs). Confirmation of identities might involve the ERO asking a taxpayer not known to them for two forms of identification (picture IDs are preferable) that include the taxpayer's name and current address. If the ERO sees all the actual documents (especially Social Security cards), this will avoid including incorrect TINs for taxpayers, spouses, and dependents on returns. Care should be taken to ensure that all TINs are transcribed correctly. The TIN entered in the Form W-2 of the electronic return record must be identical to the TIN on the version provided by the taxpayer unless otherwise allowed by the IRS. TINs that are not correct, the same TIN used on multiple

Chapter 21 – Circular 230, Due Diligence & Fraud Protection

returns, or associating an incorrect name with a TIN cause the largest number of returns to be rejected.

Additionally, the TINs for taxpayers, spouses, and dependents are identified by a Name Control. *A Name Control is the first four significant letters of an individual taxpayer's last name or a business name as recorded by the Social Security Administration (SSA) or the IRS.* [1] The IRS will match the name control with the TIN of each person on the return (taxpayer, spouse, and dependents). During this matching process, the IRS often will reject the return due to a mismatch between the name control and the TIN. This reason for a rejected return is quite common. In many of these cases, the mismatch involves a newly married taxpayer. After marriage, the spouse needs to update the records with the Social Security Administration (SSA) to reflect the name used in the marriage. Until this is done, the SSA's records will show the spouse's previous name. Thus, the tax return may be filed with the correct SSN, but the name control will not match because the new married name is on the return, but the spouse's previous name is in the SSA's records. This problem can be minimized if the ERO sees the actual Social Security card of everyone on the return before submitting the electronic return to the IRS. This will indicate whether the name change has been reported to the SSA.

Be Aware of Non-standard Information Documents

Questionable Forms W-2 have been identified by the IRS as a primary indicator of possibly abusive and fraudulent returns (see *Safeguarding IRS e-file,* covered previously). EROs should be observant when looking at Forms W-2, W-2G, and 1099-R. If the form submitted by the taxpayer appears to be suspicious or if it has been altered, this may be a sign of fraud. Other documents should also be checked closely to determine if they may have been forged or fabricated. If Forms W-2, W-2G, or 1099-R have been altered, handwritten, or typed, the "non-standard form" code should be entered in the electronic record of that income tax return. Any pen-and-ink change would be an alteration. The information must never be altered after the forms are given to the ERO.

Any tax preparer who observes or becomes aware of questionable Forms W-2 should report it to the IRS as described on the IRS website, by calling 1-800-829-0433 (toll-free), or by submitting Form 3949-A.

Be Careful with Addresses

Addresses that differ from the taxpayer's current address on Forms W-2, W-2G, or 1099-R; Schedule C or C-EZ; or on other tax forms supplied by the taxpayer must be added into the electronic record of the return. Addresses that differ from the taxpayer's current address must be input even if the addresses are old or if the taxpayer has moved. EROs should inform

---

[1] *Publication 1345, page 11*

Chapter 21 – Circular 230, Due Diligence & Fraud Protection

taxpayers that the address on the first page of the return, once processed by the IRS, will be used to update the taxpayer's "address of record." A taxpayer's address of record is used by the IRS for various notices that are required to be sent to a taxpayer's "last known address" under the Internal Revenue Code and for refunds of overpayments of tax (unless otherwise specifically directed by the taxpayer, such as by Direct Deposit).

Finally, an ERO's address must never be put in fields reserved for taxpayers' addresses in the electronic return record or on Forms 8879 or 8453. The only exceptions are if the ERO is the taxpayer or the taxpayer's power of attorney for the tax return.

Avoiding Refund Delays

Taxpayers should be advised that they can avoid refund delays by taking the following steps:

- Have all taxes and obligations paid.

- Be sure that all bank account information is current.

- Ensure that their SSA records are current.

- Make sure that information provided to the ERO is current, complete, and correct.

As an additional final step, the taxpayer should be sure to check their tax return information carefully before signing the return.

Several things can be done by EROs for clients and customers to lessen rejects and refund delays. The following are examples:

- Do not deviate from the requirement for identification and documentation of Social Security and other identification numbers for **all** taxpayers and dependents.

- Carefully enter tax return data into tax return preparation software and check the tax return information thoroughly prior to signing the tax return.

- Be very careful with taxpayers who are adamant about claiming dubious items on tax returns or present altered or suspicious documents. Avoid these taxpayers.

- Check with the taxpayer for any problems with last year's refund. If there was a problem last year, make sure that whatever caused the problem has been corrected so that the problem does not occur again.

- Monitor any client issues that result in refund delays and check for common problems. Advise taxpayers on ways these problems may be addressed.

Chapter 21 – Circular 230, Due Diligence & Fraud Protection

Signatures

As with a paper income tax return submitted to the IRS, an electronic income tax return must be signed by the taxpayer as well as by the paid preparer, if applicable. Currently, there are two permissible methods for electronically signing individual income tax returns.

The Declaration of Taxpayer must be signed and dated by the taxpayer to authorize the origination of the electronic submission of the return to the IRS before the return is ultimately transmitted to the IRS. The Declaration of Taxpayer is comprised of the taxpayer's Consent to Disclosure along with their declaration under penalties of perjury that the return is true, correct, and complete. *The Consent to Disclosure authorizes the IRS to disclose information to the taxpayers' Providers. Taxpayers authorize Intermediate Service Providers, Transmitters, and EROs to receive from the IRS an acknowledgment of receipt or reason for rejection of the electronic return, the reason for any delay in processing the return or refund, and the date of the refund.* [2]

After the taxpayers sign the declaration and the return is checked, certain electronic return data amounts may change. If this happens, taxpayers must sign a new declaration if any of the following differing amounts occur:

- More than $50 to "total income" or "AGI;" or

- More than $14 to "total tax," "Federal income tax withheld," "refund," or "amount you owe.

Electronic Signatures for Taxpayers

Two methods of signing individual income tax returns with an electronic signature can be used by taxpayers. These are the Self-Select PIN and the Practitioner PIN. Either method allows taxpayers to use a Personal Identification Number (PIN) to sign the return and the Declaration of Taxpayer.

Both methods require the IRS to be able to verify that the electronic signature submitted was selected or authorized by the taxpayer. The following lists the two methods and states the requirements of each:

---

[2] *Publication 1345, page 17*

Chapter 21 – Circular 230, Due Diligence & Fraud Protection

1. **Self-Select PIN method:** Taxpayers must provide their prior year Adjusted Gross Income (AGI) or prior year PIN for authentication by the IRS. No signature documents are required.

2. **Practitioner PIN method:** Form 8879, a signature authorization form, must be completed.

Whichever method of electronic signature is used, taxpayers may enter their PIN in the electronic return. EROs can select (or the software may generate) the taxpayer's PIN, providing the taxpayer agrees by signing an IRS e-file signature authorization, Form 8879, containing the PIN.

When taxpayers sign using the Self-Select method and enter their PIN directly in the electronic return, signature documents are not required. In all other instances, taxpayers must sign signature authorization forms. The Practitioner PIN method requires the use of signature authorization forms.

The following taxpayers are ineligible to sign individual income tax returns with an electronic signature using the Self-Select PIN method:

- Primary taxpayers under age sixteen who have never filed; and

- Secondary taxpayers under age sixteen who did not file the prior tax year.

Everyone is eligible to use the Practitioner PIN method. However, some taxpayers may also need to file Form 8453, as indicated previously.

IRS e-file Signature Authorization

In some instances, taxpayers may wish to sign electronically but are unable to enter their PIN directly in the electronic return. When this occurs, taxpayers can authorize the ERO to enter their PINs in the electronic return record by signing the appropriate completed IRS e-file signature authorization form.

*Form 8879, IRS e-file Signature Authorization, authorizes an ERO to enter the taxpayers' PINs on individual income tax returns and Form 8878, IRS e-file Signature Authorization for Form 4868 or Form 2350, authorizes an ERO to enter the taxpayers' PINs on Form 1040 extension forms. **Note:** Form 8878 is only required for Forms 4868 when taxpayers are authorizing an electronic funds withdrawal and want an ERO to enter their PINs.* [3]

---

[3] *Publication 1345, page 18*

Chapter 21 – Circular 230, Due Diligence & Fraud Protection

Form **8878**	IRS *e-file* Signature Authorization for Form 4868 or Form 2350	OMB No. 1545-0074
Department of the Treasury Internal Revenue Service	► ERO must obtain and retain completed Form 8878. ► Go to *www.irs.gov/Form8878* for the latest information.	2019

Submission Identification Number (SID) ▶

Taxpayer's name	Social security number
Spouse's name	Spouse's social security number

Part I Information From Extension Form — Tax Year Ending December 31, 2019 (Whole dollars only)

Check the box and complete the line(s) for the form you authorize your ERO to sign and file. *Check only one box.*

1 ☐ **Form 4868,** Application for Automatic Extension of Time To File U.S. Individual Income Tax Return. Amount you are paying from Form 4868, line 7 . . . . 1 _____

2 ☐ **Form 2350,** Application for Extension of Time To File U.S. Income Tax Return

a I request an extension of time until this date as shown on Form 2350, line 1 . . . . 2a _____

b Amount you are paying from Form 2350, line 5 . . . . 2b _____ 4

The taxpayer's PIN may be entered in the electronic return record before the taxpayer signs Form 8879 or 8878, but the appropriate form must be signed and dated by the taxpayer before the ERO originates the electronic submission of the return. In most instances, the taxpayer must sign and date the Form 8879 or Form 8878 after reviewing the return and verifying that the tax return information on the form matches the information on the return.

Taxpayers who provide a completed tax return to an ERO for electronic filing may complete the IRS e-file Signature Authorization without reviewing the return originated by the ERO. The line items from the paper return must be entered on the applicable Form 8879 or Form 8878 before the taxpayers sign and date the form. EROs may use these pre-signed authorizations as authority to input the taxpayer's PIN, only if the information on the electronic version of the tax return matches the entries from the paper return.

The ERO representative and taxpayers must always complete and sign Forms 8879 or 8878 for the Practitioner PIN method of electronic signature. Taxpayers may use the Practitioner PIN Method to electronically sign Form 4868, *Application for Automatic Extension of Time to File U.S. Individual Income Tax Return* if a signature is required. A signature is only required for Form 4868 when an electronic funds withdrawal is also being requested.

The ERO must retain Forms 8879 and 8878 for three years from the return due date or the date that the IRS received the return, whichever is later. EROs must not send Forms 8879 and 8878 to the IRS unless the IRS requests they do so.

---

4 *Form 8878*

Chapter 21 – Circular 230, Due Diligence & Fraud Protection

Electronic Signatures for EROs

If the taxpayer signs their return using either of the electronic signature methods, the ERO must also sign with a PIN. The same PIN must be used by the ERO for the full tax year. It may be manually input, or software generated in the electronic record in the location designated for the ERO EFIN/PIN. When the ERO enters a PIN in the EFIN/PIN field, the ERO is affirming the ERO Declaration. If the return preparer is also the ERO, the preparer is declaring under the penalties of perjury that the return was reviewed and is true, correct, and complete.

EROs are responsible for all electronic returns originated by their firms, even if the ERO authorizes members of their firms or specific employees to sign for them. If the ERO firm does not prepare a return, then the ERO that originates the electronic submission will attest that the return preparer signed the copy of the return and that the electronic return contains the same tax information as that contained in the paper return. The paid preparer's identifying information (e.g., name, address, and PTIN) must also be entered in the e-file return.

Various methods for signing Forms 8879 and 8878 are available to EROs. Permissible methods include rubber stamp, mechanical device (e.g., signature pen), or computer software, as described in Notice 2007-79. An ERO's signature must include either an exact copy of that ERO's signature or printed name. EROs are personally responsible, even if using one of these alternative means, for affixing their signatures to returns or requests for extension. In every case, taxpayers must sign Form 8879 and Form 8878 by handwritten or electronic signature. EROs must retain Forms 8879 and 8878 for three years from the return due date or the IRS received date, whichever is later. Forms 8879 and 8878 should not be sent to the IRS unless the IRS requests that the ERO do so.

Paper Signatures

The Internal Revenue Service simplified the signature process for electronically filed individual income tax returns submitted by tax practitioners. The simplification eliminates the need for a paper signature document to be sent to the IRS in support of electronically filed tax returns.

Sending Paper Documents to the IRS

Tax practitioners will no longer submit a paper signature for e-filed returns by using Form 8453, U.S. Individual Income Tax Declaration for an IRS e-file Return. Instead, a newly designed Form 8453 will be used to transmit supporting paper documents that are required to be submitted to the IRS with e-filed returns.

Chapter 21 – Circular 230, Due Diligence & Fraud Protection

Electronic Signatures for Form 8879

The IRS issued new electronic filing requirements for EROs and preparers. Tax professionals and EROs are required to validate the signature and identity of a taxpayer who signs his tax return electronically. Methods of electronic signature include, but are not limited to:

- Signature pad which allows a handwritten signature to be transferred into an electronic form.

- The taxpayer's name typed into a signature block, by the taxpayer.

- A password, code, or PIN (shares d secret) used by the taxpayer to sign an electronic record.

- A digital signature or mark captured as a scalable graphic[5].

Identity Verification Requirements

Electronic signatures will now require separate validation and authentication of the identity of each taxpayer, including a husband and wife who file a joint return. Electronic signature methods now must be able to produce evidence of the taxpayer to whom the electronic signature belongs and evidence that the taxpayer is connected with the electronic records.

The identity verification requirements must be in accordance with National Institute of Standards and Technology Special Publication 800-63, Electronic Authentication Guideline, Level 2 assurance level and knowledge-based authentication or higher assurance level. [6]

EROs are now required to:

- Examine government picture IDs
    - Driver's License
    - Employer issued ID
    - School issued ID
    - State issued ID
    - Military issued ID
    - National ID
    - Registered voter ID

---

[5] *IRS Publication 1345, page 18*
[6] *IRS Publication 1345, page 19*

Chapter 21 – Circular 230, Due Diligence & Fraud Protection

- Visa
- Passports

- Verify the applicant is the same person whose picture appears on the form of ID
- Record and verify the following details from the form of ID examined
  - Name
  - Social Security number
  - Address
  - Date of Birth
- Verify that other personal information on within the taxpayer's file are consistent with any information provided through record checks with applicable agencies, institutions or through credit bureaus or similar databases.[7]

Record checks are optional for signatures obtained in a person-to person setting. However, identity verification and authentication are still required for each taxpayer.

Acknowledgements of Transmitted Return Data

During the various stages of Modernized e-file (MeF) processing, the IRS issues several notifications to the return transmitter. For specific information, taxpayers should check with their transmitter, if applicable. The receipt of all transmissions is electronically acknowledged by the IRS and is either rejected for a specific reason or accepted. An accepted return may be questioned later since "acceptance" by the IRS just means that the return meets the MeF processing criteria. These "accepted returns" are considered "filed" as soon as the return is signed electronically.

On the other hand, rejected returns do not meet the processing criteria and are considered "not filed." When an electronic return fails MeF validation, the acknowledgment identifies the source of the problem using a system of error reject codes and form field numbers (sequence numbers). The error reject codes tell why the return is rejected, and the form field numbers refer to the fields of the electronic return data that are involved.

Other information useful to the originator is included in the acknowledgment record of an accepted individual return. This record will confirm the following:

- IRS acceptance of a PIN;
- Whether the taxpayer's refund has been applied to a debt;

Chapter 21 – Circular 230, Due Diligence & Fraud Protection

- If an elected electronic funds withdrawal paid a balance due; and

- Whether or not the IRS approved a request for a Form 4868 extension.

EROs should check acknowledgment records regularly in order to identify returns requiring follow up action. If follow up actions are required to address issues identified on acknowledgment records, the ERO should take reasonable steps to accomplish such actions. An example would be if the IRS rejects a return because a dependent's name does not match the IRS Master File. If this occurred, the ERO should contact the taxpayer to get the correct information for the dependent and resubmit the return electronically as soon as possible.

At the request of the taxpayer, the ERO must provide the Submission ID and the date that the IRS accepted the electronic individual income tax return data. A Submission ID is a unique 20-digit number assigned to electronically filed tax returns. Form 9325, *Acknowledgement, and General Information for Taxpayers Who File Returns Electronically*, may be used by the ERO to satisfy this requirement. In addition, the ERO must, if requested, supply the electronic postmark if the Transmitter provided one for the return.

Electronic individual income tax return data, if rejected, can be corrected, and retransmitted without new signatures or authorizations if changes do not differ from the amount in the electronic portion of the electronic return by more than a specific amount. These differences, depending on the item, will be limited to the following amounts:

- $50 for "total income" or "AGI," or

- $14 for "total tax," "Federal income tax withheld," "refund," or "amount you owe."

The new electronic return data must be given to the taxpayer, and new signatures are required. The taxpayer must be furnished with copies of the new signatures.

Rejected federal electronic return data due to errors may also cause the state electronic return data to reject. The reverse situation may also be true since both federal and state electronic return data must be accepted by the IRS. In the reverse situation, if the state electronic return data is rejected by the IRS  due to error, the federal electronic return data may also reject. Once both are accepted by the IRS, a subsequent rejection of state electronic return data by a state tax administration agency will not affect the accepted federal electronic return data. Once the state receives electronic return data from the Federal/State e-file Program, the state will determine whether that data is accepted as filed. The state tax administration agency should be contacted when problems or questions arise.

Chapter 21 – Circular 230, Due Diligence & Fraud Protection

Resubmission of Rejected Tax Returns

If the IRS rejects the electronic portion of a taxpayer's individual income tax return for processing and the reason for the rejection cannot be rectified, the ERO must take reasonable steps to inform the taxpayer of the rejection within 24 hours. When the ERO advises the taxpayer that the return has not been filed, the ERO must provide the taxpayer with the reject code(s) accompanied by an explanation. If the taxpayer chooses not to have the electronic portion of the return corrected and transmitted to the IRS or if it cannot be accepted for processing by the IRS, the taxpayer must file a paper return. In order to be filed timely, the paper return must be filed by the later of the due date of the return or ten calendar days after the date the IRS gives notification that the electronic portion of the return is rejected or that it cannot be accepted for processing. The paper return should include an explanation of why the return is being filed after the due date.

Due Diligence

With the Tax Relief Act of 1997 came a new challenge for tax preparers. Within the Tax Relief Act is a provision for a penalty per return for preparers who fail to exercise due diligence. The penalty is $530 per each failure to comply with Circular 230 Due Diligence Requirements. The definition of due diligence, from Circular 230, §10.22, *Diligence as to accuracy*, follows:

Each attorney, certified public accountant, enrolled agent, enrolled retirement plan agent, enrolled actuary, or registered tax return preparer shall exercise due diligence:

a) In preparing or assisting in the preparation of, approving and filing returns, documents, affidavits, and other papers relating to Internal Revenue Service matters.

b) In determining the correctness of oral or written representations made by him to the Department of the Treasury.

c) In determining the correctness of oral or written representations made by him to clients with reference to any matter administered by the Internal Revenue Service.

The IRS has decided to extend the due diligence requirements to all tax preparers as it relates to the preparation of tax returns claiming EIC. The IRS is examining these returns very closely with special emphasis on those who claim both Schedule C income and earned income credit.

Chapter 21 – Circular 230, Due Diligence & Fraud Protection

Tax preparers must meet all the following requirements to comply with the due diligence requirements:

1. The preparer must (a) complete Form 8867, *Paid Preparer's Due Diligence Checklist*, and submit it with the return in the manner required, and (b) otherwise record in the preparer's electronic or paper files, the information which would be necessary to complete the Checklist, such as the Earned Income Credit Eligibility Checklist, which follows.

2. The preparer must either (a) complete the Earned Income Credit Worksheet in the 2019 Form 1040 instructions, or (b) otherwise record in the preparer's paper or electronic files the preparer's EIC computation, including the method and information used to make that computation. The information must be provided by the taxpayer or otherwise reasonably obtained by the preparer.

3. The preparer must not know or have reason to know that any information used is incorrect in determining the taxpayer's eligibility for the EIC or in computing the EIC. The preparer may not ignore the implications of information furnished to, or known by the preparer, and must make reasonable inquiries if the information furnished to, or known by, the preparer appears to be incorrect, inconsistent, or incomplete.

4. The preparer must retain (a) a copy of the completed Form 8867, (b) the applicable worksheets used (or alternate computation record), (c) documents from the taxpayer used to determine his eligibility and amount of EIC, and (d) a record of how and when the information was obtained by the preparer, including the identity of any person furnishing such information.

   These items must be retained for three years after the later of the following dates:

   a. The original due date of the return

   b. The date the return was filed (for e-filed returns)

   c. The date the return was presented to the taxpayer to sign (for mailed returns)

It should be noted that Form 8867 was expanded and revised, beginning with tax year 2016 returns, to cover credits other than EIC. In subsequent years, additional paid preparer due

Chapter 21 – Circular 230, Due Diligence & Fraud Protection

diligence requirements were added to Form 8867. There are now due diligence requirements for tax preparers paid to prepare returns for any taxpayers claiming the EIC, the Child Tax Credit/Additional Child Tax Credit/Credit for Other Dependents (CTC/ACTC/ODC), the American Opportunity Tax Credit (AOTC), and/or the Head of Household filing status. These credits will be discussed in depth in future chapters. Due to these tax law changes, the IRS cannot issue refunds for returns that claim the EIC or the AOTC before mid-February of 2020. This applies to the entire refund. For this chapter's assignments, students will be required to complete the EIC column of Form 8867 only.

Form 8867 must be submitted with the tax return of any taxpayer claiming the earned income credit if a preparer was paid to complete the return. If the return is not being electronically filed, the paid preparer should give the taxpayer the completed form for filing.

Suggested Additional Safeguards

To protect tax preparers, every effort must be made to be certain that taxpayers qualify for the filing status they choose, the Earned Income Tax Credit, and all expenses they declare on Schedule C.

Worksheets are provided within your tax software to help determine if the taxpayer qualifies. Appropriate worksheets should be completed and kept in the taxpayer's file. As had been previously required, copies of identification cards and Social Security cards are required for taxpayers claiming Earned Income Credit. Copies of Social Security cards are also required for dependents claimed by those taxpayers.

Worksheets should be completed for taxpayers who are filing Head of Household. You should ask your taxpayers to sign all worksheets completed, acknowledging that the information provided is true and correct to the best of their knowledge.

To determine whether children can be claimed as dependents if the taxpayer is receiving TANF (Temporary Assistance for Needy Families), a Cost of Maintaining a Household worksheet should be completed. Tax preparers must develop the habit of asking clients if they are receiving TANF.

To Meet Your Four Due Diligence Requirements, You Must:

1. Complete Form 8867, Paid Preparer's Due Diligence Checklist, and submit this completed form to the IRS with every electronic or paper return or claim for refund you prepare with the EITC, CTC/ACTC/ODC, AOTC, and Head of Household .

   a. Make sure your software includes the Form 8867 and that it is transmitted with every electronic return and included with every paper return you prepare with the EITC, CTC/ACTC/ODC, AOTC, and Head of Household.

b. Answer each question on the form based on information from your client and information you know is true.

c. You must also personally answer question 12, Credit Eligibility Certification.
   Form 8867 Paid Preparer Due Diligence Checklist:
   https://www.irs.gov/pub/irs-pdf/f8867.pdf
   Instructions for Form 8867: https://www.irs.gov/pub/irs-pdf/i8867.pdf

2. Complete the applicable worksheet(s), or your own worksheet(s) with the same information, for any EITC, CTC/ACTC/ODC, AOTC, and Head of Household claimed on the return.

   a. Most professional tax return preparation software includes the worksheets.

3. Keep copies of the following either electronically or on paper for your records:

   a. Form 8867

   b. The applicable worksheet(s) for EITC, CTC, AOTC and Head of Household claimed on the return

   c. Any documents you relied on to complete the Form 8867 or to determine eligibility for and the amount of the credit(s)

   d. A record of how, when, and from whom the information you obtained to prepare the tax return and worksheet(s)

   e. A record of any additional questions you asked to determine eligibility for and the amount of the credits and your client's answers. Keep these documents for three years from the latest of:

      i. The due date of the tax return.

      ii. The date the tax return was electronically filed.

      iii. For a paper return, the date the return was presented to your client for signature.

      iv. If you are a non-signing tax return preparer, the date you give the part, for which you are responsible to the signing tax return preparer. You can keep these records in either paper or electronic format, but

Chapter 21 – Circular 230, Due Diligence & Fraud Protection

you must produce the records if IRS requests them. You should keep a backup of these records in a separate, secure location.

4. Not know, or have reason to know, that any information used to determine if your client is eligible for or to compute the amount of the credit(s) is not correct, not consistent, or not complete.

   a. You must ask your client additional questions if a reasonable and well-informed tax return preparer, knowledgeable in the law, would conclude the information furnished seems incorrect, inconsistent, or incomplete.

   b. At the time of the interview, you must document in your files the questions you asked and your client's answers.

The IRS Assesses Most Due Diligence Penalties for Failure to Comply with the Knowledge Requirement.

To meet the knowledge requirement, you should:

- Apply common sense standards to the information provided by your client.
- Evaluate whether the information is complete and gather any missing facts.
- Determine if the information is consistent; recognize contradictory statements and statements you know are not true.
- Conduct a thorough, in-depth interview with each client, every year.
- Ask enough questions to know the return is correct and complete.
- Document in the file at the time it happens any questions you asked and your client's responses.

An Employer May Be Penalized for An Employee's Failure to Exercise Due Diligence, if Any of the Following Apply:

- An employer or a principal member of management participated in, or prior to the time the return was filed, knew of the failure to comply with the due diligence requirements; or
- The firm failed to establish reasonable and appropriate procedures to ensure compliance with due diligence requirements; or

Chapter 21 – Circular 230, Due Diligence & Fraud Protection

- The firm disregarded its reasonable and appropriate compliance procedures in the preparation of the tax return or claim for refund through willfulness, recklessness, or gross indifference. This failure includes ignoring facts that would lead a person of reasonable prudence and competence to investigate.

Due Diligence Promotes Accurate EITC, CTC/ACTC/ODC, AOTC, and Head of Household Claims.

Incorrect tax returns and failure to comply with the Due Diligence requirements can adversely affect you and your client:

- The IRS can examine your client's return, and if it is found incorrect, can assess accuracy or fraud penalties on your client. The IRS can also ban your client from claiming EITC, CTC/ACTC/ODC, AOTC, and Head of Household for 2 or 10 years.
- If you fail to comply with the EITC, CTC/ACTC/ODC, AOTC, and Head of Household Due Diligence requirements, the IRS can assess a $530 (for tax year 2020) penalty (adjusted for inflation) against you and your employer for each failure. IRS can assess you up to three penalties to a return that claims all three credits. (IRC § 6695(g)).
- If you prepare a client's return and any part of an understatement of tax liability is due to an unreasonable position, the IRS can assess a minimum penalty of $1,000 (IRC § 6694(a)) against you.
- If the understatement is due to reckless or intentional disregard of rules or regulations, the minimum penalty is $5,000 (IRC § 6694(b)).
- You and your firm can face suspension or expulsion from participation in IRS e-file.
- You can be barred from preparing tax returns.
- You can be subject to criminal prosecution. Each refundable credit has different eligibility rules. Take these simple steps to avoid errors:
  - Know the tax law for each refundable credit including eligibility rules
  - Remember, software is not a substitute for knowledge of the tax law
  - Follow the Due Diligence Must Do's

Pay Attention to the Following Issues to Avoid EITC, CTC/ACTC/ODC, AOTC, and Head of Household Claim Errors:

Chapter 21 – Circular 230, Due Diligence & Fraud Protection

Most Common EITC Errors:

- Claiming EITC for a child who does not meet the qualifying child requirements. Make sure you find out if the child lived with your client for more than half the year, is related to him or her and meets the age test. You must ask how long the child lived with your client, at what address, and did anyone else live with the child for more than half the year. Also, find out how the child is related – by blood, by marriage or by law. Age is a bit easier; but if the child is a student or permanently and totally disabled, make sure your client has the documents needed to show the IRS if audited.

- Filing as Single or Head of Household when married. Ask the questions to find out if your client is married under state law, including common law, or was ever married. Also, if your client is married, make sure your client did not live with his or her spouse at any time during the last six months of the year.

- Incorrectly reporting institution income or expenses. Does the Form W-2 look like the Forms W-2 of other clients who have the same employer? Is your client saying they own a business but not claiming any business expenses? Ask enough questions to make sure your client has a true business and claims all income and deducts all allowable expenses. Publication 4687 (Rev. 8-2016) Catalog Number 51636Y Department of the Treasury Internal Revenue Service www.irs.gov Know the law Apply your knowledge Ask all the right questions Get all the facts Document as you go and keep records Most Common AOTC Errors

- Claiming AOTC for a student who did not attend an eligible educational institution. The AOTC is for post-secondary education, which may include education at a college, university, or technical school. To be an eligible institution, the school must be able to participate in the student aid program administered by the U.S. Department of Education (note: they do not have to participate but must be eligible to participate).

- Claiming AOTC for a student who did not pay qualifying college expenses. Educational expenses must be paid or considered paid by your client, your client's spouse or the dependent student claimed on the tax return.

Chapter 21 – Circular 230, Due Diligence & Fraud Protection

- Claiming AOTC for a student for too many years. The AOTC is only available for the first four years of post-secondary education and your client can only claim it for four tax years per eligible student. This limitation includes any year(s) your client claimed the Hope Credit. Most Common CTC/ACTC/ODC Errors

- Claiming the CTC/ACTC/ODC a child who does not meet the age requirement. The child must be under the age of 17 at the end of the tax year. There are no exceptions to this rule.

- Claiming the CTC/ACTC/ODC a child who does not meet the dependency requirements. The child must be claimed as a dependent on your client's return and meet all the eligibility rules for a dependent.

- Claiming the CTC/ACTC/ODC a child who does not meet the residency requirement. The child must be a U.S. citizen, U.S. national or a U.S. resident alien and the child must have lived with your client for more than half the year. If the qualifying child uses an ITIN, Individual Taxpayer Identification Number, the child must meet the substantial presence test to qualify. The Tax Preparer Toolkit on EITC and Refundable Credits Central, eitc.irs.gov, is your place for more information on Refundable Credit Due Diligence.

- Training opportunities, videos, and training modules such as the Refundable Credit Due Diligence, Schedule C and Record Reconstruction

- Interview tips and best practices

- Frequently asked questions

- More the Due Diligence Must Do's BY law, if you are paid to prepare tax returns claiming one or more of the Earned Income Tax, the Child Tax, Additional Child Tax, Other Dependent or the American Opportunity Tax credits, in addition to Head of Household, you must meet four Due Diligence requirements. The 2015 PATH Act extended the Due Diligence requirements from EITC, Earned Income Tax Credit, to both the CTC, Child Tax Credit, ACTC, Additional Child Tax Credit, ODC, Other Dependent Credit and the AOTC, American Opportunity Tax Credit. These requirements focus on accurately determining your client's eligibility for and the amount of each credit. The first three requirements have to do with completing

Chapter 21 – Circular 230, Due Diligence & Fraud Protection

forms and keeping records. The fourth, the one most often missed, is the knowledge requirement. It requires you to:

- o Know the EITC, CTC/ACTC/ODC, AOTC, and Head of Household tax laws thoroughly
- o Evaluate your client's information
- o Ask questions based on your client's information to determine each client's personal situation and eligibility
- o Document the questions you ask and your client's answers

Following are Examples of Situations When You Should Ask Additional Questions to Meet Your Due Diligence Knowledge Requirement:

- A client and spouse want to claim the CTC and the AOTC. Your client is a resident alien with one child and has higher education expenses. You should ask enough questions to determine if the child and spouse are citizens, resident aliens, or non-resident aliens. You should also ask enough questions to determine if your client is eligible for the AOTC.

- A client wants to claim his niece and nephew for EITC. You should ask enough questions to determine whether each child is a qualifying child of your client. You should also ask enough questions to find out if the child is the qualifying child of another person. And, if so, will the other person claim the child. If more than one person claims the same child, the IRS will apply the tiebreaker rules.

- An 18-year-old client with an infant has $3,000 in earned income and states she lives with her parents. She wants to claim the infant as a qualifying child for the EITC. This information seems incomplete and inconsistent because your 18-year-old client lives with her parents and earns very little income. You must ask additional questions to determine if your client is the qualifying child of her parents. If she is the qualifying child of her parents, she is not eligible to claim the EITC.

- A 22-year-old client wants to claim two sons, ages 10 and 11, as qualifying children for the EITC. You must make additional reasonable inquiries regarding the relationship between your client and the children since the age of the client seems inconsistent with the ages of the children claimed as your client's sons.

Chapter 21 – Circular 230, Due Diligence & Fraud Protection

- A client has two qualifying children and wants to claim the EITC. She tells you she had a Schedule C business and earned $10,000 in income and had no expenses. This information appears incomplete because it is unusual that someone who is self-employed has no business expenses. You must ask additional reasonable questions to determine if the business exists and if the information about her income and expenses is correct.

- A 32-year-old client indicates he has been going to college for many years and would like to claim the AOTC. He provides a Form 1098- T, Tuition Statement, showing $4,000 received for tuition and that your client was at least a half-time undergraduate student. You must ask more questions. The Form 1098-T is a good indicator that your client is eligible for the AOTC but does not contain all the information needed to determine eligibility or to compute the amount of the credit. You must also find out if your client received any scholarships, how and when the expenses were paid, if your client has a felony drug conviction, and if your client claimed AOTC or the Hope Credit previously and if so, for how many years.

- A client wants to claim the CTC for three children. Your client is a resident alien. The children all have ITINs and lived part of the year outside the U.S. You must ask questions to determine that each child is related to your client and meets the residency requirements for the CTC. You must also complete Part 1 of Schedule 8812 for each child with an ITIN to show the child meets the residency test

Conclusion

All tax preparers must strictly comply to the IRS Circular 230 and Due Diligence requirements. Failure to comply will result in severe monetary penalties. You should have written policies for your employees to follow. Tax preparers are required by the IRS to adhere to strict policies to protect the privacy of all taxpayer information. In addition, the Gramm-Leach-Bliley Act requires that a privacy notice be posted in your office. Tax preparers must report any suspected fraud to the IRS Criminal Investigation Division (CID). Any tax preparers that you may employ must receive complete training in IRS Circular 230 and Due Diligence requirements, and supervision to ensure compliance.

Chapter 22

Helping Your Client Deal With the IRS

"People who complain about paying their income tax can be divided into two types: men and women."

- Anonymous

Chapter 22 – Helping Your Client Deal With the IRS

Given the choice, most taxpayers would rather not deal directly with the IRS. They are content to file their tax returns, settle their tax bill each year, and hope that is the end of the matter. Many taxpayers are intimidated by the IRS and get upset when they receive correspondence from the agency, especially if it infers an audit.

Some taxpayers are so fearful they will not open letters from the agency. It is not uncommon for a taxpayer to bring to the practitioner a stack of unopened letters he has received over a considerable period of time on a tax matter. Invariably, some of these letters will have required action on the part of the taxpayer by a certain date. By the time the tax practitioner receives the information, the response dates have passed, and a relatively simple matter has become a more serious issue.

As most experienced tax practitioners know, it is very important to deal with IRS problems in a timely manner. Procrastination and failure to adhere to IRS deadlines can sometimes turn a relatively small problem into a more complicated matter that will be more time-consuming, as well as expensive, to resolve. In some cases, failure to adhere to deadlines can result in the inability of a taxpayer to refute a proposed tax adjustment. Additionally, penalties and interest accrue on amounts due.

Examination of Returns

A taxpayer's return may be examined for different reasons. The IRS will examine or audit a return to determine if all income, expenses, and credits are recorded accurately. Returns are selected for audit by computerized screening, by random sampling, or by income document matching.

The IRS's computer program, the Discriminant Inventory Function System (DIF), assigns a numeric score to each individual and some corporate returns after they have been processed. If the taxpayer's return is selected due to a high score on DIF, an examination of the return will normally result in a change in the taxpayer's income tax liability.

The taxpayer's return may also be selected for examination due to information:

- Received from third parties, e.g., Form W-2s and 1099s that do not match documents that were filed by the taxpayer.

- Recorded in a questionable manner; or

- Received from other sources citing potential noncompliance with tax laws or inaccurate filing.

Chapter 22 – Helping Your Client Deal With the IRS

An examination usually begins when the IRS notifies the taxpayer by mail that his return has been selected for audit. If the taxpayer receives a telephone call and the caller indicates that he is from the IRS, the call could be a scam. The IRS will only make calls if they are currently working on a case with a taxpayer, and the taxpayer will know who that person is at the IRS. They will not make random calls demanding information or payment, nor initiate email contact without taxpayer consent; the IRS will always notify the taxpayer by mail first. The notice will tell the taxpayer which records he will need for the examination of his return. The changes proposed by the IRS will be explained to the taxpayer and/or his authorized representative. This information will need to be provided to the IRS in writing.

If You Agree

If the taxpayer and or his authorized representative agrees with the proposed changes, the taxpayer can sign an agreement form and pay any additional tax that may be owed. The taxpayer will be liable for any interest due on the additional tax. If the taxpayer is due a refund, he will receive interest on the refunded amount. If the IRS accepts the tax return as filed, the taxpayer will receive a letter in a few weeks stating that the examiner proposed no changes for the return. The taxpayer should keep this letter with his tax records for the tax year in review.

If You Do Not Agree

If the taxpayer and/or his authorized representative do not agree with the proposed changes, the examiner will explain the appeal rights available to the taxpayer. The taxpayer should respond to the notice that he does not agree with all or some of the proposed changes and submit documentation to prove his position. The taxpayer can request a telephone conference or a meeting with the examiner's supervisor in an IRS office. If an agreement is reached with the supervisor, the taxpayer's case will be closed.

If an agreement is not reached with the supervisor or the taxpayer did not meet in an IRS office, the examiner will write up the case explaining the taxpayer's position as well as the IRS's position. The taxpayer's case will be forwarded for further processing. If the taxpayer agrees with the examiner's changes after receiving the examination report, he can sign and return the examination report or the waiver form. The taxpayer should always keep a copy for his records.

IRS Notices

As mentioned above, many taxpayers will receive a notice of some kind from the IRS during their lifetime. These notices can range from notifying a taxpayer of a math error on a return to the notice of their selection for a comprehensive examination of a tax return. Notices of any type, other than a refund check, are likely to cause apprehension to the taxpayer.

Chapter 22 – Helping Your Client Deal With the IRS

Many computer-generated notices are sent to taxpayers addressing different issues. While they follow certain formats, they are sometimes difficult for many taxpayers to understand. Becoming familiar with the more common notices generated by the agency will make it easier for the taxpayer to understand the notice and the action, if any, that is required.

"CP" notices are the most common notices sent to taxpayers. The CP notices have a CP number and a title. The IRS has redesigned its correspondence with taxpayers to achieve better clarity, effectiveness, and efficiency. The new format includes plain language used to explain the reason or nature of the correspondence. The letter will clearly state the steps that the taxpayer must take to resolve the issue.

Taxpayers should refer to *www.irs.gov/Individuals/Understanding-Your-IRS-Notice-or-Letter* in the event they receive an IRS notice or letter. They may enter the CP number in the "Notices & Letters Search" box to obtain more information, including answers to many notice-related questions. Some of the more common notices are listed and described in the following tables.

Some of the more common notices include:

Notice Number	Description	Topic
CP11	*We made changes to your return because we believe there's a miscalculation. You owe money on your taxes as a result of these changes.*	*Balance Due*
CP11A	*We made changes to your return because we believe there's a miscalculation involving your Earned Income Credit. You owe money on your taxes as a result of these changes.*	*Balance Due*
CP11M	*We made changes to your return involving the Making Work Pay and Government Retiree Credit. You owe money on your taxes as a result of these changes.*	*Balance Due*
CP12	*We made changes to correct a miscalculation on your return.*	*Return Error*
CP14	*We sent you this notice because you owe money on unpaid taxes.*	*Balance Due*
CP31	*Your refund check was returned to us, so you need to update your address.*	*Refund*
CP49	*We sent you this notice to tell you we used all or part of your refund to pay a debt.*	*Overpayment*
CP53	*We can't provide your refund through direct deposit, so we're sending you a refund check by mail.*	*Direct Deposits*
CP501	*We have a balance due (money you owe the IRS) on one of your tax accounts.*	*Balance Due*
CP504	*You have an unpaid amount due on your account. If you do not pay the amount due immediately, the IRS*	*Levy*

	will seize (levy) your state income tax refund and apply it to pay the amount you owe.	
CP523	*This notice informs you of our intent to terminate your installment agreement and seize (levy) your assets. You have defaulted on your agreement.*	*Levy* [1]

Notice Number	Title
CP161	*Request for Payment or Notice of Unpaid Balance (Business Return): Informs the recipient there is an unpaid balance due on their account.*
CP90	*Final Notice Before Levy and Notice of Your Right to a Hearing (Individual Return): Informs the recipient they still have a balance due on their account and that the IRS intends to levy on certain assets unless they take appropriate action within 30 days.*
CP297	*Final Notice Before Levy and Notice of Your Right to a Hearing (Business Return): Informs the recipient of the IRS's intent to levy and of the recipient's right to receive appeals and consideration.*
CP91	*Final Notice Before Levy on Social Security Benefits (Individual Return): Informs the recipient they still have a balance due on their account and that the IRS intends to levy on their Social Security benefits unless they take appropriate action within 30 days.*
CP298	*Final Notice Before Levy on Social Security Benefits (Business Return): Informs the recipient of the IRS's intent to levy on their Social Security benefits.*
CP2000	*Notice of Proposed Adjustment for Underpayment/Overpayment: Informs the recipient that the IRS is proposing changes to their tax return based on different information reported to the IRS by their employers, banks, and other payers. The CP2000 provides detailed information about the differences, the changes proposed, and what to do if the recipient agrees or disagrees with the proposal.* [2]

Refer to http://www.irs.gov/Individuals/Understanding-Your-IRS-Notice-or-Letter to see the full list of CP notice numbers and the explanation for each number.

While it should be obvious that some of these notices are merely to notify the taxpayer of an error found on his tax return or to remind him of a balance due, others are more serious in nature and require timely action on the part of the taxpayer.

---

[1] *www.irs.gov/Individuals/Understanding-Your-IRS-Notice-or-Letter*
[2] *www.irs.gov/Individuals/Understanding-Your-IRS-Notice-or-Letter*

Chapter 22 – Helping Your Client Deal With the IRS

CP2000 Notice

Undoubtedly, the most common notice that taxpayers receive is the CP2000 notice. In most cases, this notice results from a mismatching of payer information that the agency has received regarding the taxpayer. Common problems in this area are W-2 and/or 1099 income omitted from the return or possibly the omission of a significant amount of interest and/or dividend income.

Generally, the actions to take when a CP2000 notice is received are to review the information carefully and determine if it is correct. Pay close attention to the tax year the notice references. The changes the agency is proposing will usually result in an increase in the tax liability but could also result in a refund.

The taxpayer can either agree or disagree with the proposed adjustments. If disagreeing, the taxpayer will need to submit an explanation of why he disagrees. In many cases, the taxpayer will need to provide documentation to support his position. If that does not result in the taxpayer's satisfaction, the Taxpayer Advocate Service (TAS) may be able to assist.

The taxpayer should pay attention to the date that a response is requested. In most cases, the taxpayer has **30** days from the date of the letter to respond. If a response cannot be formulated by the due date, the taxpayer should call the IRS and request an extension.

CP504 Notice

The CP504 notice, "Notice of Intent to Seize (Levy) Your Property or Rights to Property," is another common notice that requires immediate attention. It involves IRS intent to levy on certain assets. This notice follows a previous notice of a balance due on a return. If the taxpayer cannot pay the taxes owed, the correct response is not to ignore the notice, but to contact the IRS and inform the agency of the inability to pay. It is very probable that a payment plan will be offered to the taxpayer, depending upon the size of the tax bill and the financial resources of the taxpayer.

CP90 Notice

The CP90 notice, "Intent to Seize Your Assets and Notice of Your Right to a Hearing," is very serious, as the title implies. This notice is usually delivered as a certified letter, requiring the taxpayer's signature. In the case of joint filers, a copy is delivered to each spouse. If the CP90 notice is ignored, the taxpayer should not be surprised to discover that his bank account has been levied or his wages garnished. Employers are required to garnish wages until they receive notification from the IRS to stop. The employee must deal with the IRS directly to stop the wage garnishment.

Chapter 22 – Helping Your Client Deal With the IRS

CP523 Notice

The CP523 notice, "Intent to Terminate Your Installment Agreement," is also significant. This informs the taxpayer of the IRS's plan to end the installment agreement and levy their assets. When setting up an installment agreement, the taxpayer should be careful to set the payments in an amount that the taxpayer can reasonably make. However, circumstances can occur that can cause severe financial stress to the taxpayer, making it impossible to make a payment. The recommended action is to notify the IRS before the payment is due, apprising them of the change in financial condition. Defaulting on an installment agreement is a serious situation and may make it impossible to obtain a future installment agreement should one be needed. It is always the best policy to be proactive in these situations; in many cases, the IRS will work with a taxpayer if it is obvious, he or she is really trying to pay their tax bill.

Other Notices

These are just a few of the notices generated by the IRS. Some are merely a request for more information on a tax return. Missing forms from a tax return that explain an entry on Form 1040 can trigger a request for that information. The taxpayer should realize that most of the schedules are designed to explain the entries on Form 1040. In some cases, the agency itself misplaces an accompanying form. This is one reason the taxpayer's name and Social Security number should be entered on all forms on the tax return. Taxpayers should also file electronically whenever possible to minimize the risk of missing forms.

In some cases, a taxpayer might have a certain situation that needs to be further explained on a tax return. Submitting a detailed explanation with the original tax return could prevent the need for such a notice from the agency.

A taxpayer might receive a notice that the IRS has not received a tax return for a given year. The taxpayer may have mailed the return, but the IRS never received it, or it was lost in the processing. In this case, the taxpayer should submit a copy of the return. With more returns being electronically filed, this is becoming less of a problem and is another good reason to e-file.

Additionally, there is the notice that some taxpayers receive which informs them of an examination of their tax return or a portion of the tax return. This will be covered in a later section.

Chapter 22 – Helping Your Client Deal With the IRS

Tips on Responding to the IRS

1. When responding to an IRS notice, be sure to keep a copy of all correspondence sent to the agency.

2. When sending documentation, keep the original and send a copy, since it could be lost in the mail.

3. When speaking with IRS representatives on a matter, be sure to record the date of the conversation, the person with whom the taxpayer spoke, and the basic points of the conversation.

Be Patient

All taxpayers should keep in mind that the IRS is very slow in responding to information submitted. One should not expect a problem to be resolved in a couple of days. Even the simplest matter will likely take six to eight weeks.

Call the IRS if You Don't Receive a Response After Several Weeks

If several weeks pass and the taxpayer does not receive a response on a particular problem, assumptions shouldn't be made, and consideration should be given to calling the representative that is handling the problem.

Taxpayer Advocate Service (TAS)

If several weeks pass and the taxpayer does not receive a response regarding a problem, the taxpayer or representative should contact the IRS for a status update.

If the taxpayer cannot get satisfactory resolution of a problem, the Office of the Taxpayer Advocate might be a solution. However, they will usually not get involved in a matter until several attempts have been made to resolve the issue directly with the agency.

The Taxpayer Advocate Service (TAS) is an independent organization within the IRS. They provide assistance to taxpayers with differing issues, such as:
- The taxpayer may be experiencing economic harm.
- The taxpayer is seeking help in resolving tax problems that have not been resolved through normal channels; or
- The taxpayer believes the IRS system or procedure is not working as it should.

The taxpayer can call the TAS at 1-877-777-4778 or TTY/TDD 1-800-829-4059 or visit their website at *https://www.irs.gov/taxpayer-advocate*. Assistance is always free for those who qualify. See Publication 1546 *"Taxpayer Advocate Service: We Are Here to Help You"* for more information about contacting the Taxpayer Advocate Service.

Payment Plans and Issues

If the taxpayer can pay the taxes that are owed, he should do so as soon as possible. This will reduce the amount of penalties and interest as well as stop most letter and levy threats. If he cannot pay them, it is possible to set up a payment plan with the IRS. Taxpayers should consider other means to pay off the debt such as credit cards and installment loans. If the taxpayer uses the payment plan/installment plan, he will have to pay penalties and interest to the IRS on the taxes that are due while there is a balance on the account.

A taxpayer can request a payment plan by filing Form 9465, *Installment Agreement Request*. There is a one-time setup fee for an approved payment plan. Set up fees are as follows:

	Applicable Fees		
Payment Method	*Using online payment application*	*Not using online payment application*	*Low-income*
Direct Debit	$31*	$107*	$43
Check, money order, credit, or debit card	$149**	$225**	$43
Payroll deduction fee using Form 2159	N/A	$225**	$43
*Low-income taxpayers may have received a fee waiver or reimbursement. **Low-income taxpayers may be eligible for reduced fees, a waiver, or reimbursements.			

Reduced setup fees apply if the taxpayer uses the online payment application to apply for a payment plan. The taxpayer should provide the IRS with an amount he can reasonably pay each month. There are no penalties for paying more than the monthly payment to extinguish the debt earlier but becoming delinquent on a payment plan will usually lead to the entire balance becoming due. It is recommended to complete the

---

[3] *Form 9465, Instructions*

Chapter 22 – Helping Your Client Deal With the IRS

payoff as soon as possible since penalties and interest will continue to accrue until the payoff is completed.

Taxpayers whose most recent tax year's adjusted gross income is at or below 250% of the federal poverty guidelines are considered low-income taxpayers. Taxpayers who meet this criterion are eligible for reduced, waived, or reimbursed installment fees. Low-income taxpayers who agree to pay their installments agreement payments through direct debit from a checking account qualify for a waiver of the installment agreement fee.

If you can pay the full amount you owe within 120 days, then you can avoid paying the fee to set up the installment agreement. Use the online payment agreement (OPA) application at irs.gov/OPA or call the IRS at 800-829-1040.

Effective January 1, 2020, taxpayers who need to reinstate or restructure an installment agreement arrangement can do so through an OPA and pay a reduced fee of only $10. Prior to January 1, 2020, the fee to reinstate or restructure an installment agreement arrangement was $89 ($43 for low-income taxpayers).

Taxpayer owes $10,000 or less in taxes

Upon filing a tax return, if a taxpayer discovers he owes but cannot pay the taxes in full, he can apply for an installment agreement. Applications for an installment agreement are made by completing Form 9465. Generally, a guaranteed installment agreement will be accepted if the tax owed is $10,000 or less and the following conditions are met:

- Returns for the past 5 years have been timely filed, any tax due has been paid, and the taxpayer has not entered into an installment agreement for payment of income tax.

- The IRS determines that the taxpayer cannot pay the tax owed in full when it is due; and

- The taxpayer agrees to pay the entire amount owed within three years and to comply with the tax laws while the agreement is in effect.

Interest and penalties

The taxpayer will be charged interest and may be charged a late payment penalty on any tax that the taxpayer did not pay by its due date, even if the IRS has granted the taxpayer's request to pay the amount due in installments. The interest and penalties will be charged on the outstanding balance until the balance is paid in full. The taxpayer can limit his interest and penalties by filing his return on time and paying as much of the tax owed with his return as possible.

Chapter 22 – Helping Your Client Deal With the IRS

Payment Methods

The taxpayer can make payments by check, money order, or credit card. The taxpayer can also utilize IRS Direct Pay, IRS2go, and the Electronic Federal Tax Payment System. As discussed earlier, there are fees associated with setting up an installment agreement. The taxpayer can refer to IRS.gov/payments for a list of all the available payment options.

The IRS sends notices to taxpayers on installment plans. Taxpayers who mail installment payments to the IRS will receive notices of payments received. The notice will show the remaining balance, the due date, and the amount of the next payment. If the taxpayer has the payments automatically withdrawn from his checking account, he will not receive a notice from the IRS. The bank statement will be the taxpayer's receipt of payment. The IRS will send an annual statement showing the beginning balance, payments made throughout the year, and the ending balance.

The taxpayer can apply online for a payment installment agreement instead of filing Form 9465 if he owes up to $50,000. The taxpayer can set up a monthly installment plan via the Online Payment Agreement. Payments can be spread over a period of 72 months.

If the taxes owed are greater than $50,000 or the taxpayer needs longer than 6 years to pay, he will need to provide the IRS with a financial statement. In addition to Form 9465, a Collection Information Statement, Form 433-A or Form 433-F, may be required by the IRS.

The IRS notifies the taxpayer in writing informing him if the installment agreement has been accepted, or if it needs to be modified.

If the taxpayer gets into financial difficulty and is unable to make a payment, he should notify the IRS as soon as possible to work out a solution. Failure to make timely payments could default the agreement, resulting in the IRS filing a Notice of Federal Tax Lien and/or an IRS levy action, neither of which are desirable for the taxpayer.

Generally, the period of collectability on federal tax debts is 10 years from the date the return was filed. If the taxes are not collected during that period and the statute has not been extended by an action of the taxpayer, the debt is extinguished. Certain events will cause this period to be extended. The taxpayer needs to be careful that he does not unknowingly sign an agreement that extends the statutory time for collecting the taxes.

Chapter 22 – Helping Your Client Deal With the IRS

Statutory Collection Period

In order to receive a credit or a refund, the taxpayer must file a claim within 3 years from the date that his original return was due (including extension), or 2 years from the date he paid the tax, whichever is later. The statutory collection period is generally 10 years from the date the return was due or the date the return was filed, whichever is later. The statutory period does not begin until the return is filed, and the tax is assessed. That is one reason it is important for taxpayers to file their returns in a timely manner.

By law, the time-period may be suspended while:

- an installment agreement request or OIC request is being considered

- the taxpayer lives outside of the U.S. continuously for at least 6 months

- the tax periods being collected on are included in a bankruptcy with an automatic stay

In some cases, the IRS will file a return for a taxpayer based upon the information they have. In many cases, this results in the taxpayer owing substantially more than if he had filed his return with all the deductions and exemptions to which he is entitled.

The taxpayer might opt for letting the statute run out when much of the statutory period on a tax debt has elapsed and the IRS has been unable to collect. In these cases, the taxpayer should be prepared for stepped-up collection procedures by the IRS. The taxpayer is likely to receive letters threatening collection actions. Except for certain allowances, once the ten years are up, the IRS must stop its collection efforts.

Bankruptcy

Bankruptcy is rarely considered a viable alternative for removing a federal tax debt. However, in certain cases, federal taxes can be discharged via bankruptcy. Generally, the assessed taxes must be over three years old. There might be other considerations as well.

The most common type of bankruptcy for individuals is Chapter 13. Before the taxpayer considers filing Chapter 13, he should be aware of the following requirements:

- The taxpayer must file all required tax returns within four years of his bankruptcy filing.

- The taxpayer must continue to file all tax returns during the bankruptcy period.

- The taxpayer should pay all current taxes as they come due during his bankruptcy period.

- The taxpayer's case may be dismissed if he fails to file returns and/or pay current taxes during his bankruptcy period.

Chapter 22 – Helping Your Client Deal With the IRS

The taxpayer should consult a competent bankruptcy attorney when considering this alternative.

EIC and Head of Household Questionnaires

A significant number of IRS audits are targeted to the recipients of the Earned Income Tax Credit (EITC). Since many of these filers also claim Head of Household Filing status and most have at least one dependent, these issues are also included in these audits.

The IRS will send the taxpayer a letter informing the taxpayer that:

- The taxpayer may qualify for EITC, so he should file and claim the credit,
- The IRS needs to verify that the taxpayer can claim EITC; or
- The IRS disallowed or reduced the taxpayer's EITC previously; therefore, the taxpayer must file Form 8862, *Information to Claim Certain Refundable Credits After Disallowance*, to claim EITC.

The taxpayer must complete Form 8862 or Form 8862 (SP) and attach it to his tax return if **both** the following are true:

- The taxpayer's EITC was reduced or disallowed for any reason other than a math or a clerical error for a year after 1996; and
- The taxpayer wants to take the EITC and he meets all the requirements.

The taxpayer does **not** have to file Form 8862 or Form 8862 (SP) to claim the EITC if he meets **all** the EITC requirements and:

- After the taxpayer's EITC was reduced or disallowed in an earlier year, he filed Form 8862 and the IRS allowed him the EITC. The IRS did not reduce or disallow it again for any reason except a math or clerical error; or
- The taxpayer is taking the EITC without a qualifying child and the only reason the IRS reduced or disallowed the taxpayer's EITC in an earlier year was because it was determined that the child on the taxpayer's Schedule EIC was not the taxpayer's qualifying child.

The taxpayer should **not** file Form 8862 and **not** take the EITC for:

Chapter 22 – Helping Your Client Deal With the IRS

- The 2 years after the most recent year that the IRS determined that the taxpayer's EITC claim was due to reckless or intentional disregard of the EITC rules; or

- 10 years after the most recent tax year that the IRS determined that the taxpayer's EITC claim was fraudulent.

Most of these audits begin with the taxpayer being notified by mail that his return is being examined for a specific issue. Included with the correspondence are the proposed changes to the return if the EIC, Head of Household filing status, and dependency exemptions are not allowed. In addition, instructions are enclosed providing information to the taxpayer regarding documents to be submitted if he wants to appeal the proposed changes. The size of the packet sent to taxpayers from the IRS can often be intimidating.

In dealing with these audits, it is important to recognize that there are usually three major issues involved: the Earned Income Credit, Head of Household filing status, and claiming dependents. Separating the audit into the three issues allows one to attack each issue individually to ensure it is adequately covered in the response. This concept is often difficult for taxpayers to understand and often hampers their efforts to respond to such an audit successfully.

Some documentation will be relevant to more than one of the issues; e.g., proving that the dependent being claimed resided with the taxpayer for the required period of time also provides evidence for the other two issues, since one of the requirements for claiming HOH filing status and EIC is for the qualifying person to reside with the taxpayer.

In conclusion, audits often take several months to complete. The key to proving the taxpayer's case is to provide the information requested by the examiner in a timely fashion. In many cases, the process is so time-consuming and frustrating that the taxpayer will just give up, but it is essential that they do not do so.

Proving Requirements for Earned Income Credit (EIC)

Major emphasis must be placed on proving that the qualifying person has met the requirements for it. It should be kept in mind that a child can qualify a person to receive EIC without the child qualifying as a dependent or qualifying the taxpayer as HOH. To claim EIC, the taxpayer must prove the qualifying person resided with the taxpayer for the required length of time.

Chapter 22 – Helping Your Client Deal With the IRS

In proving that the taxpayer is entitled to EIC, he must also prove that the qualifying person, usually a child, was either related to the taxpayer or, in the case of a foster child, was placed with the taxpayer by an authorized agency.

If the taxpayer is a parent of the child, the fact that the child is related to the taxpayer can be proven by a birth certificate, provided the taxpayer's name is on the document. In cases in which the qualifier is related in other ways, proof becomes more difficult.

Proving to the IRS's satisfaction that the qualifying child resided with the taxpayer for the required length of time is more problematic. Documents that can be used for such proof include school records, medical records, receipt of mail by the child at the taxpayer's address, name of the child on a residential lease, etc. The more items of proof that can be furnished to the IRS, the stronger will be the taxpayer's case for EIC.

Proving Requirements for Head of Household (HOH)

For HOH filing status, the taxpayer must prove that he provided a home for a qualifying child. This usually entails providing a list of household expenses, and proof that the taxpayer paid more than half the total cost for the year. In many cases, because of limited income, the claiming of HOH filing status does not increase the tax refund for the taxpayer.

Proving dependency is another issue that is often difficult to prove to the IRS's satisfaction. In addition to proving that the taxpayer qualifies for EIC, the taxpayer must prove that he provided over half the total cost of support for the dependent(s). This is often very difficult since many people in the income category that qualify for EIC do not use checking accounts or other methods of paying for goods and services which provide documentation that verifies support.

Tips for Clients Who are Likely to be Audited

When preparing returns for EIC recipients, practitioners should make the taxpayers aware of the possibility of an audit and the documentation they might want to keep to be prepared for such an audit. Providing them with a written checklist of records they should keep documents the practitioner's attempt to create awareness on the part of the client that the possibility of an EIC audit exists.

The tax practitioner must ensure that he asks enough questions to determine the taxpayer does qualify for EIC, HOH filing status, and the dependency exemption. By applying due diligence, the practitioner protects both the taxpayer and themselves in contending with these issues on a tax return.

Practicing Due Diligence

There is a required form to ensure due diligence is performed in determining if a taxpayer qualifies for EIC. Form 8867, *Paid Preparer's Due Diligence Checklist*, is a checklist that

Chapter 22 – Helping Your Client Deal With the IRS

the preparer completes, files with Form 1040, and keeps on file for the period that the return is open for scrutiny by the IRS. The revised checklist covers the EIC due diligence and has been expanded to offer the Child Tax Credit (CTC), Additional Child Tax Credit (ACTC), Credit for Other Dependents (ODC), the American Opportunity Tax Credit (AOTC), and Head of Household (HOH) filing status. The practitioner should ensure that he retains these forms to prove that due diligence was practiced in preparing the return. Failure to practice due diligence in preparing EIC returns can subject the preparer to a $530 fine for each occurrence on a 2019 return. Practitioners should inform their clients that refunds including the EIC or ACTC are legally delayed until mid-February of the tax filing season by the PATH Act, which gives the IRS extra time to block identity thieves and prevent fraudulent claims for this credit.

These audits often take several months to complete. The key to proving the taxpayer's case is to provide the information requested by the examiner in a timely fashion. In many cases, the process is so time-consuming and frustrating, the taxpayer will just give up.

Supporting Documents

The IRS will request that the taxpayer provide supporting documentation to prove that he is able to claim EIC (Form 886-H-EIC), Head of Household (Form 886-H-HOH), and the dependency exemption (Form 886-H-DEP). The IRS will mail the relevant Form 886-H with the audit letter. The following lists and forms indicate the types of supporting documents a taxpayer may be requested to supply to the IRS.

Form **886-H-EIC** (October 2019)	Department of the Treasury–Internal Revenue Service **Documents You Need to Send to Claim the Earned Income Credit** **on the Basis of a Qualifying Child or Children for Tax Year 2019**	
Taxpayer name	Taxpayer Identification Number	Tax year

To get Earned Income Credit (EIC), the child must have lived with you, be related to you and be a certain age.

Para recibir el Crédito por Ingreso del Trabajo (EIC, por sus siglas en inglés), el niño tiene que haber convivido con usted, ser su pariente, y tener una edad específica. Visite IRS.gov/espanol para buscar la versión en español del Formulario 886-H-EIC (SP) (Rev. 10-2019) o llame al 1-800-829-3676.

Visit IRS.gov/eitc to find out more about who qualifies for EIC.

1. **Each child that you claim must have lived with you for more than half of 2019* in the United States. The United States includes the 50 states and the District of Columbia. It doesn't include Puerto Rico or U.S. possessions such as Guam.**

   *Count time that you or the child is temporarily away from home due to special circumstances as time the child lived with you. Examples include illness, college, business, vacation, military service or detention in a juvenile facility.

To prove the child lived with you in the United States, the document(s) must have:	You can send one or more of the following documents to prove the child lived with you for more than half of 2019:	Or, send dated statements on letterhead from:
• your U.S. address, your name, and the child's name. (If you use a P.O. Box as your mailing address, you must send a completed Form 1093, *P.O. Box Application* stamped by the Post Office) • the dates in 2019 the child lived at the same address as you must cover more than half of 2019 • if the document has the child's name and your address but not your name, you need to send in another document with your name showing the same address	• school records (you may need to send one or more school records) • Medical records from doctors, hospital or medical clinic (immunization records may not include all the necessary information) • adoption or child placement documents • court records	• the child's school • the child's childcare provider (not a relative) • the child's health care provider, doctor, nurse or clinic • a social service agency • a placement agency official • your employer • an Indian tribal official • your landlord or property manager • a place of worship • shelters
2. Each child that you claim must be related to you in one of the ways listed below. If the child is:	**Then, send in copies of:**	
Your son or daughter (including an adopted child)	Nothing at this time, go to Section 3. If your name is not on the child's birth certificate, send us other records or documents proving you are the parent such as adoption records, court decree or paternity test results. If the child was not born in the United States, we need a copy of the birth certificate or immigration papers in English or a copy of the legal translation.	
Your grandchild or great grandchild	One or more birth certificates or other legal documents proving how you are related. For example, if you are claiming your: • Grandchild, send your child's and grandchild's birth certificates • Great grandchild, send your child's, your grandchild's and your great grandchild's birth certificates If the names aren't on the birth certificates, you need to send another type of document such as a court decree or paternity test results.	

Table continued...

Catalog Number 35113Q	www.irs.gov	Form **886-H-EIC** (Rev. 10-2019) [4]

---

[4] *www.eitc.irs.gov/EITCCentral/f886-h-eic.pdf*

2. Each child that you claim must be related to you in one of the ways listed below. If the child is	Then, send in copies of:
Your niece or nephew	One or more birth certificates or other legal documents proving how you are related. For example, the child's birth certificate, showing your brother as the father, your brother's birth certificate showing your mother's name and your birth certificate showing your mother's name. If the names aren't on the birth certificates, you need another type of document such as a court decree or paternity test.
Your brother, sister, half brother, or half sister	One or more birth certificates or other legal documents proving how you are related. For example, If you are claiming your half-brother, you need your brother's birth certificate with the name of your mother or father and your birth certificate with the name of the same mother or father. Both birth certificates must have the name of the parent in common. If not, you need another type of document, such as a court decree or paternity test results.
Your stepson, stepdaughter, step-brother, step-sister, step-grandchild, or step-great grandchild	One or more birth certificates or other legal documents, such as court papers or marriage licenses, proving how you are related. If the birth certificate doesn't have the name of the parent to prove how you are related, you need another type of document, such as court decree or DNA test results.
A child pending adoption	If the adoption is not final, you need a statement on letterhead from an authorized adoption agency.
Your foster child placed with you by an authorized placement agency	A statement on the letterhead of the authorized placement agency or the court document placing the child with you during 2019.
3. Age of each child that you claim is:	**Then, send in copies of:**
Under age 19 at the end of 2019 and younger than you (or your spouse if filing a joint return)	Nothing at this time.
• age 19 but under age 24 at the end of 2019, and • a full-time student for any part of 5 calendar months during 2019, and • younger than you (or your spouse if filing a joint return)	• School records showing the child was considered a full-time student for any part of five months of the tax year. It can be any five months of the year. The months do not have to be consecutive. • The school records must show the child's name and the dates the child attended school during 2019.
Any age and permanently and totally disabled at any time during 2019	A letter from a doctor, other health care provider, a social service program or government agency verifying the person is: permanently and totally disabled. To be permanently and totally disabled for EIC purposes, the condition must last or be expected to last continuously for at least a year or is expected to result in death; and the person can't work or perform other substantial gainful activities.

We must have proof for all three: you are related to the child, the child lived with you and the child's age. If you don't have or can't get the legal documents that we ask for, you can't claim EITC with that child. But, you may still be eligible for EIC without a qualifying child.

Important things to check before sending copies of your documents to us:

☐ Your records and documents prove all three: the child lived with you, is related to you and is a certain age. If not, we cannot allow your claim for EIC.

☐ Your documents are for 2019 not the current year.

☐ If your documents are not in English, you are sending a legally translated document.

☐ We cannot accept documents signed by **someone related to you** for example, your sister takes care of the child while you work. You can't send a statement signed by your sister as the childcare provider to prove the child lived with you.

☐ You are using the same record or document to prove different things. For example, you use a school record to show the child attended school from January to May and then another record showing the same child attended from September to December during 2019. If the records show your address and list you as the parent, you can use the records to prove the child lived with you for more than half the year in 2019 and that the child is related to you. If the child is age 19 but under age 24, the records also prove the child is the right age.

Catalog Number 35113Q   www.irs.gov   Form **886-H-EIC** (Rev. 10-2019)   5

---

[5] *www.eitc.irs.gov/EITCCentral/f886-h-eic.pdf*

Chapter 22 – Helping Your Client Deal With the IRS

Form **886-H-DEP** (October 2019)	Department of the Treasury–Internal Revenue Service **Supporting Documents for Dependency Exemptions**	
Taxpayer name		Taxpayer Identification Number / Tax Year

If You Are:	And:	Then please send photocopies of the following documents:
Divorced, legally separated, or living apart from the other parent of the child claimed on your return.	Both parents *(together)* provided more than half of the child's **total support** for the tax year. **and** One or both parents have custody.	Entire divorce decree, separation agreement, decree of separate maintenance. If you are living apart from the child's other parent, but you are not divorced or legally separated, send proof that you did not live with the child's other parent for the last six months of the year. Current custody order, completed *Form 8332, Release of Claim to Exemption for Child of Divorced or Separated Parents* or a similar statement as applicable for 2019. You may need to send more than one document.

If the Person Is:	And:	Then please send photocopies of the following documents:
Your qualifying child	The child is: your son, daughter, adopted child, a child lawfully placed with you for legal adoption, stepson, stepdaughter, brother, sister, stepbrother, stepsister, foster child placed with you by an authorized placement agency or by court order, or a descendant of any such person *(for example, a grandchild, a niece, or a nephew)*, **and** The child lived with you for more than half of 2019; *(temporary absences away from home, such as the child going away to school, count as time lived at home)*, **and** The child did not provide half of his or her own support for 2019, **and** At the end of 2019, the child is under age 19, or a full time student under the age of 24, or permanently and totally disabled regardless of age.	Birth certificates or other official documents of birth, marriage certificates, letter from an authorized adoption agency, letter from the authorized placement agency, or applicable court document that verify your relationship to the child *(send these documents only for a qualifying child who is not your natural or adopted child)*. To show both you and your child lived together at the same address or addresses for more than half of 2019, send either: · School, medical, daycare, or social service records. · A letter on the official letterhead from a school, medical provider, social service agency, or place of worship that shows names, common address and dates. *(If you send a letter from a relative who provides your daycare, you MUST send at least one additional letter that provides proof.)* **You may need to send more than one document** to show that the child lived with you for more than half of the year.

If the Person Is:	And:	Then please send photocopies of the following documents:
Your qualifying relative	Your relative is any of the relatives listed in the box above or any of the following: father or mother and their ancestors, step-father or step-mother, aunt or uncle, brother- in-law or sister in-law, **and** You provided over half of his or her support in 2019, *(except for children of divorced or separated parents)*, **and** Can not be claimed as a qualifying child by any other person in 2019.	Birth and marriage certificates that verify your relationship to the qualifying relative. If you claim a non-blood related person as a qualifying relative, send proof the person has lived in your home for the entire 12 months of the year. To show both of you lived together at the same address or addresses for all of 2019, send either: · School, medical, daycare, or social service records. · A letter on the official letterhead from a school, medical provider, social service agency, or place of worship that shows names, common address and dates. *(If you send a letter from a relative who provides your daycare, you MUST send at least one additional letter that provides proof.)*

Catalog Number 35111U   www.irs.gov   Form **886-H-DEP** (Rev. 10-2019) 6

---

[6] *http://www.eitc.irs.gov/EITCCentral/f886-h-dep.pdf*

Chapter 22 – Helping Your Client Deal With the IRS

*** Note - Send Us Copies of the Following Documents as Proof You Provided More Than Half of Your Dependent's Total Support: ***

- A statement of account from a child support agency.

- A statement from any government agency verifying the amount and type of benefits you and/or your dependent received for the year.

- Rental agreements or a statement showing the fair rental value of your residence *(proof of lodging cost)*.

- Utility and repair bills *(proof of household expenses)* with canceled checks or receipts.

- Daycare, school, medical records or bills *(proof of child's support)* with canceled checks or receipts.

- Clothing bills *(proof of child's support)* with canceled checks or receipts.

---

[7] *http://www.eitc.irs.gov/EITCCentral/f886-h-hoh.pdf*

Chapter 22 – Helping Your Client Deal With the IRS

Non-Filers

The tax practitioner may receive requests for help from "non-filers." These are individuals who have either never filed a return or have not filed for a considerable period of time. The number of people who fit this category is very surprising.

How does an individual become a non-filer? It starts when a person has an unusual situation (illness, death, or accident) and finds it difficult to get the return filed on time or by the required extension date. After missing a year or two, the non-filer will be unable to find all his records and may end up not filing for many years. Often it reaches the point that the taxpayer dreads the thought of dealing with the overdue tax filings.

Some non-filers become fearful of getting the returns filed; afraid to face the fact that they could owe substantial sums of money, they just ignore the situation. Of course, failure to file required tax returns compounds the problem, since substantial penalties and interest will be due on returns in which the taxpayer owes taxes. Some non-filers are unaware that in the case of refunds, they will not receive refunds on returns that are more than three years overdue.

Until recent years, the IRS was somewhat lax in notifying non-filers that the returns were delinquent. It was common for the taxpayer to get one or two notices, then no more. Sometimes they might not even get a notice, especially if they had moved to another residence. The situation has changed now, with more emphasis being placed on bringing non-filers into compliance.

A large percentage of non-filers owe money. The penalties for failing to file and pay by the due date, plus the interest that accrues, can really add up over a period of years. A rather small tax bill can turn into a large one in a few short years. In fact, the penalties and interest can add up to substantially more than the original tax bill since the interest is compounded daily.

Sometimes, the first hint of trouble for a non-filer is the discovery that his wages have suddenly been garnished. Another possibility is that a tax lien is discovered when selling a piece of real estate, which the taxpayer was not aware existed. While the IRS sends certified letters to the taxpayer when these actions occur, they are sometimes not accepted by the recipient or do not reach the taxpayer because he has moved.

The non-filer will often show up at the office of a tax practitioner for advice and assistance with his situation. The necessary documents for filing an accurate tax return may be either missing or incomplete, making the preparation of an accurate tax return difficult. In these

Chapter 22 – Helping Your Client Deal With the IRS

cases, taxpayer transcripts should be obtained from the IRS prior to completing the return to ensure all income is reported. In many cases, the IRS will send transcripts to non-filers when they are notified that tax returns are needed for previous years.

In the case of non-filers, the IRS will sometimes prepare a tax return for the taxpayer and send a bill. In these cases, the taxes calculated by the IRS are often more than the taxpayer owes, since he may have exemptions or deductions that are not taken into consideration by the agency.

Many non-filers will find themselves in the position of owing substantial sums of money and lacking the funds to pay the taxes plus the interest and penalties that have accrued.

In cases in which a non-filer has reasonable cause, consideration should be given to requesting that penalties be abated for the late returns. If this is the first time for such a request by the taxpayer and he generally has a good record of filing and paying prior to the late-filed return(s), there is a good chance the IRS will be willing to abate all or a portion of the penalties, provided there is reasonable cause. It is certainly worth making the request.

The next section will cover the options available to the taxpayer for paying his delinquent taxes.

Offer in Compromise

An Offer in Compromise (OIC) is an agreement between a taxpayer and the Internal Revenue Service that allows the taxpayer to pay less than the full amount owed on his tax debt. The IRS normally accepts an OIC if it is unlikely that the taxpayer will be able to pay the tax liability in full. The offer must reflect the full collection potential of the taxes owed. The OIC is designed to provide a  way for taxpayers who are not able to pay the taxes owed to settle for a lesser amount. The OIC also allows the IRS to collect money that might not otherwise be collected.

Quite often, a taxpayer who owes a substantial sum will see advertisements in the news media that a firm is able to settle an outstanding IRS debt for "pennies on the dollar." These firms claim to have ex-IRS agents and other knowledgeable experts who can settle

Chapter 22 – Helping Your Client Deal With the IRS

taxpayer debts for much less than owed. These claims are often greatly exaggerated, giving the taxpayer false hopes. The companies usually charge large fees and no guarantees are offered.

The taxpayer may submit an offer without going through a third party. The OIC application forms and instructions are available from the IRS or can be obtained via the internet. The Offer in Compromise Booklet contains Form 656, Form 433-A (OIC Individuals), and Form 433-B (OIC Business) which includes worksheets, checklists, and instructions required to prepare an accurate and complete Offer in Compromise. Accompanying the forms are detailed instructions for preparing and submitting an offer. All forms should be completed carefully and accurately, and documents to verify the entries on the forms should be submitted with the offer.

Three Types of Offer in Compromise

Offers in Compromise can be submitted for three reasons:

1. Doubt as to Collectability
2. Doubt as to Liability
3. Effective Tax Administration (ETA)

Doubt as to Collectability

Most offers are submitted because doubt exists that the taxpayer will ever be able to pay the full amount of the taxes owed within the remainder of the statutory period for collection. To be successful, the offer must demonstrate that the taxpayer does not have the ability to pay the taxes in full either by liquidating assets or through current installment agreement guidelines.

> **Example:** A taxpayer owes $20,000 for unpaid tax liabilities and agrees that the tax he owes is correct. The taxpayer's monthly income does not meet his necessary living expenses. He does not own any real property and does not have the ability to fully pay the liability now or through monthly installment payments.

Doubt as to Liability

This avenue is used if doubt exists that the assessed tax is correct. A detailed written explanation must accompany the offer detailing why a taxpayer believes he does not owe the taxes. Possible reasons to submit a doubt as to liability offer include:

1. the examiner made a mistake interpreting the law,
2. the examiner failed to consider the taxpayer's evidence, or
3. the taxpayer has new evidence.

Chapter 22 – Helping Your Client Deal With the IRS

> **Example:** The taxpayer was vice president of a corporation from 2017-2018. In 2019, the corporation accrued unpaid payroll taxes and the taxpayer was assessed a trust fund recovery penalty as a responsible party of the corporation. The taxpayer was no longer a corporate officer and had resigned from the corporation on 12/31/2018. Since the taxpayer had resigned prior to the payroll taxes accruing and was not contacted prior to the assessment, there is legitimate doubt that the assessed tax liability is correct.

Effective Tax Administration

In this case, the taxpayer can pay the taxes, and believes the taxes assessed are correct. However, an exceptional circumstance must exist for the IRS to consider the offer. The taxpayer must demonstrate that collection of the taxes by the IRS would create an economic hardship or would be unfair and inequitable.

> **Example:** Mr. and Mrs. Taxpayer have assets sufficient to satisfy the tax liability and provide full-time care and assistance to a dependent child, who has a serious long-term illness. It is expected that Mr. and Mrs. Taxpayer will need to use the equity in assets to provide for adequate basic living expenses and medical care for the child. There is no doubt that the tax is correct.

Most offers fall into the first category, Doubt as to Collectability. In these cases, the taxpayer must submit detailed financial statements with the offers. All assets and liabilities must be listed. If there are sufficient assets that can be liquidated to pay the taxes, or if the taxpayer has sufficient borrowing capability to borrow the money to pay the taxes, the offer will likely not be accepted.

The taxpayer also must complete a monthly cash flow statement detailing total income and expenses. This provides a basis for determining the amount of monthly payments the taxpayer will be able to make. If it is determined the taxpayer can pay the tax debt over the statutory collection period, the offer will usually not be accepted.

The Fresh Start Program expanded access to installment programs and streamlines the OIC program. The IRS has more flexibility when analyzing a taxpayer's ability to pay. This makes the OIC program available to a larger group of taxpayers. Individuals who owe up to $50,000 can pay through monthly direct debit payments for up to 72 months.

Once a taxpayer's OIC is accepted, the taxpayer must comply with all federal filing and payment requirements, including estimated tax and tax deposits, for five years. If the taxpayer defaults under the OIC, or fails to file a tax year, the IRS can immediately sue the taxpayer for the balance due under the OIC agreement.

If the taxpayer's OIC application is rejected, he can appeal the rejection to Appeals within 30 days of the rejection. If the taxpayer does not receive a rejection notice for the OIC application from the IRS within two years from the date of submission, it is deemed that the IRS has accepted the OIC.

Offer in Compromise Payment Options

Beginning April 27, 2020, a $205 (this is up from $189 prior to April 27, 2020) nonrefundable fee must accompany the OIC application (Form 656, *Offer in Compromise*) unless the taxpayer's income is below the poverty level. The fee is nonrefundable but will be applied to the taxes due if the offer is not accepted. The taxpayer must also include 20% of the offer amount. In recent years, the IRS has accepted fewer and fewer offers.

When the offer is submitted, it will be checked for completeness and to determine if there is sufficient information to process the offer. In many cases, the taxpayer is requested to submit additional information prior to the offer being considered. The taxpayer must respond to such requests in a timely fashion. If the dates are not strictly adhered to, the offer will be returned without being processed.

The instructions for submitting an offer are very explicit in determining the offer that is likely to be accepted. Worksheets should be completed accurately to determine a reasonable offer.

Taxpayers must select one of two payment options:

1. **Lump Sum Offer** – Payable in nonrefundable installments. A nonrefundable payment of 20% of the offer amount along with the $205 application fee is due upon filing the Form 656. The 20% nonrefundable amount will be applied to the taxpayer's tax liability if the offer is not accepted by the IRS. If the offer is accepted, the remaining balance must be paid in five or fewer payments within five or fewer months from the date of acceptance.

2. **Periodic Payment Offer** – Payable in nonrefundable installments. The first payment along with the $205 application fee is due upon filing the Form 656. The remaining balance is to be paid within 6 to 24 months in accordance with the offer.

The offer amount must include the realizable value of assets plus the total amount the IRS could collect through monthly payments during the remaining life of the statutory period for collection.

The IRS is not obligated to accept either the offer amount or the terms offered by the taxpayer and may negotiate a different offer amount and terms, when appropriate. The OIC investigator may determine that the amount offered is too low or the payment terms

Chapter 22 – Helping Your Client Deal With the IRS

are too drawn-out, and he would not recommend accepting the offer. The OIC investigator may advise the taxpayer as to what amount or different terms would likely be recommended for acceptance.

OICs generally take from two months to over a year to complete. The speed at which the offer is processed depends upon several factors. The complexity of the taxpayer's financial situation is certainly a major consideration. A taxpayer's situation that consists only of W-2 income is less complicated than the taxpayer with income from multiple sources. Another factor is the responsiveness of the taxpayer for additional information. A third factor is the person who is processing the offer.

The taxpayer should keep in mind that the statutory collection period is suspended during the time the offer is being considered. That could add several months to the time during which the IRS can collect a tax debt. If the offer is accepted, the taxpayer must agree to remain in compliance with all federal taxes during a period of five years. Failure to do so will allow the IRS to cancel the offer.

Some taxpayers try to submit an offer in a year in which they might be temporarily unemployed or have substantially less income than normal. In such cases, the IRS may accept an offer but retains the right to renegotiate if the taxpayer's situation changes substantially during the five-year compliance period

Audit Preparation

For most taxpayers, the chances of being audited by the IRS are rather small. Most of the inquiries that taxpayers receive are merely proposed adjustments of their tax returns because of some information that was submitted to the IRS on an informational document by an employer or other payer that does not appear to be on the tax return. While comprehensive IRS examinations or audits of taxpayer returns are relatively rare, they do occur.

Taxpayers are often curious about what might trigger an audit. Some audits are purely random as part of the efforts of the IRS to monitor taxpayer compliance with the tax laws. Substantial deductions that seem out of line with the norm or the income level of the taxpayer could trigger an audit. An "unusual" item on a tax return could be the determining factor. Other audits are the result of information the IRS might gather from several other sources, such as newspapers, public records, and individuals.

Chapter 22 – Helping Your Client Deal With the IRS

When tax returns are submitted to the IRS, they are put through a series of computerized screens that score the returns. A computer program called the Discriminant Inventory Function System (DIF) assigns a numeric score to each individual tax return. These scores are designed to allow the selection of returns that will have a high probability, upon examination, of items that will likely result in significant changes to an individual's income tax liability.

It is an accepted fact that certain items on tax returns are more susceptible to audit than others. Schedule C (sole proprietorships) filers are more likely to be audited since they are often a source of unreported cash transactions. In addition, many sole proprietors do not maintain all the records they should be keeping proving legitimate expense deductions. Another ripe area for audit is Schedule A contributions, both cash and non-cash, especially when they are rather large when compared to total income. The home office deduction has always been an area that is subject to challenge. When used for business, automobile expense is an area that might be targeted, since many people neglect to keep the required mileage logs to document the expense.

Normally, items that are well documented, such as wages or mortgage interest reported by a third party, will not be audited. Mismatches between what a third-party report and what is on the return can trigger an audit, but it is usually a simple one. Although there are triggers to audits, anything on a return can be audited. As a result, taxpayers should maintain their documents for anything reported on the return for the mandatory statutory period.

The examinations of returns may be done:

- Through the mail
- At the examining representative's office
- In the taxpayer's home or business
- At the location of the taxpayer's personal representative

The reviewing agent will try to schedule the interview at a time and place convenient to the taxpayer in cases of personal examinations. The IRS makes the final determination about where, when, and how the examination will take place.

An IRS examination of a tax return is not to be taken lightly, especially if it is a comprehensive examination. When a taxpayer is notified of an upcoming audit, certain preparations should be made. Preparation for an audit should begin long before the audit, i.e., the taxpayer should maintain records so that he is always ready for an audit.

If the examination is pertinent to a specific issue, the taxpayer should gather all relevant documentation on the issue being questioned. The letter the taxpayer receives will list the items being questioned. If more time is needed to gather the required information, a request should be made well in advance of the examination date.

Chapter 22 – Helping Your Client Deal With the IRS

If the examination is such that the entire return is being examined, the documentation requirement will be more extensive.

Auditors will perform a bank deposit analysis on business returns. It is important that taxpayers have a separate bank account for the business. This business bank account should be used to deposit all business income and pay legitimate business expenses from this business account. Unexplained deposits are often the basis for an examiner to claim unreported income, but these deposits could be perfectly legitimate, such as proceeds from business loans, gifts, insurance proceeds, etc.

Unless the taxpayer is thoroughly knowledgeable on the issues to be examined, it is recommended that the taxpayer obtain representation from a third party to assist with the examination, particularly in the case of comprehensive examinations. The representative may be an attorney, certified public accountant, certified actuary, enrolled agent, or the person who prepared and signed the tax return. These professionals can assist the taxpayer in preparing for the examination, accompany him to the examination, and/or represent him. The additional fee spent in obtaining representation could prove to be a good investment.

If you want your representative to appear in your absence, you must provide a properly completed power of attorney to the IRS. Form 2848, *Power of Attorney and Declaration of Representative* or any other properly written power of attorney or authorization may be used for this purpose.

Choosing to represent himself, the taxpayer will often unintentionally provide information that may cause the examining agent to review areas that he might not have been considering before. In addition, because of the complexity of the tax laws, the taxpayer may unintentionally provide information that will be harmful to a particular argument.

Examinations that take place in the home are particularly dangerous to the taxpayer. This allows the revenue agent to obtain some information on the relative standard of living of the individual taxpayer that might be inconsistent with the tax return that was filed. In addition, it gives the agent an opportunity to examine items such as the "office in the home" which might have been taken as a deduction. Non-business items located in the room or area designated as the home office certainly will not help a taxpayer's case in defending the home office deduction.

Dealing with an IRS examiner is likely to be a bit stressful at best. Proper preparation can lessen the stress and increase the chances of the taxpayer owing little or no additional taxes, or possibly getting a refund.

In preparing for the audit, it is recommended that the taxpayer or his representative put themselves in the auditor's shoes. Examine thoroughly the items that are likely to be brought up in the audit. Make sure there is documentation to prove a deduction or item

Chapter 22 – Helping Your Client Deal With the IRS

of income. If there are questionable deductions that cannot be proven, it is likely they will be disallowed. It might be possible to come up with some deductions that were missed in the preparation of the original tax return to replace the disallowed ones.

The taxpayer or his representative should be familiar with the full tax return that is being examined and be able to explain each item on the tax return. For "gray area" items, certainly one should have a basis in tax law to explain the reasoning behind the handling of the items. If any deductions were missed on the original return, they can be used to offset some of the ones that are disallowed.

It is recommended that records be provided to the auditor in an organized manner. Taking unorganized boxes of receipts to the audit will not impress the auditor and will only lengthen the time required for the audit. Only provide documents needed to prove a deduction or income.

It is wise to establish a good understanding with the examiner. If the examiner turns out to be uncooperative, abusive, or unfair, the taxpayer can request a different one. This usually entails speaking to the auditor's supervisor and providing solid, concise, and pertinent reasons for the request.

Taxpayers should keep in mind that the examining agent will be trying to obtain additional tax revenue. Auditors do not like to spend their time auditing a return without obtaining additional revenue.

Post-Audit Action

After an audit is completed, the examining agent recommends one of four determinations:

1. Acceptance of the return as filed and closing of the case
2. Assertion of a deficiency or additional tax
3. Allowance of an overassessment, with or without a refund claim
4. Denial of a claim for refund that is determined to be without merit

If the return is accepted as filed, the IRS will issue a "no change letter," and no further action by the taxpayer is required.

A few weeks after the taxpayer's closing conference with the examiner and/or supervisor, the taxpayer will receive a package containing:

- A letter (referred to as a 30-day letter) informing the taxpayer of his right to appeal the proposed changes within 30 days;
- A copy of the examiner's report explaining the proposed changes;
- An agreement or waiver form; and

Chapter 22 – Helping Your Client Deal With the IRS

- A copy of Publication 5 (*Your Appeal Rights and How to Prepare a Protest If You Don't Agree*).

The taxpayer has 30 days from the date of the 30-day letter to let the IRS know if he will accept or appeal the proposed changes. The 30-day letter states the proposed changes and is accompanied by a copy of the examining agent's report. The taxpayer is given the option of agreeing to the proposed changes. If the taxpayer does not agree, information is provided regarding protesting and appealing the results of the audit.

If the taxpayer does not respond to the 30-day letter in a timely manner, a statutory "notice of deficiency" (90-day letter) will be issued. The notice of deficiency will be postponed if the taxpayer submits a protest within the 30-day period.

A statutory notice of deficiency allows the taxpayer 90 days to file a petition to the Tax Court (150 days if the taxpayer is outside the United States). The 90-day period must be strictly adhered to and begins on the date of the 90-day letter. If no action is taken at this time, the taxes will be assessed, and no appeal is available.

Glossary

- **CP Notice and Number**

  The most common notice received by a taxpayer from the IRS, which can range from notifying a taxpayer of a math error on a return to a notice of their selection for a comprehensive examination of a tax return. Each type of CP notice has a CP Number and a title.

- **Discriminant Inventory Function System (DIF)**

  The IRS's computer program, which assigns a numeric score to each return after it has been processed by DIF. If a return is selected because of a high score under the DIF system, the potential is high that an examination of the return will result in a change to income tax liability.

- **Form 866-H-DEP**

  A form taxpayers use to support their claim to the IRS that they are entitled to claim a dependency exemption.

Chapter 22 – Helping Your Client Deal With the IRS

- **Form 866-H-EIC**

  A form taxpayers use to support their claim to the IRS that they are entitled to claim the Earned Income Credit.

- **Form 866-H-HOH**

  A form taxpayers use to support their claim to the IRS that they are entitled to claim Head of Household filing status.

- **Form 8862** – Information to Claim Earned Income Credit after Disallowance

  If a taxpayer's Earned Income Tax Credit (EIC or EITC) has been reduced or disallowed since 1996 (except for math or clerical errors) and he wants to take EIC again, he must complete Form 8862 and attach it to his tax return.

- **Form 8867** – Paid Preparer's Earned Income Credit Checklist

  A tax preparer is required to complete and submit this form with all electronic and paper returns to meet IRS due diligence requirements for taxpayers claiming EIC.

- **Form 9465** – Installment Agreement Request

  A form used to request a monthly installment plan for a taxpayer who cannot pay the full amount of tax owed shown on his tax return.

- **Levy**

  An administrative action by the IRS, under statutory authority, to seize property by any means to satisfy a tax liability.

- **Non-Filer**

  Individuals that have either never filed a return or have not filed for a considerable period of time.

Chapter 22 – Helping Your Client Deal With the IRS

- **Offer in Compromise (OIC)**

  An agreement between the taxpayer and the IRS that settles the amount the taxpayer owes for less than the full amount.

- **Statutory Collection Period**

  As a general rule, there is a ten-year period of time in which the IRS must collect a tax debt.

- **Taxpayer Advocate Service (TAS)**

  An independent organization within the IRS that is designed to help taxpayers resolve problems with the IRS.

A Note about Representing Taxpayers

Unless you are an attorney, Certified Public Accountant, Certified Actuary, Enrolled Agent, have an Annual Filing Season Program Record of Completion, or are the person who prepared and signed the tax return, you cannot represent the taxpayer in an IRS audit.

Conclusion

One of the main reasons taxpayers use the services of a tax professional is to have peace of mind. Your clients feel comfort and safety in knowing that you will be there to help them if they should receive a letter from the IRS or other taxation authority. You should stress to your clients the importance of notifying you immediately if they receive any correspondence from the IRS or any state or local taxation authority. Addressing the problem without delay is essential. Most IRS audits can be resolved by mail and will not require you and your client to visit the IRS office. It is recommended that you do not charge your clients for assistance unless taxpayer representation services requiring an EA, CPA, or attorney, or attending an office visit with your client, are necessary. Being well prepared to communicate with the IRS is important and you should strive to establish a rapport with all IRS agents with whom you must interact on behalf of your clients.

Chapter 23

Peer Support and Tax Professional Associations

"We may not have it all together, but together we have it all."

- Unknown

Chapter 23 – Peer Support and Tax Professional Associations

Seeking Support and Assistance

There is no need for you to develop and build your business in a vacuum. In 1624, English poet, John Donne said, "No man is an island; entire of himself..." John Donne's sage advice is as valid today as it was more than 400 years ago. You should seek advice and support from others to ensure that you are not making costly mistakes and to capitalize on ideas and experience of others to maximize the growth and profitability of your business. These sources of support and assistance include tax professional associations, tax professional conferences, social media tax professional and tax business owner groups, business advisors, small business support agencies and, of course, this book.

Other independent tax business owners should be viewed as colleagues rather than competitors. The only tax business owners who are competitors are those operating in the same market where you operate, and even they can be considered "friendly competitors" rather than foes. Collectively, independent tax business owners compete with the national tax firms that have proven systematic operating methods and the number of locations and the financial resources to effectively use mass-media advertising. Independent tax business owners have the opportunity to collaborate to help one-another to succeed and you should take advantage of this opportunity.

Keep Abreast of Tax Industry News

As a professional in the industry, you must look up from your piles of forms and receipts occasionally, to stay in tune with what's going on in the industry. It's hard to be in touch with the outside world when there are so many returns to file, but there is still news to pay attention to, client newsletters that need to be sent, and social media content that needs to be written. Hopefully, you're on social media.

How do you stay on top of all of this content that needs to be created and consumed? Below is our "Go To" list of industry resources.

Chapter 23 – Peer Support and Tax Professional Associations

1. **IRS.gov**

   Believe it or not, the IRS is pretty on top of things when it comes to communication. You can sign up for several different types of email alerts and let the IRS news and tax tips come to you. https://www.irs.gov

   Here are some of the alerts you can sign up for.

   - **IRS Tax Tips**

     Receive tax information via email from the IRS daily during the tax-filing season and periodically the rest of the year.

     http://www.irs.gov/uac/Subscribe-to-IRS-Tax-Tips

   - **IRS Newswire**

     Receive news releases as they are issued by the IRS National Media Relations Office in Washington, DC.

     http://www.irs.gov/uac/Subscribe-to-IRS-Newswire

   - **GuideWire**

     Receive notifications by e-mail when the IRS issues advance copies of tax guidance such as Regulations, Revenue Rulings, Revenue Procedures, Announcements, and Notices.

     http://www.irs.gov/uac/Subscribe-to-IRS-GuideWire

   - **Tax Statistics**

     Receive information about the most recent tax statistics.

     http://www.irs.gov/uac/SOI-Tax-Stats-Join-the-Tax-Stats-Dispatch-Mailing-List

   - **Here's where you can find the full list of IRS alerts**

     https://www.irs.gov/newsroom/e-news-subscriptions

2. **Accounting Today**

   Bookmark Accounting Today at https://www.accountingtoday.com/. They are on top of breaking news in the industry, their columns are on point and informative and they have lots of great content to help guide you as a tax professional. You can subscribe to Accounting Today at no cost.

Chapter 23 – Peer Support and Tax Professional Associations

3. **Tax Business Owners of America on LinkedIn**

   Where can you go to get news and information from close to 9,000 tax industry professionals? LinkedIn Group: Tax Business Owners of America. It can be found here: https://www.linkedin.com/groups/1868452. This group is extremely active posting discussions, asking questions, and posting information to share with the rest of the group. Additional information about TBOA is provided later in this chapter.

4. **Tax Industry Blogs**

   Accounting Today cites posts at least weekly from their "Favorite Blogs." Below are two examples.

   - The Income Tax School blog, https://www.theincometaxschool.com/blog/ posts weekly with valuable and unique timely posts on topics of interest to tax preparers and tax business owners.
   - Kelly Phillips Erb writes weekly about taxes for Forbes at https://www.forbes.com/sites/kellyphillipserb/ and manages to make it entertaining. She also has an excellent series going on right now for tax season called Taxes A to Z, which is on her own blog: https://www.taxgirl.com/, where she also covers major tax news and other interesting topics related to the industry.

5. **Make Google do the Work**

   If you're not using Google Alerts, you're doing too much work searching the Internet. Go to https://www.google.com/alerts and set up alerts for tax related keywords, your competitors, yourself and your company. Google will crawl the Internet for you and serve you up digests of alerts in a nice, neat email.

6. **Twitter**

   The tax industry is on Twitter and they are Tweeting away! Here are some great Twitter Handles to follow:
   - @IRStaxpros

Chapter 23 – Peer Support and Tax Professional Associations

- @taxgirl
- @AccountingToday
- @NJSCPA
- @CPALetter_Daily
- @taxfoundation
- @AICPA_JofA
- @NSAtax
- @SoCalTaxProf
- @TaxSchool

Ways Tax Preparers Can Stay on the Cutting Edge

Tax preparation is a constantly changing industry. While many of the principles and processes stay the same, there are laws, deductions, exemptions, and policies that change each season. This is one of the main reasons why tax preparers are expected to take Continuing Education (CE) Courses.

Education is not the only way a tax preparer can stay on the cutting edge and compete with National Tax Firms. There are many other ways to stay sharp, up-to-date and on point.

Keep a Pulse on the Industry

You should always know what's going on and what's changing in your industry – no matter what industry you're in. For tax preparers, this means paying attention to IRS news releases, reading industry publications, following tax related news sources, and listening to what's being said by influencers in the industry.

Attend Workshops/Seminars

Seminars and workshops are great refreshers and a great way to learn new tricks, tips and laws. If you are not an EA and have not yet taken the IRS Annual Filing Season Program in order to gain your Record of Completion, you should make that a priority. All tax preparers who have completed this program are listed in a National Database where

Chapter 23 – Peer Support and Tax Professional Associations

taxpayers can search for tax preparers who have credentials or have completed the program. If you are not on this list, you are not on the cutting edge. In fact, not being on this list could be detrimental.

In order to compete and earn more money, you should also be taking Continuing Education. The more complicated returns you learn to prepare, the more money you will make. CE courses are also important to stay on top of any changes to the law. The Income Tax School offers dozens of affordable online CE seminars.

- https://www.theincometaxschool.com/continuing-education/ce-seminars/

You should also attend seminars. Seminars keep you up-to-date with changes in the industry. Seminars also allow you to gain the perspective of, and learn from, veterans in the industry. The IRS Tax Forum and the tax professional associations provide many seminar opportunities.

Attend One of the Annual IRS Nationwide Tax Forums

Each Summer the IRS presents the Nationwide Tax Forums in five cities throughout the country. The Tax Forums consist of 3 days of Continuing Education (CE) seminars presented by the IRS. In addition, there is an Exhibit Hall where dozens of tax industry vendors have displays. The Exhibit Hall is typically open for about one and one-half days. The IRS Commissioner is often the keynote speaker of the first seminar.

Join your colleagues for three days of informative education sessions, training, and networking, featuring a full agenda of the latest tax law information, networking opportunities and exhibits of the latest products and services for your business needs. The IRS Nationwide Tax Forums launched a Virtual Expo in 2020 due to Covid-19.

Chapter 23 – Peer Support and Tax Professional Associations

Benefits of the IRS Nationwide Tax Forums Include:

1. **Obtaining Continuing Education (CE)**

   Attending one of the IRS Nationwide Tax Forums provides an excellent opportunity for you to obtain Continuing Education (CE) from dozens of seminar classes.

2. **Peer to Peer Interaction**

   With thousands of tax professionals attending these seminars each year, you can interact with fellow tax professionals and tax business owners from various other parts of the country. Where else can you do that? Having peers to talk to about the challenges you face in the industry is extremely valuable for growth and sanity.

3. **Learning about the Latest Products and Services**

   The IRS does a great job of wrangling up tax vendors from across the country. Attending the forums gives you an opportunity to visit with multiple tax industry vendors, all in one place, for you to obtain detailed product and service information, compare options, and see demonstrations. Where else can you learn about the latest products and get to test them in person? Among the exhibitors, are the major tax software vendors and tax professional associations, and, of course, The Income Tax School!

Pay Attention to What Your Competition is Doing

It's so important to pay attention to your competition. They may be filling an unmet need that you could also fill, they may be attacking your brand, or they may be able to provide you with some insight or inspiration.

Here are some ways to pay attention to your competitors:

- Follow them on social media
- Read their blogs
- Sign up for their newsletters
- Visit their websites
- Create Google Alerts for them
- Talk with them at the IRS Nationwide Tax Forums

Chapter 23 – Peer Support and Tax Professional Associations

Pay Attention to What Other Industries are Doing

Don't look at your tax business in a vacuum. There are other industries that you could take notes from. For example, if you want to be better at marketing, why not keep an eye on the industry as a whole? What are the influencers saying and doing? What about the tech industry? What are the trends there?

Being on the cutting edge means you're trying new things, breaking the mold, and stepping out of the normal tactics that have been used for years.

Learn from Your Peers

Keep your friends close and your enemies closer. It's important to know what your peers are saying and doing. You can do this by engaging in forums like LinkedIn Groups or other places where tax professionals chat.

Tax Professional Associations

Independent tax business owners are empowered by tax professional associations including the National Association of Tax Professionals (NATP), the National Association of Enrolled Agents (NAEA), the National Society of Tax Professionals (NSTP) and the National Society of Accountants (NSA). If you are a CPA, consider joining the American Institute of Certified Public Accountants (AICPA). You should join at least one of these tax professional associations. If you can't afford the dues to join the national association, you may be able to join a state chapter at a significantly discounted price, at least until you can afford the national dues. These tax professional associations provide valuable resources to help you increase your tax knowledge and build your tax practice. They also provide tax industry products and services at group discounted pricing. One of the most valuable benefits is the opportunity to interact with other tax business owners. The benefits of being a tax professional association member far exceed the membership dues.

National Association of Tax Professionals (NATP) - https://www.natptax.com/

NATP's mission is simple: They exist to be the most reliable resource for gaining and developing professional tax expertise. They strive to support their members through cutting-edge knowledge and resources, effective advocacy, and the relationships they need to succeed professionally and personally.

Chapter 23 – Peer Support and Tax Professional Associations

National Association of Enrolled Agents (NAEA) - https://www.naea.org/

NAEA is the organization powering enrolled agents, America's tax experts®! NAEA provides the networking, educational opportunities, programs and services that enable enrolled agents and other tax preparers to excel beyond their peers. Membership in NAEA is a key building block of success for enrolled agents seeking to provide the highest level of representation for their clients and for preparers thinking of advancing their careers by becoming enrolled agents.

National Society of Tax Professionals (NSTP) - https://www.nstp.org/

NSTP is committed to helping its members attain the greatest expertise, proficiency, and competency in all areas of the tax profession. NSTP exists to equip its members to be qualified to effectively provide professional tax preparation services for their clients. It is their vision that the National Society of Tax Professionals is the nation's premier organization providing educational benefits, which has enhanced the competency of the tax professional community.

National Society of Accountants (NSA) - https://www.nsacct.org/

NSA provides national leadership and helps its members achieve success in the profession of accountancy and taxation through the advocacy of practice rights and the promotion of high standards in ethics, education, and professional excellence.

American Institute of Certified Public Accountants (AICPA) - https://www.aicpa.org/

Founded in 1887, the AICPA represents the CPA profession nationally, regarding rule-making and standard-setting, and serves as an advocate before legislative bodies, public interest groups and other professional organizations. The AICPA develops standards for audits of private companies and other services by CPAs; provides educational guidance materials to its members; develops and grades the Uniform CPA Examination; and monitors and enforces compliance with the profession's technical and ethical standards.

Tax Business Owners of America (TBOA) - https://www.linkedin.com/groups/1868452

Finally, you should consider joining LinkedIn groups for tax professionals, especially Tax Business Owners of America (TBOA), the only LinkedIn group that is dedicated specifically to provide a  forum for independent tax business owners to support one-another. TBOA was founded by the author of this book, Chuck McCabe. TBOA currently has almost 9,000 members who are engaged in numerous discussions on topics of interest to independent tax business owners.

Chapter 23 – Peer Support and Tax Professional Associations

Through communication and cooperation, members share intellectual capital, become aware of best practices, develop new best practices, address key common issues, forge strategic alliances and gain strength in numbers.

Collective buying power may be possible through collaboration. Together, independent tax business owners can also have a voice before Congress and IRS alongside the national tax firms on issues affecting the tax industry. No one understands the challenges faced by a tax business entrepreneur better than a fellow tax business entrepreneur. TBOA provides a forum for tax business entrepreneurs to share their experiences and knowledge and to learn from one-another.

Membership is open to independent tax business owners who realize the majority of their revenue from income tax preparation services. Membership is also open to IRS employees, and select tax industry executives. Select tax industry vendors may be admitted by invitation only, provided that promotion of their products and services is limited to responses to requests for information by tax business owner members. Only individuals who are identified by their legal names may be members. Non-individual entities may not be members.

Free Resources for Tax Preparers and Tax Business Owners

At The Income Tax School, our mission is to empower people with a professional career to fulfill their dreams and serve others as industry leaders. That's why, along with all of the materials and support we provide to students, we also strive to write informational blog posts and provide other free sources of information.

The Income Tax School has lots of free, downloadable white papers among other valuable information. Simply visit https://www.theincometaxschool.com/ to access them from the website.

Conclusion

As an independent tax business owner, you can compete with national tax firms by using proven best practices and by capitalizing your strengths. Creating value beyond your client base requires that you recruit, hire and train qualified employees and adopt proven systematic methods of operation. Advice from experienced operators and experts should be sought out by you in making key business decisions such as expanding, tax office site-selection and leasing. You can collaborate with other independent tax business owners to realize strength in numbers and thereby level the playing field. Due to the limited resources you have available, you must employ neighborhood and targeted marketing tactics to succeed. Fortunately, there is no need for you to reinvent the wheel. Valuable information and resources to help you succeed as an independent tax businesses owner are available from a number of sources.